The Technological Woman

The Technological Woman

Interfacing with Tomorrow

edited by Jan Zimmerman

PRAEGER

PRAEGER SPECIAL STUDIES • PRAEGER SCIENTIFIC

Library of Congress Cataloging in Publication Data

Main entry under title:

The Technological woman.

Bibliography: p.
Includes index.
1. Women — Addresses, essays, lectures. 2. Technology — Addresses, essays,
lectures. 3. Home economics — Addresses, essays, lectures. 4. Women — Employment — Addresses, essays, lectures. 5. Human reproductions — Addresses,
essays, lectures. I. Zimmerman, Jan.
HQ1154.T38   1983   305.4   82-14033
ISBN 0-03-062829-6

To my parents
To Sandy
for making this possible

Published in 1983 by Praeger Publishers
CBS Educational and Professional Publishing
A Division of CBS Inc.
521 Fifth Avenue, New York, New York 10175 U.S.A.

456789   052   9876543

Printed in the United States of America

Acknowledgments

When I started to compile the list of people to whom gratitude is due for their assistance in preparing this book, I quickly realized that to do so properly would require an acknowledgments section almost as long as the text. Since the publisher would never have stood for that, I must apologize to those many people who remain anonymous to the public, but whom I thank, like Jimmy Carter, in my heart.

This project would never have taken place without the support of the California Council for the Humanities, a state program of the National Endowment for the Humanities, which funded the *Conference on Future, Technology and Woman* at San Diego State University in March 1981. **The Technological Woman** grew directly from that conference and from the **Conference Proceedings**, which were published six months later. By the way, the findings, conclusions, and opinions presented herein do not necessarily represent the views of either the California Council for the Humanities or the National Endowment for the Humanities.

The many organizations that supported the conference also deserve credit here: the San Diego Center for Women's Studies and Services, the San Diego chapters of the Society of Women Engineers and the Coalition of Labor Union Women, women's student organizations and individual students at San Diego State University (SDSU), and especially the SDSU Women's Studies Department. I would particularly like to thank Pat Huckle, department chair, for her continuing support and participation in this effort.

Artist/photographer Suda House, who teaches and exhibits fabric xerography in San Diego, and designer Bob Wolf, at the SDSU Design Center, are responsible for the spectacular cover and sophisticated design of this volume. I am most appreciative of their creative efforts and advice. Also at SDSU I would like to thank Annette Goodman of the SDSU Foundation for handling our financial records and Robert Detweiler, Dean of the College of Arts and Letters.

Among the many who took a direct hand in producing this book, which was typeset and pasted up in a high-tech variation of cottage industry, I wish to thank Sandra Forest for doing all the text entry on our Apple II computer, Kim McAlister and Jean Habenicht for paste-up, Rich Hand of Dream Electronics for figuring out how to typeset from a personal computer, and Nancy Koontz, Allison Rossett, and Rob Cavanaugh for back-up hardware and software.

My appreciation also extends to the design staff at Praeger and to Lynda Sharp, sociology editor, whose patience I sorely tried with all my questions. And boundless thanks, of course, go to all the contributors to this volume, without whom there would have been no book and no acknowledgments to write.

Since every project I undertake ultimately becomes a collective one, I must thank my patient and willing friends, relatives, and colleagues for their contributions, research, and proofreading: Karen Zimmerman for devotion beyond the call of sisterhood, Dot Logan, Beth Sherman, Sandy Boyer, Edie Kuven, Sheila Pinkel, Corky Bush, Raquel Scherr, Bonnie Zimmerman, Becky Allen, Shelley Savren, Idelfha Loyola, Doris Davidson, Catarina Martinez, Alida Allison, Kim Herber, and Wendy McBride. With all this help, I can only plead that whatever errors or faults remain are mine.

It is also customary in this space to thank one's lover, spouse, housemate, or any other intimates on whom the author has inflicted the tortures of production. It is relatively easy to thank my cat for the solace she offered, her "willingness" to be petted on my nights of dark despair. But how can I thank the woman with whom I share a house and a computer for all she has done? How can I thank her for putting up with my elation ("Oh boy, oh boy, Praeger's going to do the book!"); exhilaration ("Wait 'til you see all the terrific authors!"); depression ("We can't afford typesetting, not in this town."); desperation ("It'll never be done on time; no way."); 3 a.m. panic ("Wake up, quick! The computer just ate my file — and then it lost its cookies!"); exhaustion ("I can't read another word — ever."); and finally relief ("Not to worry. I shipped the paste-up out this morning."). I ask you, how can I thank such a woman? How do I tell her I'm planning to write another book? Give her a hug and do the laundry? It's not enough.

Jan Zimmerman

Contents

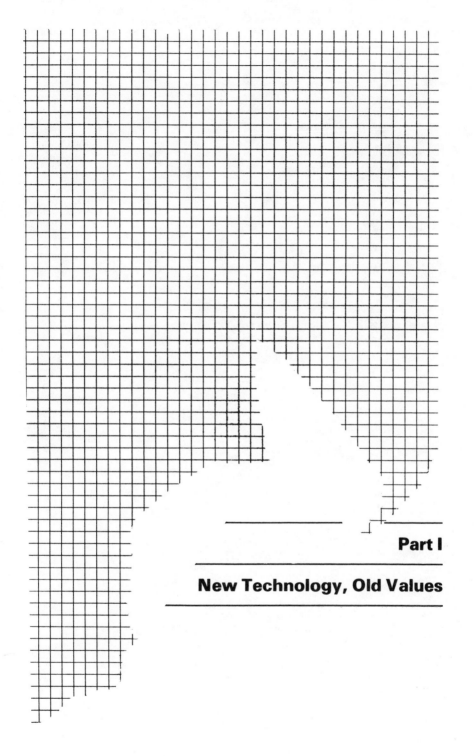

Part I

New Technology, Old Values

Chapter 1

Introduction

by Jan Zimmerman

One of the great asymmetries of our relativistic universe is the fact that time, unlike space, moves in only one direction — forward. We can run films or videotapes in reverse, but in reality it is impossible to put Humpty Dumpty's egg back together or to return a giant, blooming sunflower to its former state as a seed. In a not-so-funny-joke, however, new technology seems to be doing the impossible. It is running backward — back to a period before the current Women's Movement, back before the growth of multinational corporations, before the expansion of government-sponsored research, back before the suffragist era, back to the Industrial Revolution, to the Scientific Revolution, back perhaps to the early roots of capitalism and rationalism in the Middle Ages. The net result, as the articles in **The Technological Woman** show, is a future that can be read in women's history books — skip the crystal ball.

To find sexism, racism, classism, and a host of other values running as rapidly as electrons through the microcircuitry of tomorrow comes at first as a bit of a shock. Certainly we ought to be able to change the future, even if the present is proving a bit recalcitrant to our efforts. And if we acknowledge, as it is by now becoming fashionable to do, that technology is not neutral or value-free, then certainly we should be able to design new technologies that predispose society in desirable directions of social change.

And there, in that sentence, lie all the problems of determining the shape of tomorrow. Who is "we"? How does "design of new technology" take place? Who decides what is "desirable"? Can technology actually suggest a direction, or make some choices more probable than others, or must changes in political theory precede material change? Who wants "social change" anyway? Like every other human activity, technology reflects the values, thoughts, ideologies, beliefs, and biases of its creators. Sometimes it happens consciously, more often unconsciously, but inevitably the creators of tomorrow encode their value systems into the design, development, and marketing of their inventions. In this time (the next to the last decade before the twenty-first century) and in this place (Western postindustrial nations), those creators are almost all men. (Fact: in 1980 only 4 percent of the engineers in the United States were women.)

Not too long ago, in a more trusting age, advertisers besieged us with promises of "better living through chemistry"; assured us that "progress is our most important product"; promoted "atoms for peace" as our path to glory. Now sadder, if not wiser, from a growing awareness of the hazards of unexamined technological growth — toxic waste sites; cancer-causing chemicals in workplaces and homes; the Three Mile Island nuclear power plant failure; privacy-invading computer mailing lists — the public has become more wary of tomorrow's brave new worlds.

Yet public concern remains diffuse, easily distracted by media sugarplums of "golly, gee whiz" technology that will somehow get us out of the "mess" we've gotten ourselves into. Relatively little attention is paid to those ostensibly benign technologies, like dishwashers, buses, light bulbs, tractors, or calculators, that seem to have found their way into North American life. And even the most strident critics of technology seem oblivious to the idea that technology may have very different impacts on women's lives than it does on men's.

How else can we explain the deafening silence several years ago that greeted a commercial for the "office of the future"? It took a mere 60 seconds for women to be forbidden the use of a typewriter reserved for a single male, grudgingly admitted to the secretarial profession, forced into large, impersonal typing pools, confronted with electric and electronic memory typewriters that reduced the number of workers needed, and finally replaced by a single male running a computer-driven "paperless office." When women's future starts to look so disquietingly like their past, then it is time, as **The Technological Woman** insists, to make a critical, feminist assessment of technology as a force in women's lives.

Consider some horrifying possibilities (future scenarios in the lingo game). Women isolated at home, trapped in electronic cages, using cable TV, computers, and touch-tone phones for video shopping and telephone banking. Women reading **Family Circle** magazine on the TV screen to see which recipes they should pull from their home computer file, while daughter Jane plays with her voice-synthesized doll and son Dick plays computer chess. Women forced to do data entry or circuit board assembly from home for piecework pay, so they can work and care for children at the same time.

Consider women pushed out of the few jobs in which they predominate, as computers replace secretaries, bank tellers, and telephone operators. Women out of work because they were "allowed" into nontraditional, skilled crafts jobs in the 1970s, not realizing those jobs were slated for automation in the 1980s. Imagine women training for computer programming jobs, so they can march in the electronic revolution, only to find their place reserved, as usual, at the back of the line as programming becomes less skilled, less creative, and less well-paid.

As low-woman on the energy totem pole, women may find their time- and labor-saving home appliances the first victims of an energy shortage. They may lose second-car mobility (if, in spite of their relatively low earnings, they can afford one) for those "non-essential" trips to the nursery school, laundromat, and grocery store. And if some appropriate technologists have their way, women will use their spare time to grow their own food and build their own solar-solution houses.

Or dream the nightmare: women left out of the future altogether as genetic and reproductive engineering discoveries pair cloning with artificial wombs to make women extraneous even to biology. But nothing in the laws of nature decrees the banishment of women from offices, factories, or delivery rooms. As **The Technological Woman** states, it is politics, not electrons, that determine the path of progress.

This point is stressed in the first section, *New Technology, Old Values*, which uses the tools of history, linguistics, anthropology, mythology, and economics to consider how broad social forces influence the development of technology, and in turn how social value systems emphasizing differences in gender, race, and class become encased in technical developments. By contrast, the second section of the book, *Ladies' Home Technology*, travels from theory to reality, focusing on the particular potency of everyday technologies to structure the pattern of women's day-to-day lives in the private sphere. Far too many "daily use" technologies, from mass transit to frozen foods, have become invisible parts of an infrastructure whose elements serve to support existing power relationships.

In a complementary fashion, *A Living Wage* considers women in the public sphere as workers in technical environments, from blue collar to upper management. Sketching out both job opportunities and job loss from technological change, this section also acknowledges that pervasive patterns of exploitation, job segregation, and discrimination can be written into the future even as the Women's Movement seeks to expunge them from the present. Finally, *The Politics of Tomorrow* draws our attention to the ways that women can control technology to create a future that meets their needs and celebrates visions of a better world. Recognizing that control of one's body is central to the political dialogue of our time, this part emphasizes once again that social values are integral to debates over technological control.

The intertwining of politics and technology could easily lead us into endless arguments over the proper strategy for change: do we seek a technological "fix" or a socio-political one? Is technology itself so corrupted by its rational, distancing language and its historical thrust of dominating and exploiting nature that it cannot ever find positive expression? Is social change too weak to hold its center against the forces of the status quo without making specific efforts to embed new values into the design of an alternate material reality? The contributors to **The Technological Woman** do not agree on the solution; they only open up the discussion.

But they would all concede the truth of of the question posed by Rebecca Harding Davis, author of **Life in the Iron Mills**, who asked, "What are rights without means?" It is one thing to have the right to ride on the front of the bus, but what if the bus doesn't travel from home to work? It is one thing to have the right to enter technical careers, but what if childcare facilities are not available to make it feasible? **The Technological Woman** urges us to recognize that *means*, in fact, must also become *ends*; the struggle for change is more complicated than we thought.

What does this really imply for women in concrete cases? What can we learn from the authors in the section on *New Technology, Old Values* about women's role in invention and their relationship to the technological enterprise? Can this knowledge break down the mystique of technology, born partly out of ignorance and partly out of fear, that has set technology apart from feminist analysis?

The authors in this section would undoubtedly say "yes." Marian Lowe describes the social and political intent of biological theories used to "prove" women incapable of scientific thought, pointing out similarities between nineteenth century craniology and twentieth century sociobiology; Robin Tolmach Lakoff shows how the quantifying, distancing language of technology itself attempts to preclude women's participation. Two contributors delve into history: Carolyn Merchant draws parallels between women and nature as objects of domination during the Scientific Revolution of the seventeenth century, while Autumn Stanley searches for the common circumstances of black women inventors from 8000 b.c. to the present — anonymity, lack of validation, lack of money and technical knowledge, and achievement in spite of hardship.

Three authors look to current events for evidence of value systems embedded in technological development. In a stinging indictment of the "global assembly line," Maria Patricia Fernandez Kelly cites both the racist and sexist practices of high technology companies in the Third World. Margaret Benston finds evidence in North America of computer programming technologies that mirror the practices of the assembly line and set up women for failure through "blame the victim" strategies and emphasis on individual solutions to collective, social problems. Judy Smith, on the other hand, takes a close look at appropriate technology as an alternative to "high tech" and doesn't like the sexism she sees.

To be sure, this section is far from comprehensive in its coverage of consequences of technology that do not *have* to be. Age discrimination and heterosexual biases are two that seem to wend their ways into technology, although they are not mentioned in these pages. Nor does this section pretend to provide a detailed analysis of capitalism as a central force directing technological "progress."

Still, each of these writers, in her own way, writes an epitaph to the myth of technological determinism. This myth, which would have us blame the whims of Mother Nature rather than the hands of man for technical development, has protected technology from the critical scrutiny of feminists and others committed to the use of technology for human liberation, not enslavement to material reality. We begin.

Chapter 2

Sex Differences, Science,

And Society

by Marian Lowe

No one contests that men dominate most professions, especially scientific and technical fields. This, however, is almost the only aspect of sex and the professions about which there is agreement. Why the numbers of women and men in science, for example, are so different and how, or even whether, to change the situation are hotly debated issues. This, of course, is part of a larger debate about women's unequal representation in most professions, a debate which increasingly revolves around biological explanations for these observed inequalities. Since such ideas have important implications for women, just as they do when used to explain racial and class differences, we need to be aware both of the theories and of their potential impact.

Sex differences in abilities are said to arise from differences in biology: from genetic differences, sex differences in the brain, or hormonal differences. These differences are then said to result in different social roles, including participation in science and other male-dominated professions. All of these theories turn out to be unscientific, politically-loaded, fact-free speculation. Nevertheless, they may have important effects on efforts to change women's and men's roles in society and to change society itself.

The influence of these theories, in spite of their inaccuracy, can be seen from the incredible amount of attention they have been receiving. Books on them, such as Desmond Morris' **The Naked Ape** or E. O. Wilson's **On Human Nature**, have been best sellers and even have received Pulitzer prizes. Articles have appeared in an extremely wide range of publications, from professional journals to **Home and Garden** and **The National Observer**. Sunday newspapers that reach millions of people regularly carry the latest claims of the biological determinists, with prominent attention given to social and political implications, including women's lack of participation in high prestige occupations.

In an article in the New York **Times Sunday Magazine**, E. O. Wilson, a Harvard biologist, wrote that because of sex differences developed in the course of evolution, "even with identical education and equal access to all professions, men are likely to continue to play a disproportionate role in political life, business and science." Recently, the Sunday Boston **Globe** carried an article on brain differences that began, "Boys think differently than girls. Recent research on brain behavior makes that conclusion inescapable . . . . Social equality for men and women really depends on recognizing these differences in brain behavior." The article then went on to point out that in order to create social equality, there must be differential schooling for females and males. **The Canadian**, a Sunday newspaper supplement billed as Canada's largest circulation magazine, also recently carried an article on brain differences that states, "There is mounting evidence that the brain does possess natural male and female characteristics. . . . Biological differences in the brain may account for the fact that the majority of engineers . . . are men and the majority of secretaries are women."

The idea that biology is destiny is prominently displayed in all of this work. Stereotypes of masculine and feminine behavior and roles are reinforced, and perhaps even created, by giving them the legitimacy of natural law. In order to understand fully the way in which the sex role stereotypes portrayed by biological theorists keep women out of a large number of professions, it is useful to take a look at the connection between gender and science, or more specifically, scientific rationalism, the philosophical basis of the modern view of the world.

Scientific Rationalism

Science is seen as male, as an essentially masculine activity, not only because historically almost all scientists have been men, but also because the attributes of science itself are defined as the attributes of males. Modern science stands back from nature, to observe, quantify, and ultimately control it. Science is thus seen as objective instead of subjective, active instead of passive, logical instead of intuitive, rational instead of emotional. Under capitalism in particular, the goal of the scientific enterprise has been to understand how the physical world works in order to dominate it; in turn, scientific rationalism has become the dominant way of looking at the world throughout Western industrial society. Then, since science and the scientific world view deal with power, science is seen as masculine. Its attributes have come to be equated with the attributes of men, while the opposite attributes have come to be associated with women.

Masculine and feminine characteristics were seen as distinct long before the rise of modern science, of course. In all cultures in which women lack power, they usually have been seen as deficient in intellect in some way. However, the domination of scientific rationalism in Western society has meant that the specific traits assigned to women and men in our own culture have been strongly influenced by the definition of traits necessary to think "scientifically."

By the late nineteenth century, the scientific world view had become dominant and the particular characteristics ascribed to women and to men took on their modern form. Scientists naturally turned to the question of the origin of these sex differences in behavior which they took to be universal, and looked for their basis in natural law. Their belief that society was founded on biological or physical laws made it reasonable to look for biological explanations for women's nature as the emotional, subjective nurturer and men's nature as the rational, objective doer. It is useful to look at these theories of the past century since many of the arguments we see now are direct descendants of these ideas.

The Nineteenth Century: Evolution, Hormones, and the Brain

In the nineteenth century there were two basic biological theories abut the origins of human behavior. The first approach was an evolutionary one, called Social Darwinism, based on Darwin's theory of evolution through natural selection. Social scientists and biologists attempted to root differences in behavior in differing evolutionary pressures on the sexes. The second approach tried to find direct biological causes of behavior by demonstrating a connection between some biological feature, such as brain size, and a given trait, such as intelligence.

Evolutionary theories were generally based on one of the central themes of evolutionary literature, the increasing sexual division of labor. As one went up the evolutionary ladder, female and male behavior patterns increasingly differentiated. Scientists claimed that males, in general, became more aggressive and more intelligent, while females devoted more time to maternal behavior. Among humans, the culmination of evolutionary progress, women's primary function was said to be raising children, a task for which intelligence and the power of abstract reasoning were not necessary. Specifically, it was claimed that women's physical evolution had actually stopped at an earlier stage than had men's, in order to conserve energy for reproduction, so that women showed less development of the nervous system. This resulted in a smaller mental capacity. There was little or no evidence put forward for any of these claims. In general, scientists just assumed that whichever behavioral difference they were interested in, existed and that it was biologically determined. Their theories then dealt with why such a difference might have made evolutionary sense.

The evolutionary theories provided a framework for the second kind of work — the search for direct biological evidence of the differences presumably created by evolution. One important area involved studies of sex differences in the brain. Much of the early work was done on race, but eventually scientists, fearing that demands for women's rights threatened "to divert the orderly progress of evolution," decided to examine the position of women "rationally and objectively," using the tools of science. Scientists believed that social reformers' ideas about the intellectual equality of women violated nature and would have a "most baneful effect in unsettling society." The science of craniology or skull measurement became a promising tool for demonstrating what scientists saw as the misguided thinking of social reformers who advocated equality for women.

Craniologists assumed that intelligence was directly related to brain size. Results on different racial groups had already seemed to bear this out. Whites appeared to have bigger brains than Native Americans, Orientals or Blacks. (We now know that the measurements came out this way only because the craniologists expected them to do so; they manipulated their data to fit their ideas, in some cases, quite unconsciously). It was clear to craniologists that if brain size were correlated with intelligence, men must have bigger brains than women, since they were sure that men were smarter. In this case, the data did not have to be manipulated to get the expected answer, since on the average, women do have smaller brains than men. However, it was also apparent that women have smaller bodies than men and this created a dilemma. If sheer size of the brain, independent of body size, were to be directly related to mental capacity, whales and elephants ought to be a lot smarter than human beings. The "elephant problem" eventually led to the disappearance of craniology as a serious scientific field. No one could find an obvious way of taking body size into account that convincingly demonstrated male intellectual superiority. The most obvious way of dealing with differences in body size was to take the ratio of brain weight to body weight, but, unfortunately, women came out ahead by this measure.

At the same time that craniologists were struggling with sex differences in whole brain size, other scientists were working with specific areas of the brain trying to show that one lobe or another was different in size in women and men. This work ran into difficulties of the same sort as craniology and it, too, was eventually abandoned. Still other scientists, particularly in the medical profession, used observed differences in social behavior as evidence of differences in biology, such as differences in the nervous systems of women and men or differences in energy levels. These postulated biological differences were then cited as independent proof that sex differences in behavior were innate.

By the beginning of the twentieth century, most of these theories were no longer important as science. They were abandoned not because they were seen as unscientific, however, but because they did not work. They did not produce convincing evidence of biological causes for assumed differences between groups. Craniology, for example, failed to produce an index that could be tied to differences in average intelligence between groups, one which would consistently put white men ahead, where everyone knew they belonged.

In the early twentieth century, work on newly discovered sex hormones appeared for a time to offer a new approach. It was thought initially that sex hormones were specific to the sexes, that the male hormones (androgens) were produced only by males and female hormones (estrogens) only by females. It was assumed that these hormones were responsible for the development of the characteristics of each sex. Thus it appeared that sex differences could once and for áll be reduced to straightforward biological differences. Eventually, however, hormonal theories went out of fashion when it became clear that both hormones occurred in both sexes and, furthermore, that there was no simple relationship between hormone levels and behavior. At this point in history, biological theories lost their prominence. From the demise of the hormonal theories until the 1970s, discussions of sex differences have been dominated by the ideas of Freud, which are implicitly rather than explicitly deterministic.

With the entrance of large numbers of women into the wage labor force in the last few decades and with a vocal Women's Movement demanding equal access to male-dominated professions, including science, the question of the origins of women's inequality has become a major social issue. The response has been a resurgence of explicitly biological theories of the origin of sex differences. Assertions of biologically-based sex differences in mathematical ability, aggression, and nurturance have been used to explain the under-representation of women in most aspects of public life. Contemporary theories follow the same two basic approaches as nineteenth century biological determinism. There is an evolutionary approach, which claims that certain sex differences are genetically determined and asks *why* these alleged differences arose. And there is a great deal of work on the second approach, which searches for direct biological causation.

The Twentieth Century: Evolution, . . .

Like nineteenth century theories, twentieth century evolutionary explanations of human social behavior rely heavily on sex differences. The most influential version appeared in 1975 with the publication of E. O. Wilson's book, **Sociobiology**. Wilson defines sociobiology as "the systematic study of the biological basis of all social behavior." The theory tries to use Darwinian natural selection to explain the origins and basis of social behavior in all species, including humans. Those organisms which can pass on the most genes are *assumed* to be those that will be most successful in evolutionary terms. They are the fittest. The genes can be passed on directly by reproducing, or indirectly by helping close relatives, who share genes, to reproduce. Genetically determined behaviors which lead to more reproduction, that is, which are "adaptive," either for the individual or for relatives, will be those passed on from one generation to another.

It is critical for the sociobiological argument that behavior be genetically determined. However, it is extremely difficult to say how much of any animal's behavior is due to genes and how much is environmentally influenced. This is particularly true for human beings, with our large capacity to learn and to pass on behavior by learning from one generation to another. This means that being able to show that a behavioral trait is adaptive is not a sufficient demonstration that it is genetically determined. Wilson's theory has been formulated in such a way that *any* behavior can be explained as adaptive. But clearly, not all human activities are directed by genes. Human culture, a product of the human mind, must be involved in at least some human activities. Then how can we figure out how or whether it is biology or environment that contributes to behavior? Everything seems to have both a biological and a cultural explanation. Sociobiology offers no guidelines for choosing one kind of explanation over another.

Sociobiology, then, like nineteenth century theories, offers no evidence within the theory itself that behavior is genetically determined. It does try to use other evidence to demonstrate that the behaviors it treats are indeed biologically determined. Major weight has been given to comparisons between human and other primate societies. For example, Wilson looks for "conservative" traits, any traits which are observed in all primates, since he claims that these are "the ones most likely to have persisted in relatively unaltered form into the evolution of *Homo* ." In addition, universals in human behavior are looked for across culture, under the assumption that if a trait is observed at least to some degree in all human cultures, it must be, at least in part, genetically determined. Social traits that are both universal and conservative are then to be taken as genetically determined and used to develop sociobiological arguments.

Because a case is made in this particular way for a genetic basis for behavior, sex differences turn out to be fundamental to the theory. David Barash, in his popularized version of sociobiology, **Sociobiology and Behavior**, acknowledges this when he says, "Sociobiology relies heavily upon the biology of male-female differences and upon the adaptive behavioral differences that have evolved accordingly. Ironically, mother nature appears to be a sexist." We see the role played by sex differences when we look at the social traits listed in Wilson's book as both universal and conservative: "aggressive dominance systems with males generally dominant over females; scaling of responses, especially during aggressive interaction; intensive and prolonged maternal care, with a pronounced degree of socialization in the young; and matrilineal social organization." Since Wilson argues that males are naturally more aggressive than females, we can see that all of these traits are based on sex differences, not on species universals. Other social traits that are then said to be universal are derived from these more fundamental traits, including a hierarchically-structured society and of course, a sexual division of labor which follows current sex role stereotypes.

There has been extensive criticism of sociobiological demonstrations of innate behavior in humans; a close look at the assumptions and data on which the conclusions rest suggests that they are no better than those of the nineteenth century. For example, it has been shown that the traits listed above, which Wilson uses as the basis of his theorizing, are neither conservative nor universal, and it was only selective use or misrepresentation of data and ambiguous definitions of terms, probably caused by his own prior expectations, that allowed this list to be compiled. Other critics have questioned the use of *any* animal studies for theories of human behavior. In addition, it has been pointed out that even if behavior were observed universally in all human societies, we could not necessarily conclude that the behavior arose because of evolution. In the end, sociobiology fails to demonstrate that human social behavior is subject to evolutionary pressures, or that a genetically-based human nature or genetically-based sex differences exist. As a number of critics have pointed out, the extent to which genes or biology influence complex social behavior is probably unknowable, at least at the present time. Nevertheless, sociobiology has been heralded as a major breakthrough by the media, and popularizations emphasize its social implications. Remember Wilson's assertion that even with equal opportunity women will never achieve equality. David Barash writes, ". . .women have almost universally found themselves relegated to the nursery while men derive their greatest satisfaction from their jobs," while a film entitled, **Sociobiology: Doing What Comes Naturally**, lays heavy emphasis on sex role differences, arguing against the "assertions of the women's liberation movement."

. . . Hormones . . .

The evolutionary theory makes no direct statement about intelligence differences, since it emphasizes women's maternal role and men's competitiveness and drive for power over others. The biological causal theories focus on differences in intellectual abilities as well as differences in aggression and nurturance. The sheer variety of theories offered is rather overwhelming and the general tendency is clear. Scientists, convinced that behavioral sex differences exist and are biologically determined, simply look until they find some biological factor that appears to be correlated. Sex differences in the brain, genetic differences, and sex hormones have all been claimed as biological causes for behavioral sex differences.

Hormonal differences have been a favorite candidate for causing supposed differences in aggression. One theory, based on the male sex hormone, testosterone, outlined in a book called **The Inevitability of Patriarchy** by Steven Goldberg, makes the following (unsubstantiated) connections: male equals testosterone, testosterone equals aggression, aggression equals dominance and political power. Therefore men will inevitably, in any social setting, have power and women will not. This, of course, implies the exclusion of most women from all professions that involve significant amounts of power, including science.

Somewhat more sophisticated, and much more widely publicized, is a group of theories that suggest that the human brain is programmed before birth by sex hormones, so that males and females show different degrees of aggressiveness and different reproductive behavior. The only direct evidence for permanent effects of sex hormones on the brain comes from studies of animals, primarily laboratory rats. It has been concluded by manipulating rodent hormones that female and male hormones have an "organizing" effect on the fetal or newborn brain. This effect originally was thought to cause appropriate female and male mating behavior, although it now appears that the causal relationships may not be quite so absolute.

The original causal model of rodent brain programming has provided the basis for theories about the sexual differentiation of brains in general, even though the model is probably too simple even for rodents and even though the same effects are not seen in all animals. In nonhuman primates, our closest relatives, experiments with sex hormones simply do not show the same results, and there is no reason to expect that they would be seen in humans if the experiments could be done. Nevertheless, the rat results are widely cited as evidence for programming of the *human* brain.

Furthermore, indirect evidence for such preprogramming of the brain by hormones has been claimed. These studies have involved people with various genetic and hormonal abnormalities: females exposed while still in the womb to unusually high levels of the hormone androgen, either because of malfunctioning adrenal glands or administration of hormones to their mothers, for example. The most important of many problems with these human behavioral studies is that they have failed to control for any environmental differences encountered by people with and without the observed abnormalities. In the end, the studies simply do not allow the conclusions that are drawn about programming of the human brain. Nevertheless, like craniology in its day, the idea of sex differences in the brain brought about by the action of sex hormones is widely accepted, both within and outside the scientific profession.

. . . and the Brain . . .

Current theories of innate sex differences in intellectual abilities, unlike their nineteenth century counterparts, usually do not claim that women are less intelligent than men. Instead they focus on tests of different types of mental abilities, and use these tests to explain why women are not good at mathematics and science. Women do better on questions identified as verbal on IQ tests, while men do better on more mathematical ones and on questions involving visual-spatial ability. The magnitude of the differences and the age at which they appear are matters of some disagreement. In general, there is a great deal of overlap in the distribution of scores, while the sex differences in average scores are quite small compared with their spread and vary from one culture to another. Some studies of verbal and mathematical ability even find no differences.

The difference in visual-spatial ability has received a tremendous amount of attention, and the theories about its origin are overwhelmingly biological. Significantly, the difference in verbal ability, where males seem to do less well, is more often given an environmental explanation.

One theory of visual-spatial sex differences offers a genetic explanation. It is hypothesized that a recessive gene for visual-spatial ability is carried on the X-chromosome. This is dubious genetics, at best, since simple recessive-dominant arguments do not necessarily apply to X-linked characteristics, but in any case, studies of the relationship between visual-spatial ability of parents and children find nothing that is in accord with such a theory.

Another group of theories takes up the idea of preprogramming the brain by sex hormones and suggests that this not only causes differences in aggressive behavior but also differences in intellectual abilities. One rather tortuous speculation starts with the assumption that levels of female and male hormones affect the brain at puberty and that both types of hormones are negatively related to visual-spatial ability; that is, the lower the level of hormone, the higher the visual-spatial ability. But, the theory says, the effect is greater for testosterone (the male hormone) than for estrogen (the female hormone). Thus females with low estrogen levels and males with low testosterone levels should do best on visual-spatial tests, but males overall should do better than females. Just recently, in fact, a study appeared (and made headlines in a number of newspapers) showing just the opposite: men with high levels of testosterone seemed to have high visual-spatial ability. However, this study, like previous ones, failed to control for any effect of environmental differences found by those with and without the abnormalities.

A third explanation given for sex differences in visual-spatial abilities (and also for verbal differences) is provided by theories suggesting that innate sex differences exist in the way the two halves, or hemispheres, of the brain are used. In humans, although the interactions of the two sides of the brain are complex, the right and left halves are to some extent specialized for different tasks, a phenomenon called lateralization. The left hemisphere in most people appears to be more involved in performing verbal tasks and tasks that involve analytical thinking, while the right hemisphere seems more active during visual-spatial tasks or when thinking intuitively or associatively.

A number of studies have claimed to show a connection between sex differences in brain lateralization and sex differences in visual-spatial and verbal abilities, but such claims are largely fact-free speculation, since there is no evidence for simple, clear-cut sex differences in brain lateralization. Even if such evidence existed, it would not necessarily mean that the differences were innate. Studies show that brain lateralization can be affected by environment and behavior, and that it is by no means a fixed aspect of the brain. The type and degree of differential use of the hemispheres appears to be affected by mood, motivation, and training. For example, after biofeedback training, people are able to produce more or less asymmetry at will on tasks for which they previously preferentially used one side or the other of the brain.

A little thought shows that there is going to be a great deal of difficulty in trying to connect sex differences in abilities with brain lateralization in any straightforward way, since the way the two halves of the brain appear to be specialized for skills is not the same way sex role stereotypes divide up skills between women and men. The left half of the brain is thought to be specialized more for both verbal and logical skills, but women do better on verbal tests, while men are widely held to be more analytical and logical. The right half of the brain, on the other hand, appears to be more involved in visual-spatial ability, at which men are better, and in intuitive thinking, a trait usually assigned to women. The contortions that some investigators have gone through to try to handle this problem are reminiscent of those of the craniologists.

The tendency to look for biological bases is so strong that at times simply an observation of a behavioral difference is seen as enough evidence that a biological difference exists. An important example of this occurred recently with an article on sex differences in mathematical ability by C. Benbow and J. Stanley in **Science**. They examined scores on the mathematical part of the Scholastic Aptitude Test and reported that seventh and eighth grade students showed significant differences by sex on the exam. The average scores were different and there were significantly more boys at the high end of the distribution — the proportion of girls and boys scoring above 600 was very different, and each year the highest score received by a girl was considerably lower than the highest boy's score. They point out that the number of math courses taken was the same for girls and boys. They suggest that other environmental differences may not be too important, and conclude, with some caution, that perhaps one should consider a genetic explanation. An editorial in the same issue of **Science** ignores the caution of Benbow and Stanley and highlights the statements about biological causes. Furthermore, the study was immediately picked up by newspapers and weekly news magazines, which headlined their stories with words like "math genes." The study was cited in Senate hearings as a reason why programs designed to bring more women into science should not be funded.

Biology As Politics

Ideas about biologically-based differences in behavior between women and men are very widespread at the present time, even though there is no better basis for them today than there was in the nineteenth century. The attention given by the media to any study which claims to have demonstrated a biological cause for sex differences in behavior (or race differences or class differences) indicates the political nature of such theories. They end up reinforcing social stereotypes and suggesting that our social structures are "natural" and that we should be very careful about trying to change them. The net effect of theories about such things as female and male brains, sex differences in aggression, or math genes is to reinforce the already widespread belief that women simply do not have a mind that is compatible with success in male-dominated occupations, especially science and technology.

This belief, which may even be growing in spite of the increasing numbers of women entering science and other professions, is one of the major factors keeping women out of these occupations. The evidence is clear that women behave, think, and produce pretty much like male scientists when they are in similar situations. Nevertheless, these women are seen as exceptions and the belief persists that women are not really suited for scientific, or rational, logical thinking. The stereotypes continue in spite of the fact that women and men are in general much more alike than different, and the magnitude of observed average differences in behavior or abilities, which may be overestimated, is much smaller than are the differences between women's and men's social roles. For example, differences in mathematical ability are often cited as the reason for the small number of women scientists and engineers. But the differences in participation rates of women and men in scientific fields in our society are so much larger than the reported sex differences in mathematical ability, that differences in ability could not begin to account for the different numbers of women and men scientists. In general, observed sex and race differences in behavior, biologically-based or not, would explain only a small part of our social hierarchy, even if merit and ability were the most important factors.

We need to be conscious of both the direct and indirect effects of these theories on behavior. Any theory which discusses the origins and theoretical limitations on human behavior has the potential for affecting behavior, and even biology itself. It can become a self-fulfilling prophecy, creating the very differences it purports to explain. If some children are told that they are not as capable of doing mathematics as others, then they will probably end up worse at it. If women are told that nature made them less aggressive than men, we should not be surprised if they end up acting in less aggressive ways.

Finally, biological theories about sex differences — differences that in at least some cases may not exist — reinforce the perception that such divisions in female and male qualities are natural. They reinforce sex roles and, ultimately, justify the whole power structure of society. As a consequence, we end up spending a great deal of time arguing about the origins of sex roles, not about their appropriateness.

Notes

R. Arditti, P. Brennan, and S. Cavrak, eds., *Science and Liberation* (Boston: South End Press, 1980).

Brighton Women and Science Group, eds., IAlice Through the Microscope (London: Virago, 1980).

R. Hubbard, M. S. Henefin, and B. Fried, eds., *Women Look at Biology Looking at Women* (Cambridge, MA: Schenkman, 1979).

R. Hubbard and M. Lowe, eds., *Genes and Gender II: Pitfalls in Research on Sex and Gender* (New York: Gordian, 1979).

Special issue on "Women and Science," *International Journal of Women's Studies* 4 (September/October 1981).

Special issue on "Women and Science," *Signs* 4 (Winter 1978).

Chapter 3

Gender and Industry on

Mexico's New Frontier

by Maria Patricia Fernandez Kelly

Less than a decade ago it was still fashionable to ponder the extent to which the use of machines would free women's time and enable them to participate more fully in the flow of social and economic life. During the 1950s and 1960s, the proponents of modernization were able to assert with optimism that, thanks to technological progress, women would be relieved from the burdens of housework and childrearing, and would be able to participate in the public sphere. Nevertheless, during the following decade, many writers came to a different conclusion; they found that the impact of technology upon women's socioeconomic status has been far from uniform throughout the world.[1]

The relevance of questions regarding the relationship between sophisticated machines and gender is no longer confined to established industrial nations such as the United States. Advanced technology has made possible the further integration of the world system of production and the transformation of manufacturing processes being carried out overseas. Therefore, it is necessary to explore not only the connection between gender and machines inside U.S. households, but also the ways in which refined technology designed by industrial powers is affecting employment opportunities and the quality of worklife for women in developing nations.

One of the consequences of modern technological development has been the incorporation of vast numbers of women from developing countries into Export Processing Zones (EPZs) where electrical and electronics goods are assembled. As a concrete instance this paper examines the proliferation of electronics assembly plants under the Mexican Border Industrialization and *Maquiladora* Programs.[2]

A basic premise underlying my argument is that it is impossible to gain full insight into some of the most interesting trends in international production without giving attention to the part that women are playing all over the world. Both as operators or consumers of electronics goods inside or outside the home and as active participants in their manufacture, women at various points of the geopolitical spectrum are deeply affected by the extension of sophisticated machinery.

18

International Capital, and Manufacture

The movement of assembly work to Third World EPZs cannot be seen in isolation from the major transition from manufacturing to services that has occurred in the United States. In the last 20 years there has been a gradual drop in blue collar employment and a rapid expansion in the number and range of services offered in this country. This phenomenon has affected not only light and competitive branches such as textiles and garment manufacturing, but also highly capitalized industries such as steel and automobiles.

Several causes explain the movement toward a service economy. In part the reduction of employment in manufacturing has been due to higher educational levels and higher expectations. A major recession has sent shock waves into heavy industry. Foreign competition has contributed to reduce employment in automobile production. Nevertheless, another factor has played a paramount role in this shift: the transfer of production to low-wage areas of the world. The electronics industry has been at the forefront of this last trend.

Stirred by constant innovation, scientific breakthroughs, and the need to remain competitive in the international market, electronics firms have sought to maximize their profits by locating operations in areas of the world where productivity is high and the cost of labor low. Thus, such well-known manufacturers as RCA, Sylvania, IBM, National Cash Register, Intel, and Texas Instruments have opened subsidiaries in EPZs located in various parts of the globe.[3]

According to figures collected by the United Nations Industrial Development Organization, there are at present approximately 120 EPZs in developing countries.[4] More than a clearly defined territorial category, Export Processing Zones flow from government-sponsored incentive packages meant to stimulate foreign investment in export-directed manufacturing. Accordingly, host countries have offered multinational corporations looser customs restrictions, tax exemptions, and a variety of infrastructural advantages (ranging from industrial parks to improved communications and transportation facilities) in exchange for the creation of jobs.

For large corporations the benefits from investment in manufactures for export are a consequence of large international wage differentials and other factors that substantially reduce the costs of production. Thus, while borders continue to have political significance, from an economic point of view they have grown increasingly permeable.

A good way to understand this is to say that the world is rapidly moving toward a highly centralized arrangement in which advanced industrial nations such as the United States retain control over research and development, technological expertise, decisions affecting production, and the distribution of financial outflow. Simultaneously, developing countries have become the source of cheap labor for the manufacture of exportable goods, many of which are electrical and electronic gadgets. In advanced and Third World countries, this arrangement has been the result of innovations in the nature and velocity of international investments.

In consonance with this scheme, electronics manufacturing, for the most part, is being carried out in the EPZs of Asia, Latin America, the Caribbean Basin, and Africa. Thus, in the same way that the transition from manufacturing to services indicates changes in the role of the United States, the growth of manufactures for export in developing countries portends complementary transformations. And as the expansion of world-wide corporate investment has accelerated, the integration of the international system of production has become a vibrant reality.

Export Processing Zones have also represented a net shift of economic emphasis in many developing countries, whose mode of insertion into the world economy has shifted from a base relying mostly on the exploitation of primary resources and labor to one in which assembled goods have gained preponderance. Latin America is no exception to this trend. Several recent studies on the subject point out that the region has shifted in the last 15 years from a stage of inward-directed growth to a stage of outward-directed expansion. In the words of Anibal Pinto this may represent "an unequivocal opening to the exterior."[5]

In Latin America the focus on manufactures for export follows a long period during which countries struggled to consolidate their national economies on the basis of "import substitution." After centuries of colonialism and dependency on central economies, Latin American nations attempted during the 1930s and 1940s to gain political and economic autonomy. Countries like Mexico tried to curtail their dependence on imported manufactured goods by producing them internally, while expanding markets for their own exports. Nevertheless, several decades of import substitution proved, for the most part, unsuccessful. Rather than reducing poverty, industrialization exacerbated of migration, widened internal income differentials, accentuated urban poverty, and generated other related problems.

Since the 1960s many Latin American countries have been complementing their efforts towards the consolidation of a national industry by offering incentives to multinational corporations involved in manufacturing for export. The precursor of this new trend was Puerto Rico. In the 1950s this country embarked in a developmental project similar to the ones that were to boom a decade later in Asia and along the U.S.-Mexican border. But while in Puerto Rico the emphasis was on the manufacture of garments, in Asia and Latin America it has been on electrical and electronics assembly.

The Global Assembly Line

During this same period the semiconductor industry established a unique form of international production which observers have labeled the "integrated global assembly line."[6] Fairchild opened the first "offshore" semiconductor assembly plant in Hong Kong in 1962 and then transferred operations to Korea in 1966. General Instruments moved microelectronics assembly to Taiwan in 1964. Similarly, assembly subcontractors, that is, independent companies that do assembly processes for manufacturers, began working in Indonesia and the Philippines in 1972. Other firms have established plants in India, Mauritius, and Latin America. Nonetheless most semiconductor assembly is still carried out in Southeast Asia. Approximately 300,000 women — half the workforce in Asian manufacturing plants — are employed in electronics assembly.

The effects of EPZs in Asia have been far from uniform. In places like Singapore, Hong Kong, and Taiwan they have created a veneer of prosperity and generated hundreds of thousands of jobs. However, in countries like Sri Lanka and Philippines, export processing has caused considerable dislocation by exacerbating rural-urban migration, transforming arable land into industrial parks, forcing the relocation of large human contingents, and accentuating cultural tensions.[7]

In addition, the growth of EPZs has been made possible in some places only through the implementation of martial law and the perpetuation of highly authoritarian governments. Such is the case in the Philippines, Korea, and Taiwan. In these countries violations of human rights are commonplace, unionization and other forms of worker organization are prohibited by law, and hourly wages average 35 cents.

But what makes the growth of export manufacturing in developing countries particularly interesting, from the point of view of this essay, is its heavy reliance on female unskilled and semiskilled labor; between 85 and 90 percent of those employed in Export Processing Zones throughout the world are women, the majority of whom are young and single. About 2 million women in Asia and Latin America share this form of employment.[8] And rather than diminishing in size, this number is growing. Thus, while the economic significance of women's employment in EPZs may still be limited when seen in the broader international context, it also points to a trend which will become more important in the coming years.

Why are women preferred for this kind of employment? The conventional wisdom among government officials and personnel managers is that because of their patience and manual dexterity, women are well suited for minute, monotonous operations. But, is it not true that in both the past and the present men have partaken of occupations requiring high levels of manual skill? Brain surgeons, pianists, and miniature painters come to mind. Thus, while it is true that women historically have been employed in poorly paid, repetitive, unskilled or semiskilled work, the emphasis on dexterity contains only an element of truth. When the productive system is examined as a whole, it becomes apparent that women are hired to perform the tedious and unrewarding operations that accompany assembly work for reasons that are political and economic, not psychological or anatomical.

Because of their behavior, expectations, and attitudes (which are the result of socialization processes in which gender plays an important part); because of their comparative youth; and because of their subordinate position in their own households, these women constitute a highly vulnerable, docile, and manipulatable workforce. Their employment in low-paying unskilled and semiskilled jobs offers distinct advantages from industry's point of view.

The *Maquiladora* Program

A good example of the conditions that surround women's employment in EPZs is found along the U.S.-Mexican border, where a booming assembly plant (*maquiladora*) program has been in existence since the mid-1960s. The growth of the *maquiladora* industry is consistent with capitalist logic: *maquiladoras* have enabled international capital to penetrate local economies in search of low wage scales, the availability of what appears to be an inexhaustible supply of unskilled and semiskilled labor, high levels of productivity, and a tractable workforce.

Historically, the birth of border industrialization followed the termination of the *Bracero* Program by unilateral decision of the U.S. Congress at the end of 1964. The dramatic rise in unemployment that ensued made it convenient to contemplate efforts aimed at neutralizing the political risks posed by large contingents of idle agricultural workers (the majority of whom were male). In addition, two crucial sections of the U.S. Customs Code[9] and stimuli granted by Mexico to foreign investment[10] also played a part in facilitating the expansion of *maquiladoras*.

The official implementation of this industrializing experiment was forced by the informal transactions carried out between multinational corporations and local border entrepreneurs. Even prior to the regularization by government, business representatives in border cities were actively involved in the provision of infrastructure for multinational assembly plants. For example, in Ciudad Juarez (whose talented business representatives claim to be the cradle of the *maquiladora* industry), the Jaime Bermudez Industrial Park dates back to 1968. Since then, Mexican investors have been subsidizing international investments by financing infrastructural facilities.

By 1972 the points for the legitimation of the *Maquiladora* Program had been clearly articulated by government. They had also been extended beyond the 12.5-mile border belt to cover all but three areas of the country. In this manner the juridical bases were established to transform all of Mexico into an Export Processing Zone. In this case, as in some others, the state intervened to rationalize and sanction the growth of a phenomenon that had been made inevitable by large international economic and political forces. In combination with a local class of entrepreneurs and foreign corporate investors, the Mexican government took a decided turn-about from traditional industrial policy.[11]

As in the case of other countries where EPZs have flourished, Mexico's dependence on the *Maquiladora* Program has been limited. Nevertheless it has gained enough importance to be regarded by public officials as a central aspect of Mexico's strategy for development. At present, the *Maquiladora* Program accounts for 25 percent of Mexico's manufactured exports and 10.5 percent of total exports. It is also the fastest growing sector of the economy (including petroleum-related activities) and it employs approximately 156,000 persons. In a manner similar to that which has prevailed in the Orient, 60 percent of all goods manufactured under the *Maquiladora* Program are assembled in electrical and electronics plants.

Among the stated goals of Mexican public officials in their support for *maquiladoras* were three that are particularly relevant to this essay: (1) the creation of jobs; (2) the upgrading of skills; and (3) the transfer of technology of potential importance to national industry. Without serious empirical evaluation, it has been assumed that while the *Maquiladora* Program has imposed some social costs, it has on the whole, met these goals. To substantiate this impression a finger is pointed at the more than 100,000 jobs that the program has generated in less than 15 years. It is also sometimes assumed that by providing jobs, the program is establishing the basis for the growth of a border middle class and furthering the cause of women by allowing them to gain autonomy through remunerated work.

Women on the Industrial Frontier

In order to obtain a balanced view, it is necessary to explore the meaning of export manufacturing in the light of research, not assumptions. Border industrialization has had a peculiar, unintended result: far from providing occupational opportunities for those who had been most affected by the elimination of the *Bracero* Program (i.e., male agricultural workers), instead it precipitated the entrance of formerly "unemployable" women (particularly those who are young and single) into the workforce. In this manner, a new contingent of highly vulnerable, docile, and easily replaceable laborers emerged; 85 percent of the *maquiladora* workers in Cuidad Juarez are female. The equivalent figure for similar plants in all of Mexico is 75 percent.

In the same vein, when only the number of *maquiladora* jobs is considered, the program seems like a success. Nevertheless, when the nature and length of employment are taken into consideration, sobering doubts disturb the calm surface of self-congratulatory appraisals. It is known that the average stay of *maquiladora* workers on their jobs is less than three years. While many young women leave their jobs prompted by cultural notions regarding marriage and motherhood, many more do so as a response to the many disincentives of *maquiladora* work.

Low wages (averaging less than 90 cents an hour), long work weeks (48 hours), numbing manual work, and high production quotas combine to deter permanent employment. Asseblers often leave their jobs temporarily in order to "rest," and then rejoin the workforce at a later point in time. While this may be a salutary palliative to assuage tedium, it also prevents women from achieving the benefits of seniority. Thus, the trend is toward temporary and unstable employment. There are also indications that because managers believe women to be "supplementary" wage earners whose main responsibilities are in the home, they do not encourage permanence on the job.

But *maquiladora* workers cannot be considered "supplementary" wage earners. They contribute, on the average, more than half of their weekly wages to family expenditures and use a substantial amount of what is left to pay for meals in the workplace and job-related transportation. In Ciudad Juarez women work as members of households for whose subsistence their wages are vital. Since 49 percent of the population in that city is 14 years of age or younger, it obvious that the need to provide for the needs of children — either offspring or siblings — is a contributing factor in precipitating women's search for employment.

From a personal standpoint, the rationale that often compels young women to seek wage employment is best illustrated by a statement from Teresa, whom I met while standing in line for a job interview at a *maquiladora* :

> I am single, thanks be to God! But my sister Beatriz married when she was only 15. Now she is divorced and has three children to support. All of us live with my parents. Beatriz and I are the oldest in the family, you see, that's why we really have to find a job.

Perhaps more important in this respect is the scarcity of viable occupational alternatives for men in the families of *maquiladora* workers: the majority of men who share households with female assembly operators in Ciudad Juarez are either unemployed or underemployed. In order of importance the occupations of these men were unskilled construction worker, petty clerk, general unskilled worker, and street vendor.[12]

The potential advantages derived from unemployment are not overlooked by firms. For example, according to top management at Electro Componentes de Mexico, the subsidiary of General Electric in Ciudad Juarez, "because of the high levels of unemployment and underemployment, which in this city surpass 30 percent, we can be highly selective with the personnel we employ."[13]

There is, therefore, a convergence between labor market conditions and familial needs that facilitates the flow of women as suppliers of labor for *maquiladoras* . The result of this has been the rapid transformation of women into the main providers of a stable and regular income (however small this may be) for their families.

The case of the Mexican border demonstrates that an abundance of women in search of jobs can be made possible by men's inability to gain access to gainful employment. This is not to say that the desire for an independent income and personal fulfillment do not play a part in the search for a job. But in countries like Mexico, where for better or worse women aspire and are encouraged to become mothers and/or housewives, female factory work does not necessarily indicate an expansion of alternatives. In fact, some of the worst stereotypes of female roles are reproduced in the factory environment through subtle and overt mechanisms.

For example, Sandra, a 25-year old *maquila* worker whom I met while working at a garment *maquiladora*, knew many women who had been seduced and then deserted by engineers and technicians. Other women felt they had to comply with the sexual demands of fellow workers because they believed that otherwise they would lose their jobs. According to Sandra, things are especially difficult for very young women at large plants like RCA. During the first years of the *Maquiladora* Program sexual harassment was blatant. There were supervisors who insisted on having only the prettiest workers under their command, thus developing a sort of factory "harem." Sandra knew a man who wanted as much female diversity as possible. All the women on his crew, at his request, had eyes and hair of a different color. Another man boasted that every woman on his line had borne him a child. There were also scandals, widely covered by the city tabloids, about the spread of venereal disease in certain *maquiladoras*.

Another advantage of female employees for electronics manufacturers is their easy replacement. Given the nature of *maquiladora* work, firms prefer to hire new personnel than to incur the responsibilities that a long-standing workforce might demand. After only a few years of work, a woman may literally be replaced by a younger sister. Understandably, this can happen only in areas such as the U.S.-Mexican border, where there is an abundant supply of female labor and where unemployment rates are high.

The same factors make possible high levels of selectivity on the part of firms hiring new personnel. Throughout the world, electronics assembly (particularly the manufacture of integrated circuits) is associated with highly discriminatory employment policies which favor very young, single, and childless women. In "help wanted" ads printed in local dailies, RCA of Ciudad Juarez called for female workers between 17 and 25 years of age, single, childless, with a minimum level of schooling of six years and a maximum of ten, and with at least six months of residence in the city. Walking about the industrial parks while following job-seekers can be especially informative. Very young women between 16 and 17 often go with their mothers. One mother told me she sold *burritos* at the stadium every weekend. Her husband worked as a janitor, but their combined income was inadequate for six children. Her daughter Elsa was 16. "I can't let her go alone into the plants," the mother explained. "She's only a girl and it wouldn't be right. Sometimes girls working in the plants are molested. It's a pity they have to work . . . .. I want to be sure she'll be working in a good place."

After 25 a woman may be superannuated, that is, too old to be employed in stable electronics manufacturing firms. If she has youngsters to support and/or is married, her possibilities for work in this sector diminish even more substantially. Most of these older women enter the labor force after many years dedicated to domestic chores and childcare. Frequently, desertion by their male companions forces their entry into the paid labor force. A 31-year old mother of six explained:

> I have been looking for work since my husband left me two months ago. But I haven't had any luck. It must be my age and the fact that I have so many children. Maybe I should lie and say I've only one. But then the rest wouldn't be entitled to medical care ence I got the job.

Women need jobs to support their children, but they are often turned down because they are mothers.

Young women are not only easy to replace and discard, they are also docile. Managers see them as a controllable group whose members are not easy to unionize. According to one manager, "We prefer to hire young girls who haven't been spoiled by experience in other factories. They are more responsible, patient, and agile than men. And you also find fewer troublemakers among them." Another one thought that unexperienced young women "come to us without preconceptions about industrial work. Women such as these are easier to shape to our own requirements." To encourage docility, firms often transfer familial authority patterns into the workplace, replicating in the public sphere conditions with which workers are well acquainted in their own households.

Women: The International Labor Force

Another important and typical feature of the *Maquiladora* Program in Mexico has been its extreme reliance on labor-intensive operations which are officially classified as unskilled labor. A brief clarification of terms is necessary at this point. The definition of skill is a historical and dynamic process, rather than a static and mechanical one. Level of skill is frequently deduced from definitions imposed by producers in a position of control, and not from the quantity or complexity of the work performed. To put it crudely, unskilled labor is often distinguished from other forms of labor by the wage attached to it. Poorly paid work always is "unskilled labor"; the smaller the wage, the less skilled a particular job is assumed to be. Unskilled labor is typically performed by females, the young, and the racially different. Therefore, it is not only the size of the wage, but also the race, age, and gender of the workers that determine the definition of the level of skill.

In the case of the electronics industry these factors have been compounded by significant changes in the manufacturing process itself. The history of manufacturing has been, in large part, the saga of how artisans lost control over their crafts as a result of the needs imposed by automation, mass production, and a perpetual fragmentation of the labor process. The electronics industry has carried this development to its ultimate consequence by reducing most operations to their smallest possible denominator. Therefore, the bulk of the assembly work performed in Mexican-border *maquiladoras* and Export Processing Zones throughout the world consists of minute, monotonous, repetitive, manual movements.

By deskilling operations, firms have achieved three complementary advantages. First, they have reduced training periods for the majority of workers. This, in turn, curtails dependence on the workforce and affords maximum flexibility in recruiting strategy.[14]

Second, this strategy has evolved logically from the internationalization of capital investments, for it allows the geographical dispersion of discrete subprocesses which are later combined as a single, integrated manufacturing process. Thus, women linked halfway throughout the world by the same corporation may be participating in the assembly of the same products. Under such well-known brand names as IBM, National Cash Register, United Technologies, Hewlett-Packard, Fairchild, and Texas Instruments, Asian and Mexican Women are turning out videogames, digital watches, computers, pocket calculators, and word processors.

Third, deskilling and its corollary, geographical dispersion, afford corporations maximum flexibility in their dealing with labor. In fact, it has become common policy on the part of foreign firms to invoke a polite but effective type of economic blackmail by threatening to leave a host country in search of more hospitable areas of the world whenever discontent or grievances are expressed, or when political turmoil is imminent. In some parts of Asia this has been translated into an accentuation of repression and a flourishing of martial law.

Nevertheless, even in cases like those found along the U.S.-Mexican border, where political stability has been maintained and where social turmoil has been expeditiously arrested, firms may abruptly close their doors even after relatively lengthy periods of continued operation. In part due to their extreme dependence on the U.S. economy, scores of border *maquiladoras* were forced to close their doors during the recession of 1975. Tens of thousands of jobs were lost. A similar situation is currently taking place as a new recession curtails employment both in the United States and in its southern neighbor.

All these factors afford corporations an important edge in their negotiations with labor. By operating in various parts of the globe, firms diversify political and economic risks. But the same factors translate into a weakened capacity on the part of workers to bring employers to the bargaining table. Export Processing Zones deflate organizational efforts such as unionization and hamper the possibilities for higher wages, improved working conditions, and stable employment.

Finally, for the reasons stated above, it is doubtful that the *Maquiladora* Program and similar forms of industrialization on the basis of manufactures for export are adequate vehicles for upgrading skills and transferring technology. Paradoxically, the same technological advancements that account for the creation of some of the most imaginative and creative gadgets in the history of humankind have also spun a web of international production whose advantages are highly asymmetrical.

Nonetheless, this new form of industrialization has opened new possibilities for women. Throughout the world women recognize that although far from a suitable form of employment, multinational assembly plants often represent a badly needed alternative for subsistence in areas of the world where options are meager. Many admit that a bad job is better than no job at all. The possibility of earning an income on their own may open paths for individual autonomy and reduce economic dependence. Perhaps more importantly, the internationalization of production and the extension of complex communications systems are enabling, for the first time in history, the creation of a world-wide workforce. Women all over the globe share now a common experience, the result of their similar position in the world of production. And this may yet provide the basis for new forms of organization and strengthened solidarity in the future.

Notes

1. See "Development, Women's Status and the Sexual Division of Labor," special issue of *Signs: Journal of Women in Culture and Society* 7 (1981).
2. The Spanish word *maquiladora* is used in this article to denote an assembly plant operating as a direct subsidiary or subcontracted firm for the manufacture of export-oriented goods under the Mexican Border Industrialization Program, started in 1965; since 1972 it has been known as the *Maquiladora* Program.
3. J. Nash and M. P. Fernandez Kelly, *Women, Men and the International Division of Labor* (Albany, NY: State University of New York Press, forthcoming).
4. United Nations, *Export Processing Zones in Developing Countries*, Industrial Development Organization Working Paper on Structural Change, no.19, August 1980.
5. Anibal Pinto, "The Opening Up of Latin America to the Exterior," *CEPAL Review* (August 1980).
6. R. Grossman, "Changing Role of the Southeast Asian Women: The Global Assembly Line and the Social Manipulation of Women on the Job," *Southeast Asia Chronicle* 66 (January/February, 1979).

7. L. Arrigo, "The Industrial Work Force of Young Women in Taiwan," *The Bulletin of Concerned Asian Scholars 12 (1980).*

8. *In addition, approximately another million women work in similar assembly plants in Europe and the United States. Many of the statements made here can be generalized to those groups. See Naomi Katz, "Join the Future Now — Women and Work in the Electronics Industry," in J. Nash, and M. P. Fernandez Kelly, eds., Op. Cit.*

9. Sections 806.30 and 807 of the U.S. Customs Code permit the temporary export of components and raw materials and the re-entry of finished or semifinished products after paying a tax on the value added by foreign components and/or services.

10. Among these are (1) modifications to the Mexican customs code to permit the entry on a temporary basis ("in bond") of machinery and components; (2) the possibility to own or lease Mexican land through trusts engaged with Mexican banks; (3) total control of investment by foreign firms; and (4) since 1972 the extension of these stipulations to all of Mexico.

11. Under normal circumstances Mexico has only allowed up to 49 percent of control over industrial investment to foreigners. Under the *Maquiladora* Program, however, this proviso has been set aside.

12. M. P. Fernandez Kelly, "Las Mujeres y las Maquiladoras: Paradojas de la Industrializacion bajo el Capitalismo Integral," in *Sociedad, Subordinacion y Feminismo* , ed. Magdalena Leon (Bogata: Asociacion Colombiana para el Estudio de la Poblacion, 1982).

13. R. Michel, speech delivered at the Symposium on Maquiladoras, American Chamber of Commerce, Mexico City, 1978.

14. Harry Braverman, *Labor and Monopoly Capital* (New York: Monthly Review Press, 1974).

Chapter 4

Women, Nature, and Domination

by Carolyn Merchant

For some time I have been interested in the relationship between women and nature on the one hand, and ecology and feminism on the other. I would like to give some perspectives on both these connections.

Ecology comes from a Greek word *oikos* which means house. The science of ecology is really the science of the household, the household extended to include the earth. Environmentalism involves the study of the whole earth as a household, and women traditionally have mediated between the two. Nature has been thought of as female in many cultures over long periods of time, and in our own culture for several hundred years, the house has been thought of as women's sphere.

First, let us go back to the sixteenth and seventeenth centuries and explore the interconnections between the female and nature, and then see what happens when certain types of technology are introduced during the Scientific Revolution of the seventeenth century. At that time a tremendously important change occurred in the metaphors which describe human experience.

In the Middle Ages and in the Renaissance the primary metaphor binding human life together was that of the organism. The cosmos was thought of as a living organism with a body, a soul, and a spirit; the earth was thought of as alive, as a nurturing mother.

The change that came about, which is so critical as an important root of today's environmental crisis, is the change from the organism as predominant metaphor to that of the machine. The machine, by the end of the seventeenth century, served as the root metaphor. The self, society, and the cosmos came to be thought of in terms of atoms or parts that were grouped in associations or governed by external forces.

For Descartes, one of the most important modern philosophers, the human body became a machine. Animals were merely machines that did not have souls or feelings; human beings at least had souls, but, after Descartes, the dualism between the mind and the body became a major philosophical problem in Western society.

In the seventeenth century, for political philosophers such as Thomas Hobbes and John Locke, society also became a group of individuals held together by a contract, or an external force. People voluntarily gave up certain freedoms in order to be protected by the sovereign. In Hobbes' introduction to **the Leviathan**, the sovereign was shown raising a sword with the people grouped as atoms within him. The cosmos also was cast in metaphorical terms as a machine, with God as an engineer or mathematician. God set the universe in motion at the beginning by putting forces into it that were subsequently transferred among the particles.

The critical change that took place from the time earth and nature were viewed as organisms to the time they were viewed as machines was the rise of a commercial economy, which was based on technology, and the introduction of increasingly powerful machines. In other words, a mercantile economy based on the exploitation of nature. Metals such as gold, silver, iron, mercury, and copper were extracted from the earth and made to serve as exchange mediums. During these two critical centuries, society moved away from a hierarchical, feudal, land-based, agrarian society toward a fast-moving commercial economy.

In the Renaissance the earth was thought of as a nurturing mother, a female who felt sensation and with whom one interacted. The world had reason, otherwise how could the earth, as a mother, have produced reasonable, rational human beings? The earth, in this view, had physiological systems like those of the human being. The circulation of water and air through the veins in the earth were like fluids ebbing and flowing in the human body. The earth poured forth sweat in the form of dew, and even had its own elimination system — a volcanic eruption or an earthquake, for example, was the indignation of the sacred parent, Mother Earth, expressing herself and breaking wind. The earth had sensitivity and could react. However, as soon as the earth became a machine made up of dead, inert parts in which there was no life, worries about the earth's reactions diminished. The Scientific Revolution and the change in metaphor from the earth as organism to the earth as machine sanctioned the indiscriminate exploitation of its forests, the draining of its swamps, and the mining of its entrails for precious metals.

From Organism to Machine

With the rise of modern science in the seventeenth century, some of the so-called fathers of modern science, the giants who brought us this new world view, talked specifically about technologies affecting the earth and the female. According to Francis Bacon, technological operations on nature were to be modeled on the work of miners and smiths. The blacksmith, for example, shaped nature on the anvil, and the miner penetrated into nature's womb to extract metals. Bacon said the truth of nature lies hid in deep mines and caverns, and described the way in which the new scientists ought to study nature. The studious among them, he said, should sell all their books and build furnaces; they should forsake Minerva and the Muses as barren virgins and instead rely on Vulcan.

Now, if we examine Bacon's many volumes of letters, articles, and books for the kind of language he used to describe nature, we find some incredible examples of sexual metaphor. The new man of science, he argued, must not think that the inquisition of nature should be in any way forbidden. Nature should be made a slave, put in constraints, and molded by the mechanical arts. The searchers and spies of nature should discover her plots and secrets. This kind of language is very reminiscent of the European witch trials in which women were put on the rack and tortured to reveal their secrets and to indict other women in their immediate communities. Bacon argued that we must hound nature in her wanderings, and to lead her and drive her to the same place again and again. In a revealing statement he wrote: "Neither ought a man to make scruple of entering and penetrating into these little holes and corners when the inquisition of truth is his whole object." Moreover, there was hope that "there is still laid up in the womb of nature many secrets of excellent use." In his book **The Masculine Birth of Time**, he said, "I'm come in truth leaving to you nature and all her children to bind her to your service and make her your slave." Nature should be "taken by the forelock, being bald behind."[1]

This language is not just archaic seventeenth century metaphor. It is used today in discussing such things as "virgin lands" and "man's war against Mother Nature." Soon after the eruption of Mount St. Helens volcano in May 1980, a geologist who was interviewed on television was asked, "What is Mount St. Helens going to do next?" He answered, "We really don't know her intentions. . . . We haven't been able yet to penetrate her deeply enough with our instruments."

So, one thing we desperately need is a transformation in language and symbol structures. We can take up the earth as a new metaphor to replace the machine. There are many new publications that use the earth as a root metaphor, such as **Mother Earth News**, **Patient Earth**, **One Woman, One Earth**, and **Spaceship Earth**. All of that is critically important but, as will be argued, a mere change in language is, in and of itself, insufficient.

A second example from the seventeenth century comes from the work of William Harvey, another of the so-called great fathers of modern science, and discoverer of the circulation of blood. Harvey was involved in the midwifery controversy in the 1620s and 1630s, as one of the censors of the Royal College of Physicians. In this period, Dr. Peter Chamberlain, his son, and several others in that dynasty, had invented forceps, and were trying to get this new instrument licensed, arguing that only doctors with licenses should be able to deliver children. This undermined the time-honored monopoly that women had had over childbirth, so the women of that time put together a petition that argued against licensing male doctors as midwives. In their petition they said that Dr. Chamberlain had no experience in midwifery but by reading. (Imagine having a child delivered out of a book!) And further:

Dr. Chamberlain's work and the work belonging to midwives are contrary to one another, for he delivers none without the use of instruments by extraordinary violence in desperate occasions which women never practiced nor desired, nor have they parts nor hands for that art.[2]

Thus, at the same time that the earth was falling prey to the exploitative technologies of the machine age, women were losing power over their reproductive functions to men through a technology which males invented and controlled.

Toward the latter part of his life, William Harvey published a book on generation in which he discussed the role of the female in reproduction. His view of women comes from Aristotle, who thought of the male as active and the female as passive — the male supplied the reason and the soul, the female supplied the matter. Harvey, elaborating on this perspective, said:

. . . among animals where the sexes are distinct, matters are so arranged that since the female alone is inadequate to engender the embryo and to nourish and protect the young, a male is associated with her by nature as the superior and more worthy progenitor, as a consort of her labor, and the means of supplying her deficiencies.[3]

Many of his arguments were based on reproduction in the hen and the rooster, and he eulogized about the rooster as being the epitome and perfection of the male:

Why should we so much wonder what it is in the cock that preserves and governs so perfect and beautiful an animal, and is the first cause of that entity we call the soul; but much more what it is in the egg of so great virtue as to produce such an animal and raise him to the very summit of excellence.[4]

He also argued against Galen and his followers, that there could be a female semen produced by the genital organs of women:

I, for my part, greatly wonder how anyone can believe that from parts so imperfect and obscure a fluid like the semen so elaborate, so concoct and vivifying, can ever be produced that would be adequate to overcome that of the male. How should such a female fluid get the better of another concocted under the influence of a heat so fostering, of vessels so elaborate, and endowed with such vital energy? How should such a fluid as the male semen be made to play the part of mere matter?[5]

The Scientific Revolution, in so far as it is grounded in the machine as metaphor, has negative implications for both the environment and for women. The last two decades, however, can be viewed as the beginning of an era of liberation, for both women and nature. The rise of the environmental movement and the rise of the women's movement came about simultaneously.

Ecology and Feminism

In 1962 Rachel Carson published her book **Silent Spring**, in which she argued that all around us organisms are dying. The greatest threats to the lives of human beings and the life of the earth come first from nuclear technology and secondly from pesticides such as chlorinated hydrocarbons, such as DDT, aldrin, and dieldrin. She single-handedly brought to public attention the critical importance of what was happening to the food chain as these chemicals began circulating through it. Although this information had been available in scientific reports and articles, Rachel Carson broke the story to the public in her beautifully written book.

In the following year Betty Friedan's **Feminine Mystique** marked the liberal phase of the Women's Movement and the liberation of women from the confines of the household. Like Carson, she was concerned with life and with women's own self-development and self-fulfillment within a program for a total life plan.

Both of these women were attempting to liberate the environment and the female sex from the repressions generated in the seventeenth century, which formed the way in which the modern world looked upon the earth and upon the household.

In certain very important ways, the goals of women and the goals of the environmental movement are unified, as the theoretical connections that have come out of the ecology and women's movements of the last two decades reveal.

It is language, after all, which is used to describe both nature and human society. Many of those words are the same words, and can have repressive or unhealthy connotations for both women and nature — or they can have liberating ones. We cannot eliminate the repressive connotations without a simultaneous revolution in economic and social structures, but it is important to see the linguistic interconnections.

The connections are derived from the structure and functions of nature and society. Structurally, for both the ecology and Women's Movements, the parts of the system have equal value. In nature the components of an ecosystem are all of equal importance for the health of the whole. We need healthy air, clean water, and good, fertile soil that has not been polluted by pesticides, hazardous wastes, and toxic chemicals. And we need to preserve the whole biotic system of plants, animals, bacteria, and fungi that operate together to form the life cycle and the food chain. Every one of these elements is of critical importance and of equal value in maintaining the health of the system.

Similarly, feminism asserts the equality of both men and women. Policy, goals, legislation, and economic and household arrangements should be directed toward equalizing roles and maintaining equity for both women and men. Both ecologists and feminists will assign value to all parts of the human nature system and take care to protect each part in cases of threat.

The second idea is that the earth is our home. The earth is a habitat for all living organisms and homes are habitats for groups of humans. Each ecological niche is a position in a community, whether it is a human community or the larger biosphere. Each niche is a place in the energy continuum into which atoms, molecules, and energy enter and leave. Ecology is the study of the earth's household.

The houses in which human beings live are places wherein life is cherished and sustained just as the earth sustains living things. The household is a place where food is prepared, where clothes are repaired, and where human beings are cared for. In and out of our houses flow energy, molecules, and atoms. Some of these are life sustaining, and need to be preserved and protected. Others are life-defeating and lead to a sick planet, a sick home, and a sick body. Radioactive hazards exist in some people's neighborhoods; hazardous chemicals are permeating some people's backyards and basements. Other chemicals have invaded the kitchen.

The home is no longer a haven. We have substances such as Easy Off, which contains hazardous alkalis. Indoor air pollution is becoming a problem in apartment complexes built on top of garages where people start and stop their cars intermittently throughout the day. Carbon monoxide fumes filter up through the walls and floors and permeate people's living spaces.

Some of the insulation which has been used recently contains urea formaldehyde, which has been found to be very hazardous. In response to the general concern over energy conservation, people had insulation blown into their walls, and this particular type has been found to be a long-term health hazard. Phenols in bathroom cleaners are bad for pets, and cosmetics and shampoos can cause headaches and respiratory problems in humans. Thus, we need to be aware that chemical and energy hazards like color television and microwaves can endanger our homes.

The third parallel derives from the functions of systems, and this is the idea of the primacy of process. The laws of ecology are based on the laws of thermodynamics. The first law of thermodynamics asserts that the total energy in the universe is conserved and is exchanged through the interconnected parts of the ecosystem. Energy flows through the system of living and non-living parts on the earth in a dynamic steady-state, open-ended process. The world is active and alive, not dead. Its processes are cyclical, stabilized by cybernetic (feedback) networks.

The stress on dynamic processes in ecology has its parallel in human society inasmuch as the flow of information through the human community is the basis of decision making. Open discussion about all kinds of problems is essential for the future. We cannot just leave this to the highly trained experts, usually males, in technology or ecology. We need to work out a system in which both men and women, lawyers and workers, ecologists and technologists contribute equally. They all have equally valuable information and experience.

The final functional connection between the two movements is the notion that there is "no free lunch." "No free lunch" is the essence of the laws of thermodynamics. Each step one takes up the organized ladder of life results in the release of unusable energy, or entropy, into the surroundings. The energy that is useless for work is continually increasing in the surroundings every time a commodity is produced, or an item is manufactured for sale on the market. Nature cannot be expected to be continually available to provide free services, free goods, and free lunches. Karl Marx called this the "capitalist huckstering of the earth"; nature is considered a free resource which people take gratis in order to make profits. But profit-hungry human beings cannot continue to extract nature's free goods and services. Whenever possible, we need to recycle resources and products.

Feminists, also, are moving away from the idea of doling out free lunches and free household services. Housewives spend most of their time struggling to undo the effects of the second law of thermodynamics. They are constantly trying to recreate order out of the disorder and chaos that seems to come naturally into the household. It is necessary to break down the dualism of public and private spheres and of male and female roles. And we need cooperation and equality between men and women in all kinds of specific contexts — in daycare centers, in childrearing and household work, in productive work, and in sexual relations.

The technologies, then, which have a low impact on the environment and low impact upon the household are the ones which we need to develop in the future. Certain kinds of issues can involve women as feminists and as ecologists because they affect our own bodies and reproductive systems as well as the health of the earth. Women can put their energy as environmentalists and as feminists into issues such as nuclear technology, radioactive wastes, hazardous chemicals, pesticides, and herbicides that have long-term implications for the health of the earth and the human species. As women, we need to undertake a program of action that can lead us sanely into the future.

Notes

1 Francis Bacon, *Works*, eds. James Spedding, Robert L. Ellis, Douglas D. Heath, Vol. 4 (London: Longmans Green, 1870), pp. 296, 20; Benjamin Farrington, ed. and trans., *The Philosophy of Francis Bacon* (Liverpool, England: Liverpool University Press, 1964), pp. 62, 129-30.
2. Quoted in Irving S. Cutter, and Henry R. Viets, *A Short History of Midwifery*, (Philadelphia: Saunders, 1964), p. 49.
3. William Harvey, *Works*, trans. Robert Willis, (London: Sydenham Society, 1847), p. 362.
4. *Ibid.*, p. 321.
5. *Ibid.*, p. 299.

For more information, contact: Women in Technological History, c/o Gay Bindocci, Mining Extension Service, Bicentennial House, West Virginia University, Morgantown, WV 26506, (304) 293-4211.

Chapter 5

Doubletalk:

Sexism in Tech Talk

by Robin Tolmach Lakoff

Language use itself is a technology, if not a science — even though it is an art at the same time. Language is a tool, as piercing and illuminating as a laser beam, and with as great a potential for good or harm as nuclear fission. But language use is changing, and what these changes can tell us about our own hopes and expectations for change is rather unexpected.

Every field has its own special vocabulary of "technical terminology"; this involves not only vocabulary, but style as well. We see it everywhere — in the professions, in government bureaucracy, in the physical and social sciences, in crafts, and in industry. Technical terminology in all fields shares some salient features: either entirely new words are created, or common words are given new senses, so that the expert is sharply differentiated from the nonexpert because only the former can use and understand the language. And the language itself is specially devised, consciously (or more often not), to circumvent emotion or subjective judgment.

The final recourse in this type of language is pure intellectual logic, with the rationalization that thereby communication is rendered more direct and clear, and less subject to the confusions and ambiguities that plague discourse conducted in ordinary language. But this is only apparently so: if we look at real perception of these special languages both from without and — more surprisingly — from within, we find that far from facilitating intelligibility, technical discourse actually impedes it. We see, for instance, lawyers totally at odds with one another, unable to resolve confusion by logical strategies in determining the sense of legal documents. We see medical experts in court fencing with one another over fine points of medical parlance. We see important contemporary books written in academese so turgid that exegesis is necessary. Thus, we cannot accept at face value the justification for technical parlance that it is a clear mode of exposition. It may be, but just as often it is not.

Indeed, governmental bureaucrats make a virtue of obfuscation. If outsiders, not sure precisely of the meaning of "friendly fire" or "supply side economics" or "cultural deprivation," are present, insiders can persuade them to agree to truly horrific policy decisions. And in all these cases it is important to realize that it is the very de-emotionalization of the language, its vocabulary as well as its syntax — for instance, the use of passives or impersonal expressions like "one" — that bleeds meaning from the text and muddies the intellectual content by disavowing the emotive content of the communication.

Language Codes

In fact, technical jargons or "codes," as sociolinguists refer to these forms of language, serve three purposes which are so valuable to their users that codes persist in the face of criticism by outsiders. First, codes have a semantic use: to fulfill their ostensible function of enabling speakers to express complicated ideas more clearly, directly, and succinctly. This is certainly true to some extent. Much special vocabulary does, indeed, save time and avoid ambiguity in specialized contexts for sophisticated users. But it is far from always the case, and certainly valid criticisms are made of lexical preciousness in many codes: bureaucratese, medicalese, and educationese are among those most rightfully criticized in this regard by outsiders, but any code can lapse into murk. Further, it is hard to see what the nonlexical characteristics of the code — impersonality and hedging, for instance — contribute to understanding, yet they are virtually universal.

The other two functions of technical codes are pragmatic, rather than semantic. They concern not the message itself, but the interaction of which it is one part: the negotiation of a context, and the establishment of a relationship among participants.

Second, the "secret handshake" function of a code language tests and affirms the unity of the participants. To speak in a code to another is to say "we speak the same language, we're the same kind of people, a cohesive body." Codes, then, serve the same functions as professional society meetings; they are socializing forces, uniting members of a discipline.

Third, codes are an exclusionary mechanism, the other side of the coin of the "secret handshake." If one person's recognition of a code phrase affirms his or her membership in my group, another's nonrecognition of it tells me that person is not one of us, cannot join our secret club, and will not be told the code words.

A colleague years ago, working among many medical professionals, (himself merely a Ph.D. linguist), was concerned about a serious condition in his infant son and worried about his own physician's decision about the treatment. So he telephoned one of the medical doctor's colleagues, a specialist in the condition involved. "This is Dr. Z," he said "and I'm wondering what you would do in this case . . ." and described the situation in the medical parlance he had, by this time, learned well. He went on that the attending physician, Dr. X, had suggested such and such, did this man agree? The physician reflected briefly, then said that well, that was one possibility, but as for himself, he felt that such a decision was irresponsible, demonstrating startling ignorance of recent literature, "because Dr. Y, as you know . . ." and launched, at that point, into a spate of pure medicalese. The linguist at that moment was lost, and asked for definitions. The other doctor was shocked at such an elementary question. "But aren't you a physician?" he asked. "No," said the linguist, "just a Ph.D. in linguistics." "Well," said the medical doctor, "in that case, forget everything I've just said," and hung up precipitously. Here is the exclusionary function of the code in its purest form.

In its exclusionary function, then, a technical code creates in its users the presumption that nonmembers are not to be treated on the same level as members. It is language that makes us fully human; if you can't talk the language, you will be excluded from serious interchange with those who can. And those who do the excluding will feel morally justified in doing so.

Technologizing the Humanities

With this in mind, we can look at academic discourse as a technical code, particularly the special language of the humanities that has recently evolved. It has been unquestionably true until very recently, and at its upper levels it is still arguably true, that the academy is a male preserve not unlike the church, the army, medicine, law, or government. We would expect the chosen code of the profession to reflect this bias, and indeed it does. In Western culture, the stereotypical conventionalization of behavior toward which men are generally socialized is distancing: a power-based strategy involving impersonality and nonemotionality, the denial of the interaction and its effects on the participants.

Women, on the contrary, have traditionally been encouraged toward a deference strategy, oriented not to power, but to acceptance or love, and the fear of its loss. Hence, women's language allows for openness to others' needs and a reluctance to acknowledge one's own needs. But as a strategy concerned with acceptance and rejection, emotional expression is valued over intellectual clarity in case of conflict.

I am not suggesting here that either of these strategies is in any sense better, or that the users of either are better people; and less still that it is male and female biology or physiology that motivates us in this direction. But I do suggest that these have been, and for most people still are, the prevalent patterns. And even those of us who have struggled hardest to rid ourselves of stereotypical behavior often find ourselves confronted by a society that still holds conventional models up to our children.

What is important in all this is that technical codes, as they were described earlier, can be understood as exaggerations of masculine distancing, or power-oriented style. Hence bureaucratese and its relatives make outsiders angry precisely because they implicitly involve a power statement: "I (the user) am more powerful and valuable than you (the nonuser)." And since it is implicit in the style, not explicitly present, it cannot be negotiated. So, as outsiders faced with this kind of language, we feel impotent and resentful.

Academese is no different. As the language of the male power elite, it continues to be used in a way that excludes women — and probably those male members of minorities, where the white male stereotype is different from their own. And it does so with the hidden implication that anyone who cannot use the language is unworthy of membership in the club. What is illegitimate in this argument is that the selected language is itself exclusionary on two levels. First, it excludes, in the way any code does, those who are not yet full members and, second, since it is based upon an exaggeration of a male style of interaction, it is relatively easier for men to assimilate. This is, after all, what graduate and professional schools are largely set up to accomplish, but the burden on women is greater. This isn't deliberate racism or sexism, but it works to exclude women and minorities from positions of influence and authority on what are presented as valid intellectual grounds. Affirmative action doesn't touch this problem, which is part of what makes women tend to drop out of graduate programs, or procrastinate in them forever at a relatively high rate.

Basically then, a woman has two choices, neither comfortable, in determining how she is to use the tool of language in her scientific or academic work. On the one hand, she can accept the male model, perhaps outdoing men themselves in the use of the code. But in general, it is more difficult for a woman to use men's language comfortably than for a man. Moreover, it prevents women from using their own "native language" or natural style, which is invariably devalued in the university as unscientific, imprecise, or subjective — with the again unquestioned assumption that these are *ipso facto* negative characteristics.

Or she can, in defiance of the rules, use her own language. But, as suggested above, she is unlikely to be taken seriously if she does. If she does not use the code and her work is therefore readily accessible, readers will not feel flattered and respond with approval. Rather, since they can follow it with ease, they will assume that she hasn't had to work very hard. They could have done it themselves and probably have. Hence formal technical vocabulary, in a kind of linguistic Gresham's law, tends to drive out clear — that is, emotionally punctuated — discourse. The more formal and impenetrable the language, the more seriously the content will be taken.

In linguistics we have no end of examples. In the last 20 years formal syntax and semantics have caused the flourishing and expansion of a field that, before mathematics was introduced as the model, could hold its professional society meetings in one small room. Now the Linguistic Society of America looks more like the Modern Language Association every year, with as many as 12 simultaneous sessions. What is unintelligible to laity is gold to the elect. Or consider ethnomethodology, the study of the surface regularities in conversation. Its body of literature is well known for its unfailing turgidity of style and vocabulary. Its practitioners defend its impenetrability, of which they are aware and which they claim to consciously utilize, by saying that since they are discussing conversation, which everyone knows about and everyone knows how to do, their work would not be taken as a scientific inquiry if they did not clothe it in arcane vocabulary and style. Here we see the exclusionary force of an academic code used to give a field of study respectability quite apart from any content — like dressing a beggar in the trappings of a king.

These examples are amusing, but they are not unique or exaggerated. The technologization of discourse is rampant in the humanities now, surely more so than in the past. Writings on language and literature, until very recently, were almost always fully accessible to the literate nonspecialist. Practitioners argue that, much as they deplore it, technologization is necessary: the subject matter has gotten so complex that language must, of necessity, follow suit.

But what is curious, if we accept this reasoning, is that modern science, particularly in the most popularly celebrated fields, like artificial intelligence and atomic physics, has actually done just the opposite. While many of their concepts are exceedingly complex and not readily accessible to the untrained, their language, while they invent new technical terms, is quite the opposite of a new humanistic parlance. Scientists in these fields seem to strive quite deliberately for the allusion, the metaphor, the term that will render the abstruse at least partially intelligible to outsiders.

So where humanistic writing revels in Hellenism and Latinity, artificial intelligence gets back to basic English with terms like "input," or "feedback," and playful uses that delight as well as educate, such as "software." Atomic physics, attempting to explain the inexplicable, offers us "quarks" and "charms," and "black holes." At least, the coiners of these words seem to be saying, "if we can't explain to you what's going on, we admit to you by our playful choices that *we* really don't understand too much either." They are not playing unquestionable authority, and they are not afraid to admit that they don't know everything; their technical vocabulary deliberately invites that inference, while that of the humanities, at present, explicitly rejects such modesty.

That is the real problem of technologizing the humanities. Why has it been done? Why do we adopt this aggressively power-oriented model? What do we gain? The answer is simple: we are operating out of insecurity. We are afraid that we really aren't important or powerful anymore, and certainly there is enough evidence to that effect; look at the budgets of the National Science Foundation (NSF) and the National Endowment for the Humanities if you doubt this claim. But by deliberately cultivating obscurantism, we do not really help. In fact, as we have seen, this creates resentment and suspicion, and leads inexorably to a position of ridiculousness and total impotence, once people see through the pose.

It is, of course, ironic that at the moment at which affirmative action is becoming a force to be reckoned with in the universities, male-based language is taking over with such vigor. But perhaps it is not ironic, but just the response we would expect, for academese is an exaggeration of male style. When people are threatened psychologically, their defenses are strengthened, which means that their style is exaggerated — what they used to do a little, and under appropriate circumstances, they now do all the time. So we can understand the proliferation of academese in the humanities at present as the expression of a male power elite's insecurity resulting from the decline of cultural influence of the humanities, from their doubts about whether their work is masculine enough, since it isn't bringing home the NSF bacon, and about whether they can compete with women once the barriers are down. Therefore the style of discourse in the humanities has become scientized without any concomitant scientization of content. Hence, humanists feel still more uncomfortable — what if they are found out in their little game? So, men in the humanities are creating a secret language all their own, to shore up their own sense of being real and legitimate in the face of doubt. They draw the inner circle ever tighter, enforcing the shibboleths ruthlessly and continually raising their requirements, linguistic and otherwise, for belonging to the club.

Interestingly, the situation we are speaking of as current in the university has analogies in older cultures. In the contemporary case, the language used by both men and women is the same, English. But during the medieval period in Japan, a remarkably similar pattern seems to have existed. There was an indigenous language, Japanese, which had not long before been given written form in the Katakana syllabary. At the same time, Chinese was extremely influential in Japan, both in terms of cultural and linguistic influence, and was considered by the Japanese to be the language appropriate to literate expression. But women were not educated in Chinese during this period; this kind of literacy and familiarity with another society was considered men's prerogative. Therefore, there was no literature in Japanese written by men during this period. What men wrote were imitative and stilted exercises copying Chinese sources in inferior Chinese. But women, relegated to the vernacular, developed a lively literature in Japanese, which endures today, recognized as a much stronger form of writing than the men's, largely because it was intended as a means of communication, rather than show.

Returning to the contemporary situation, we find that this divisive and ominous trend toward the technologization of language is not limited to academic, bureaucratic, or professional parlance; sadly it is becoming characteristic of our literature as well.

Chapter 6

For Women,

The Chips Are Down

by Margaret Lowe Benston

The relationship between women and machines is not a particularly comfortable one. The industrial economies of Europe and North America are based on complex and sophisticated technology, yet the majority of people who work in these societies possess only the most rudimentary technical skills. This is especially true for women — there is an enormous distance between them and the tools they work with. Whether they work in the home or outside it, they require sophisticated and increasingly specialized training even to understand how machines work. Only a small number of elite workers, and those mostly male, have this knowledge. In the workplace, the machines one uses are owned and controlled by others. Although few women feel confident or powerful in what are perceived as the male realms of technology, machines have drastically changed women's lives and that process of change continues.

Computer technology, based on the microcircuitry of the chip, is changing the way that much work will be done in the future. Manufacturing, transportation, communications, and office work are all being transformed.

A great deal of attention is being given these days to changes that automation may bring and to the possible responses by those most affected — particularly by women workers displaced by the new technology. This involves at least some attempts to predict future trends; one of the best ways to do that is to try to understand the forces behind automation.

As Philip Kraft points out in his book **Programmers and Managers**, the lack of technical skills and the separation of people from an understanding of, or control over, their tools is basic to automation. New technology has made mass production techniques feasible in more and more areas and has, as a result, reduced the need for human skills in production. The consequence is that the work of a relatively few highly skilled workers, such as scientists, engineers, systems analysts, and the like, has been used to make "unproductive" the skills of almost all the rest. A quick historical look will help show the basic processes involved.

The Origins of Automation

Pre-industrial business differed from modern business in more ways than simply the absence of modern machinery. Until the eighteenth century production was done in relatively small household units. In such artisan households, the producers were involved in all phases of the work from start to finish. They therefore understood the production process in all of its phases. They owned the tools with which they worked and controlled the tempo and the technique of their work. Women were a crucial part of production in the artisan households, where they not only managed the housekeeping tasks but took a direct part in manufacturing whatever goods were being produced.

So called cottage industry or "putting out" was the first step on the road to modern production techniques, since it meant the direct involvement of entrepreneurs with the productive process. Textile production, with its traditionally high participation of women, was one of the first places where "putting out" became dominant. Under this system, new tools and machines, such as spinning jennies, were introduced to increase output and ease bottlenecks, but the crucial change was the control exerted over production by the entrepreneur. He owned the raw materials, the tools, and the machines, and could dictate how they were to be used. Typically he broke the process of manufacturing into its general tasks — spinning, weaving, dyeing, finishing — and "put out" these tasks to different individuals or households. This division of labor decreased, but did not totally eliminate the control that workers, spinsters, for example, had over what they did. The entrepreneurs were still dependent on workers for detailed expertise on what was actually required for each of the tasks.

With the Industrial Revolution came both the introduction of power machinery and the intensification of the division of labor that began with the "putting out" system. Both the machines and further division of labor were introduced for several reasons. First, they were intended to directly increase productivity. Such a productivity increase followed most directly from the replacement of human muscle power, by machine power but it also resulted from changing the organization of production. By dividing the work up, each task was made simpler and easier to learn. Since less skill was required for any one of the tasks involved in production, the workers could be paid less. This "deskilling" of workers, with its associated lowering of wages and shifts in labor force composition, is a continuing characteristic of the search for higher productivity.

The introduction of an ever-more detailed division of labor depended on an increased understanding of all parts of the productive process on the part of managers and bosses. No longer did workers have a virtual monopoly on the knowledge needed for the specific kind of production at issue. This situation made possible further gains in productivity, since it was now possible to exert much more direct control over worker performance than had been possible in the "putting out" system or in the early days of industrialization. In the early period, workers were often the only ones who knew enough of the details of production to speak authoritatively about the way the work should be done.

This management nightmare produced pressure for control of the productive process to move into the office. The net result was a further separation of "head" and "hand." The work of F. W. Taylor with his theories of scientific management provided the basis for attempts to increase productivity through control of worker performance. Taylor's premise was that given the chance, workers would loaf on the job and would, if they could, conceal from management the real rate at which work could be done.

According to Taylor's principles:

- There was to be strict division between mental and manual labor. Manual workers needed to understand only the specifications of the work they themselves were to do. Mental work, the overall knowledge of the labor process and the planning required for its implementation, were reserved for management.
- All production was to be reduced to its simplest and most repetitive components and each component was to be given to a different worker.
- Each of these repetitive tasks was to be timed and analyzed for potential speed and accuracy and then each worker's performance was to be monitored against these standards. Whenever possible, these performance standards were to be revised consistently upward.

These principles still form the essential basis of modern industry, although they may now occur in modified or hidden form, under pressure from workers rebelling against such work practices. It is deskilling — the reduction of the productive process to a well understood series of simple, repetitive manipulations " that makes automation possible. The assembly line is merely the logical culmination of this trend of continual deskilling.

Predictions of massive unemployment did not materialize during this phase of industrialization in Europe and North America (from the late eighteenth to the beginning of the twentieth century) for a number of reasons. Growth of education, the military, and the government were all factors, but probably the most important was the growth of the sector that handled information related to the production and distribution of goods and services.

The Growth and Automation of Office Work

As capitalism matured, there were a number of places where information needs increased. In the first place, the control that management wished to exert over production meant that much more information was required in office files and management reports. Although previously, much information had stayed on the shop floor, inside workers' heads, now it had to be spelled out and recorded for management use. Records about employee performance also became necessary. This was in addition to the growth in information handling required as a consequence of the increase in the volume of information generated simply by the growth of business, government, and financial operations.

Office work was originally done by male clerks who, like artisans, were familiar with the whole range of functions of the office. Such clerkships were often training places for future managers or even partners in the business. As the volume of information grew, this system became inadequate and, in the early part of this century, there was a large influx of women into office positions. This coincides with the introduction of the first important technological change in handling of information — the typewriter. As in earlier factory production, office work from then on was increasingly subjected to a division of labor and to increased analysis and control by management of each step in information handling.

It is not surprising then to find large businesses dividing secretarial work into a number of jobs, each requiring fewer skills. File clerks, receptionists, dicta-typists, or typing pools exist as subcategories in large offices. There has been a corresponding introduction of specialized office equipment for each of these new jobs. Machinery for posting and billing was an early installation, followed by the infamous IBM card and its associated sorters and tabulating/printing machines. The introduction of electronic data processing equipment has been continuous since the first commercial computers appeared in the early 1950s. Word processors are but the latest in the series.

The industrialization and automation of office work not only gave greater productivity by allowing fewer clerks to handle the same amount of information, but opened up the possibility for closer supervision and control of the workers involved. The monitoring possible with word processors, for example, is well known, where keystrokes, errors, and time actually worked on the terminal can all be tabulated. An increase in mechanization generally means a reduction in the variety of work activities, reduction in actual physical mobility, and reduction in control and judgment concerning one's work. As the images in **Good Monday Morning**, a new Canadian union movie about working women, show quite graphically, the office is coming more and more to resemble a factory. This is no coincidence since, as we have seen, exactly the same forces shape both the machinery and the organization of factory and office. The increase in automation in the office is having the same effect that the increase in automation in the factory had — jobs are disappearing. This time however, the jobs are being lost in an area that is of major concern to women.

New Jobs?

Where growth is possible in the economy, new jobs appear. Some of the most important areas where jobs will expand are those connected with new computer-based automation equipment itself. Women are being urged by a variety of government agencies and social analysts to respond to the loss of jobs in office work in an apparently positive way — by demanding "training" or "retraining" for these new jobs. There would seem to be two underlying reasons for advocating such a strategy.

First, there is the obviously practical idea that women should go where the jobs are. A second reason however arises from a recognition of the lack of women in technical areas and a further recognition of the lack of control that women have over the development and uses of technology. There is the feeling, I think, that if women could only enter the technical fields in sufficient numbers, they might gain some sort of power to humanize them. There are a relatively wide variety of jobs that are seen as possible openings for women, but as I will show, these openings are more mirage than oasis.

In one category, there are jobs running the new automated equipment. These, as discussed above, are mostly replacements of existing jobs and increasingly tend to resemble factory work. There will almost certainly be a smaller number of such jobs in the future, since the major reason for the introduction of such machinery is to increase productivity. These are typically women's jobs and will remain open to women.

Operation of computers themselves belongs in this category. Until recently this has been a job done by men and in the past carried with it a kind of gender-related aura of technical expertise. For reasons to be discussed below, this seems to be changing (in the United States women are approaching 60 percent of computer operators), but at present, the usual barriers limit women's entry into jobs seen as involving a high technical mastery of machines.

Second, there will be a wide variety of jobs involved in the development, maintenance, and use of computer programs (software) and databases. These are often referred to as the "large number of new jobs being created by the new technology." For example, there are predictions by various Canadian government agencies and commissions that there will be 40,000 new data processing professionals needed in Canada by 1990 (out of a workforce of just over 12 million).

This second category of jobs is a central one in any strategy that urges women to respond to these new developments by retraining and by taking responsibility for their own work destiny. Typically, when computer automation is introduced in a business, a data processing or computer section is introduced to oversee and maintain the new system. There appears to be little opportunity for displaced women to obtain these jobs, which go mainly to technically trained, male workers. The training required is often inaccessible to women in general and to working women in particular. The reasons for this involve the financial burden of technical school or university training, outright discrimination, and not least, the socialization and channeling that convinces women they are not capable of jobs that are perceived to be highly technical.

Even in the lowest programming categories, only around 30 percent of software workers are women; the number drops sharply in the higher ranks. Women are therefore urged to get their rightful share of new computer work. Even at lower levels, the work is well paid and responsible; opportunities for advancement seem relatively good (particularly given the recent heavy demand for software workers), and it would seem reasonable to expect that a job telling computers what to do would be more skilled and more satisfying than one of the jobs which computers have eliminated. It would also seem that here women might actually get some kind of control over the new technology. But just you wait, Liza Doolittle.

Since people will be required to repair and maintain the new equipment, this is the third place where jobs will increase. It is another area seen as holding out the possibility of new jobs for women. At present, and even more so than in software, these jobs are held by men. For all the reasons listed above, almost no women have access to the technical training required, even though these jobs, too, are well-paid and responsible positions compared to the office work usually done by women. There will, however, probably not be nearly as many newjbs created here as in software. In factories, these jobs will simply replace existing positions, while a data processing division in a company will require far more software workers than maintenance people.

A fourth area where jobs will be created is the manufacture of hardware. Besides the chips themselves, a wide variety of peripheral equipment, from terminals to printers to specialized control equipment and sensors, is needed to make up the complete automated system. Manufacture in Canada is limited and even in the United States, where more such jobs will be created, there is a tendency to export many of them to the Third World.

There are a number of other areas that will open up: selling computer equipment and software, and educating and training others in the new technology are two that come to mind. Women may find sales jobs difficult to get, particularly if they have a high technical component, but at least some of the educational areas may prove to be relatively open.

Given the predicted loss of clerical jobs in Canada and the United States, opening up access to new jobs being created is a necessary demand. Those who can must strive for entry into jobs now reserved for men simply as a survival tactic. Most women have no choice about working — they do so because they must. There are, however, major problems with training and retraining as universal solutions to the problems raised by automation.

The Automation of Automation

Training and retraining assumes there will be a comparable number of new jobs created to balance those that are lost. Whether or not this will happen is a matter of considerable debate, but the bulk of the evidence seems to be negative. My conclusion is that there will almost certainly be a severe *shortage* of jobs as a result of computer-based automation. A major factor here is the fact that the new jobs are subject to exactly the same forces of automation that have been operating in the factory and in the office. Let's look at this in some detail.

First of all, jobs running automated equipment are mostly deskilled ones, increasingly subject to higher levels of automation. Women who get training to be machine operators run the risk of finding their training obsolete in a short time. Keypunch operators who followed the same logic and retrained when their earlier jobs were eliminated, now find their recently-acquired skills equally out-of-date. Word processors may easily be replaced by yet more advanced equipment that responds to voice entry or optical character recognition or by procedures that force executives to enter their own material. Furthermore, simply retraining as a word processor operator does not deal at all with the questions of who controls the technology and the uses that are made of it. Nor does it address at all the exclusion of women from the shaping of machines and technology.

As far as actually tending the computers themselves goes, this, too, is being deskilled. More and more functions are being handled by operating systems and automatic controls of various kinds. As the technical expertise required decreases, it may very well be that this is an area where women will be hired, especially since the pay will go down.

The continuing trend to higher levels of automation in office jobs is nothing new. It is in the second category of jobs discussed above — software production and use — that the question of automation and productivity increases becomes more interesting. Consider the production of computer programs, for example. In the past programming has been a skilled craft in which technical expertise and the knowledge of details of the actual production of programs was a prerogative of the software workers. There is a flavor of artisan work here since programmers' procedures were largely of their own making and programs reflected the personal styles of their creators, who often used special tricks that were mysteries to both the managers and the end users of the programs.

This situation naturally tended to make managers nervous, as they found themselves dependent on individual software workers et floor, wformance of their automated systems. A friend, who developed almost all of the individual loan system for a local bank, claimed almost perfect job security since she was the only one who could reliably fix the system when it developed the inevitable bugs. Disgruntled programmers could even sabotage their own work and feel confident that no one else could fix it. Besides this problem of vulnerability, there was the problem of loafing raised by Taylor. There were no ways to set productivity standards and organize production so that workers could be monitored.

A rudimentary division of labor occurred quite early in this field with the appearance of highly skilled systems analysts at the top, program designers and programmer/analysts with somewhat lower skills in the middle, and lowly coders (who mechanically transformed a detailed design into actual computer code) at the bottom of the pile. This separation was not very successful in the beginning — often the highly paid top echelons did a great deal of low-level work. For example, the most difficult and time-consuming part of software production is debugging — finding out why the program doesn't do just what it's supposed to and fixing it. Since programs were so idiosyncratic, the highly paid software workers were the only ones capable of dealing with the problem. They would therefore spend their expensive time fixing old programs instead of creating new, profit-making ones.

Until recently then, management had no real control over the actual design and production of programs. But there have been a number of important developments recently that allow the introduction of industrial techniques into software production. First of all, the division of labor is being refined: IBM's "chief programmer team" technique is a good example of this; analysis of programming techniques has lead to a careful separation of tasks. The purely clerical function of keeping track of program listings, for example, is done by an unskilled clerical worker, thus freeing the expensive programmer to do more programming.

The use of "canned" programs is another important innovation that increases the division of labor and lowers average skills. A relatively skilled programmer writes a basic program, one to do bookkeeping operations for example. This program is designed to be suitable, with only minor modifications, for a large number of different businesses. It can be modified by "applications" programmers with relatively few skills to suit the needs of individual buyers. The result is an essentially mass-produced, standardized product. (If the program can't be sufficiently modified, then the buyer must modify appropriate business procedures to comply with the program's requirements.)

A third major development has been structured programming, with its rigidly specified programming methods. These are intended to be universal methods, understandable by all trained programmers. As Philip Kraft points out "the principle is simple: if managers could not yet have machines which wrote programs, at least they could have programmers who worked like machines." In accord with the best Taylorist principles, the work was to be made as simple, limited, and routine as possible. A highly skilled designer assigns work to lower level programmers, who create standardized program "modules" that fit together to produce a final product. Consequently, debugging is easier and can be done by workers with even fewer skills, since programming styles are no longer individual. As Kraft puts it:

> Structured programming, in short, has become the software manager's answer to the assembly line, minus the conveyor belt but with all the other essential features of a mass-production workplace: a standardized product made

in a standardized way by people who do the same limited tasks over and over without knowing how they fit into a larger undertaking.

The understanding of production techniques exemplified by structured programming has encouraged further automation of software. Since a standardized technique is involved, programmers' work can be segmented, controlled, and completely understood. At this point there is no reason why it can't be done by the machine itself. Program generators, programs that write other programs, have, in fact, been around for some time. They use what are called decision tables to produce the actual program code. A large government agency in Vancouver, well known for its assembly-line atmosphere, has been using such program generators for several years.

A more recently developed program generator uses question-and-answer routines in English to allow a program designer to specify system requirements and needs. The program generator then produces the required code in a standard computer language. Such a program is available commercially for most of the microcomputer systems widely used in business. The promotional material for such a program claims that "for the first time ever, a programmer need not shudder when a client asks for 'a few minor modifications'. Provided that the changes can be presented to the machine in a logical way, the problem of recoding is nothing more than waiting while your computer — at last — really does do the donkey work." The implication of automatically generated programs is that many of the lower level jobs in software production can now be eliminated.

Even the higher level jobs may not be exempt from automation. One large company in Vancouver now uses a program that begins to automate the work of system designers, the highly skilled software workers at the top of the heap. In their sales pitch, the company that developed this "automated systems design methodology" points out that the solutions to productivity problems lie within software technology itself and that systems analysis techniques can be applied to system analysis. A systems analyst working for the company says bitterly that "they're turning us into mechanics."

Those who are predicting the creation of thousands of jobs for software workers in the next short period in Canada and the United States clearly have not taken these new developments into account. It seems highly unlikely, given the rapid progress in productivity, control, and automation in the software industry, that anywhere near the predicted number of workers will be needed.

The third category of newly created jobs — the repair and maintenance of automated equipment — might seem immune from automation itself; not so. Here too, the trends toward deskilling and increasing productivity are clear. The new machines are designed in modular form, so that faulty sections can be easily replaced from stock. Self-diagnostic procedures, based on sensors and special chips in computers themselves and in peripheral equipment, are becoming common. An increasingly deskilled "repairman" plugs in the diagnostic outfit, pushes buttons specified by the repair manual, and replaces whole boards and modules according to the instructions he receives from the diagnostic program in the machine itself. Faulty parts may be cheap enough to throw away or they may be sent back to the supplier for repair. Fewer people with lower skills can now service the equipment. Jobs will not grow to match the growth in machines. One of the consequences of the deskilling of this work may be that it, too, will become more accessible to women, since it will no longer require heavy technical training.

The fourth major area of predicted new jobs — the manufacture of computer equipment — is also rapidly being automated in North America. This is part of a general introduction of robotics, computer-aided design, and computer-aided manufacture that will mean a rapid loss of jobs in manufacturing. These techniques and machines do not as yet dominate computer equipment production, but the trends are unmistakable. High technology areas of manufacturing are seeing the most rapid introduction of high technology automation.

The process of separating head and hand is nowhere better illustrated, incidentally, than in the manufacture of the devices which are at the heart of the new technology — the microcircuits, or chips, themselves. The two halves of this production process involve, on the one hand, the highly paid (male) technical workers in North America who design the chip itself, and, on the other hand, the very low paid women in Asia who attach, by hand, the connections that allow the chips to be plugged in.

Automation For What and For Whom?

The problematic relationship between women and technology is not going to be resolved easily. The separation between people and the tools and techniques of their work is a very deep one in this society. The control of technology does not rest with its practitioners —scientists and systems analysts — but with businessmen and bosses who use technological change for their own advantage and profit. Simply insisting that women should have equal access to high level jobs in technology does not begin to address the social use of the new machines with their expanded productive potential.

Very basic questions arise. Automation increases the possibility of a future with a much lower level of drudgery, where boring and dangerous jobs are done by machine. On the other hand, it also brings into sharp focus the problems of the present. In a society where being a full citizen is equated with having a job, what happens when there are not enough jobs for everyone? Women, as housewives, have borne the stigma of being un-waged workers in a wage-based society. As women, and men, are forced out of the labor market, will there be an institutionalized division between "the producers" with jobs and "the drones" without, as predicted as long ago as the 1920s by novelist Frederick Grove or again in the 1950s by Kurt Vonnegut? What would be the consequences of a future in which all the goods and services needed by North Americans could be produced, but couldn't be distributed because most people had no money? And, none of this even begins to take into account the relationship between the North American economy and the economies of the Third World.

These are all very hard questions. They have no quick answers. An adequate response to the problems raised by automation must involve a look at the very deep structures of society. The "training and retraining" response is a fundamentally inadequate one given the depth of the problem. Those advocating it are in effect claiming that in the face of major social changes, there are viable individual survival strategies for everyone. Since this is quite clearly not the case, it seems that this advice is as much ideological as practical. If the status quo is to be maintained, it is necessary for people to believe that what happens to them in their lives, especially their work lives, is their own individual responsibility and that it is their own fault if they somehow do not succeed.

The emphasis on individual responsibility as exemplified by self-improvement and by training/retraining is, I believe, setting the stage for another round of blame-the-victim, to which women are all too often subject. If women can't find new jobs, it is because they didn't get the proper training, didn't move with the times. None of the officials or government agencies who offer advice and conferences to working women is suggesting collective solutions. They are not urging working women to join or organize unions; they are not suggesting that we engage in a public discussion as to how and why those of us on the bottom might want to introduce or use the new technology. Short of fundamental social change, our options are limited. Unions, organizations of the unemployed, discussion, education, and research groups are all ways in which we can possibly exert some influence on the course of social change. The problem is much more than an individual one; it is unrealistic, therefore, to expect an individual solution.

Notes

Harry Braverman, *Labour and Monopoly Capital*, (New York: Monthly Review Press, 1977).

Frederick Grove, *The Master of the Mill* (Toronto: McClelland & Stewart, 1961).

Philip Kraft, *Programmers and Managers* (New York: Springer Berlag, 1977).

Heather Menzies, *Women and the Chip: Case Studies of Informatics on Employment in Canada* (Montreal: Institute for Research in Public Policy, 1981).

The CSE Microelectronics Group, *Microelectronics: Capitalist Technology and The Working Class* (London: CSE Books, 1980).

Kurt Vonnegut, *Player Piano* (New York: Holt, Rinehart, Winston, 1952).

Chapter 7

From Africa to America:

Black Women Inventors

by Autumn Stanley

If researching women's history is like looking for needles in haystacks, and researching women inventors is like looking for needles in haystacks when everyone denies that needles exist, then researching black women inventors is like looking for those nonexistent needles in haystacks that have been scattered by the wind.

But women inventors have existed from prehistory onward. In fact, if you go back far enough into prehistory, women were probably the primary technologists of the species, inventing most of the early tools, arts, crafts, and machines. African women are no exception. Evidence from mythology, anthropology, archaeology, and primate ethology supports this hypothesis about women's early technological role and can provide a new way of looking at the history of technology in general. This new view rejects male-defined criteria of significance, used implicitly in most histories of technology and invention, which consider the steam engine more important than contraception, which omit women's contributions to important inventions, and which define the technology connected with women's work as nontechnology.[1]

Let us look briefly at the available evidence for those times or stages of cultural development predating written history and patent offices, focusing here on black women, including both African Negroid women and women of the distinct !Kung and Pygmy peoples.

Mythological Evidence

Legends, stories, myths, and tales often provide insights into human activity. I would assert that if a major goddess is credited with inventing or giving to humankind some art, craft, tool, or process, women were likely to have been in charge of that activity in former times, whether they are now or not. For example, since Isis is credited with giving embalming to the Egyptians, I deduce that women were the first embalmers, but that the names of the women who originally devised the preservation procedures, and those of her successors who formalized and improved them, have not survived.

In the case of certain minor female deities or folkloric heroines credited with single inventions or advances, an individual female genius probably created the invention, and was deified or passed into folklore as a result. Such was the process with the Chinese Empress Si-ling She, who allegedly invented silk culture and silk cloth, and with Favorite, wife of Motu, in Congo myth, who brought fire from Cloud Land to Earth.[2,3]

In what I call "takeover myths," the women of a group were once in charge of a certain technology or activity and invented its tools or processes, but men stole the secrets from them. In such cases both the activity and the physical objects connected with it then usually became taboo for women. In the myths of many cultures, men steal fire not from the gods, but from women. In Pygmy myth women originally discovered or made the large horns that are central to the main religious ritual of the tribe, but men stole the instruments and took over the ceremony. Now no woman may set eyes on the instruments or be present at the ritual. Similarly, among the Ashanti of Ghana, women once made anthropomorphic images, but after a potter named Denta became barren because she molded "figure pots," women stopped making such pottery. And a Kono (Guinea) myth credits women with finding the secret of masks but losing it through fear, after which men took it over.[4,5]

Evidence from Anthropology And Archaeology

If anthropological reports show women in charge of a given activity for millennia, especially if the activity is taboo for men, as plowing and planting once were among the Greeks, then up to a certain point in the process of specialization, women probably invented the tools and processes connected with that activity. Food gathering and processing, horticulture, early agriculture, spinning, weaving, pottery (some recent evidence indicates that the world's earliest pottery may have been African, created in Khartoum (Sudan) about 8,000 B.C.), architecture, medicine, contraception, music, and probably even the beginnings of mining and metallurgy are examples of such women's activities.[6]

Division-of-labor evidence, although it must be treated with caution (since an ingenious male observer conceivably might have suggested an improvement in a women's activity), is among the most useful we have for women's early technological achievement. Many early historians and anthropologists were males who learned very little about what women did. Yet, this very under-representation of women's work in anthropological reports makes division-of-labor statistics extremely conservative, so that what I claim for women is likely to be too little rather than too much. As for the ingenious-observer theory, taboos and strict separations of the sexes for certain kinds of work make this theory much less likely in prehistory than it would be today. For instance, the beautiful quill work invented by Cheyenne women was a sacred activity performed only in the proper ceremonial manner by women initiated into the Quillworkers Society. No male would have been allowed near.

If females are buried with the tools of a certain trade or activity, or depicted on walls or vases engaging in various arts, crafts, or roles, this archaeological evidence also can be used as an indication of division of labor and a basis for qualified assumptions about the sex of the inventors of the tools. For example, grave objects in Old Kingdom Egypt indicate that women held all 22 of the Neith priesthoods, whose duties included mummifying the dead.[7]

Black women share fully in the great prehistoric record of women's inventive achievement. Like gatherers everywhere, early African women invented the carrying bag or net, the digging stick, the mortar and pestle, and other aids to finding, bringing home, and processing plant foods. The carrying bag was also, and perhaps first, a child carrier. Eventually these early African women invented horticulture — the intentional cultivation in one place of foods previously gathered wherever they grew. They transformed their digging sticks into hoes and their hoes into early plows. The first plows were modified hoes dragged across the garden or field, scratching the earth rather than turning a furrow like modern plows. Explorer David Livingstone reported from his African travels that he saw two women dragging such a primitive plow through the ground.[8]

When their gardens began to furnish crop surpluses, African women invented mud- or clay-lined storage pits, and clay or basketware granaries on stilts. The storage pits are a significant invention in their own right, but in some places they may have given rise to a more exciting innovation — an ancient people's antibiotic therapy. Researchers recently reported finding evidence that people who lived along the Nile in 400 B.C. had received large doses of tetracyclines, probably produced by mold-like organisms growing in the mud that lined the grain storage pits, and hence on the grain. It seems likely that women, in their role as storers and processors of grain, made the connection between the moldy grain and their freedom from disease, or they would have discarded the affected grain and devised new storage methods.

Like women elsewhere, African women were often the first builders of houses, inventing many of the basic forms of architecture. They are sometimes credited with inventing the dome in their clay granaries, and women builders in both African and non-African cultures could have invented the arch by bending saplings or reeds as a foundation for a tent or thatched dwelling. Masai women, for instance, build their tribe's houses of bent branches covered with skins. Women in other tribes actually weave house walls around bent pole or sapling supports, using textiles, felt, reeds, pre-woven mats, wattle, or thatch construction.

Sometimes myth and anthropology reinforce each other nicely. One African myth in which a woman builds a structure analogous to the Tower of Babel underlines women's role as house builders. In that Ila tribe story, an old woman who had known much trouble in her life decided to search out God and demand an explanation.

> She cut down some of the tall forest trees, and put them on top of one another, so as to make a ladder up to heaven. She built a great structure, but just when the topmost trees seemed to be getting near the sky the supporting timbers rotted away and the whole pile came crashing down.

The point here is not that the attempt failed — all Babel-builders are doomed to failure — but that a woman appears as the builder and seeker.

Evidence from Primate Ethology

The evidence from primate ethology is trickiest of all, and must be evaluated closely. In general, its value increases proportionally as it deals with species genetically closer to humans, especially chimpanzees. This evidence is still in its early stages, but many of the most respected researchers, who are women, are beginning to report some fascinating findings. Jane Goodall has found that among chimpanzees, with whom we share more than 99 percent of our genes, females spend more time using tools than males do. Hunting, mostly a male activity, is done with the bare hands, using no tools.

Moreover, if proto- and early-human social organization was originally based on mother-offspring units with males fairly peripheral, any social or physical inventions arising during that period, such as food sharing or the digging stick, would be far more likely to be transmitted to offspring if females invented them than if males did. With the new eyes given us by this evidence from prehistory, let us look at some likely entries in a revised history of technology.

Contraception from Prehistory to History

Contraception, from myths to history to contemporary anthropological reports, is a woman's invention. One of the most important inventions of all time, it ranks with the taming of fire, language, and the computer as a landmark in human technological development. However, it has seldom received that ranking, and most historians of technology, if they mention contraception at all, start from the nineteenth century, when male doctors produced versions of such ancient methods as cervical caps and diaphragms.

However, archaeological studies make clear, even while grossly underreporting the phenomenon, that in very ancient times women already had all the basic types of contraceptives used today, including herbal oral contraceptives and primitive intrauterine devices (IUDs). Some tribes even did ovariotomies for permanent sterilization; and ancient women may have had psychological and biofeedback methods we are only beginning to dream of.[9] On the basis of the usual division of labor on fertility issues, it seems reasonable to conclude that these were women's inventions.

African women, again, were no exception. Yao women used the sap of certain plants as a contraceptive. The Dahomey women of Central Africa invented vaginal plugs made of a crushed plant root. The Bapindas, the Bambundas, and other Central African tribes had oral contraceptives, but more often used vaginal plugs of rags or finely chopped grass. Herbal oral contraceptives would have evolved naturally from herbal abortifacients, early IUDs from early probe and foreign-body abortion techniques, and barrier contraceptives from the moss, sponges, fine grass, or other plant matter used to absorb the menstrual flow.

We would undoubtedly know more about the ancient history of contraception if more early anthropologists had been female or if males were less hostile to the idea. In an important report, Carleton Coon, studying the Riffian Hill Tribes of North Africa in the 1920s, said Rif women operated a secret weekly market where, among other things, herbal contraceptives and abortifacients were sold. Any man caught there would be severely punished. Coon learned of the market — from his wife — but could learn nothing about the antifertility formulas, since their sale and possession were secret. In fact, if a husband caught his wife practicing contraception, he would probably kill her. At the very least, it would be grounds for divorce.[10]

Middle Passage: To Invention Upon These Shores

African women, like African men, were captured by slave traders, dragged off on forced marches to the coast, crammed into stinking, disease-ridden ships and transported to the slave markets of the New World. At every stage many died, some by their own hand. Those who survived to reach North America had to improvise and make do in the manner of pioneers, only under unspeakably worse conditions. Traditional historians writing the stories of slave women, as of pioneer women, emphasize their emotionl strength in adversity rather than their technological wizardry in adapting to an alien culture on the one hand, and creating and managing farms and households without accustomed mechanical aids or support systems on the other. One example of black women's inventive adaptation is the Gullah baskets of South Carolina. Women from the Senegambia and Congo-Angola regions ("Gullah" is a corruption of "Angola") had to adapt their coil basketweaving technology to local materials — marsh grass, palmetto leaves, and long-leaf pine. They succeeded so admirably that replicas of these baskets are sold today in the boutiques of the Old Slave Market in Charleston, South Carolina.

Other impressive examples are the herbal remedies of black women healers. Some of these women's remedies were so successful that plantation owners would ask for them during plague and fever epidemics. These slave women also invented one of the most effective contraceptive devices ever known, a combination barrier and chemical method, using a spermicide far more powerful than that found in most spermicidal foams and creams today: a squeezed-out lemon half, with some juice remaining, served as a cervical cap.[11]

Later in the nineteenth century, when Mary McLeod Bethune (1875-1955) opened her first school in Florida, she made pencils out of splinters from a charred log, ink out of elderberries, and mattresses out of corn sacks stuffed with Spanish moss. In addition to this general category of improvisation and invention, there are a few examples of nineteenth century black women who patented their inventions. Even among free Blacks, a married women's invention would have been her husband's property until Married Women's Property Acts were passed late in the century. Thus many women either failed to patent their inventions or their names are lost from the records. And few single women of any race would have had the necessary money to secure a patent when working women made $3 to $6 a week, and a patent cost $100.[12] And of course a slave woman's invention would have belonged to her master. In spite of these handicaps, however, black women did invent devices to meet their needs and work roles, and a few succeeded in patenting their inventions.

On July 14, 1885, Sarah E. Goode of Chicago, Illinois, received Patent #322,177 for a folding cabinet bed. Goode is one of only two or three women inventors McKinley Burt mentions in his **Black Inventors of America**,[13] and since she is also mentioned in the Patent Office's bicentenial publication **Revolutionary Ideas**, her folding bed must have been a significant improvement.[14] Many nineteenth century inventions like this classed as "architectural" if by a man but "domestic" if by a woman, were intended to help families adapt to smaller living spaces.

Sarah Boone of New Haven, Connecticut, received Patent #473,653 on April 26, 1892, for an interesting special purpose ironing board. From the patent gazette drawing, this device seems to be a small, padded, curved, and tapered board that would fit inside a sleeve, easing the always difficult task of ironing a shirt sleeve perfectly smooth.

Ellen Eglin of Washington, DC, who worked alternately as a charwoman and a federal clerk, never patented her improved clothes wringer; instead, she sold it to an unscrupulous agent for $18 in 1888; the agent got rich. When asked why she sold the invention so cheaply after months of study, Eglin said, "You know I am Black and if it was known that a Negro woman patented the invention, white ladies would not buy the wringer. I was afraid to be known because of my color in having it introduced into the market."

Another fascinating black woman inventor of the nineteenth century was Miriam E. Benjamin, a teacher and federal clerk in Washington, D.C. On July 17, 1888, she received Patent #386,289 for a "gong and signal chair for hotels and the like." This chair had a gong or alarm controlled by a lever within easy reach of the occupant's right hand, and a silent signalling device that could be raised or lowered from the top of the chair back. Benjamin's chair enters history because the House of Representatives adopted it for use in its chambers.[15]

Twentieth Century Black Women Inventors

The most financially successful U.S. black woman inventor to date, and probably the best-known black woman of her time, Sarah Breedlove Walker, better known as Madame C. J. Walker (1867-1919) links the two centuries. Her suds-to-riches story is certainly as dramatic and worth telling as any Horatio Alger tale. Born to a Louisiana farm family, Walker was orphaned young, married at 14, and bore a daughter, A'Lelia. Widowed in her early twenties, she moved to St. Louis, where for 18 years she supported herself and her daughter by working as a washerwoman.

In 1905 she devised a method of transforming stubborn, lusterless hair into shining smoothness. Her method consisted of a shampoo, a pomade brushed vigorously into the hair, and a hot comb used to relax some of the curl. Demonstrating her method door-to-door, she won not only clients but agent-operators. The demand for cleanliness and the hygienic regime she incorporated into her agents' contracts were forerunners of the practices later required under state cosmetology laws.

By 1919 she had transferred her successful business operations to Indianapolis, where Walker products are still manufactured today. Her company has employed as many as 3,000 people, mostly female Walker agents, who make house calls all over the United States and the Caribbean. The best-selling product during her lifetime was her pomade, Madame C. J. Walker's Hair Grower, but some 16 other products appear in tin containers bearing her portrait.

When Sarah Walker became a millionaire, she also became a well-known philanthropist, endowing scholarships for young women at the Tuskegee Institute and donating money to the NAACP, homes for the aged, the YMCA, and the needy of Indianapolis. When she died in 1919, her last words were "not for me, O Lord, but for my race." Walker was the first person voted into their hall of fame by the readers of **Ebony** magazine in 1956.

Since the whole investigation of women inventors is still in a pioneering stage, only a few twentieth century names have surfaced since Madame Walker. Nevertheless, even these few names span a complete range of inventions from something as domestic as Beatrice L. Cowan's and Virginia E. Hall's embroidered wall hanging kit (#4,016,314), patented in 1977, to something as highly technical as Henrietta Bradberry's torpedo discharge means (#2,320,027), patented in 1943 during World War II.

Other women have been involved in developing cosmetic products for Blacks. Former model Carmen Murphy (1915-) first tackled the problem of the lack of good beauty salons and hairdressing systems for Blacks in Detroit in the 1940s, when she showed the operators of several small beauty shops new styling techniques for black women's hair.

Not content with her success, she addressed the cosmetic problem. Murphy worked with Irving Wexler, chief chemist of Rose Laird Cosmetics, to create a line of cosmetics that wouldn't turn dark skin ashy-looking. In 1951, after a year of work, they brought out Carmen Cosmetics in six basic colors that could be mixed to create 36 tints. Rose Laird's company manufactured the line for Murphy to distribute; when Rose Laird died in 1966, Carmen Murphy offered to buy the company.

Walker's and Murphy's stories typify women inventors' conquest over problems: even though they lacked technical expertise, they nevertheless succeeded in creating basically chemical inventions, and even though they lacked access to marketing services, they became inventor-entrepreneurs.

Less spectacularly successful, but still noteworthy in a world in which black women inventors experiencé the double discrimination of race and sex, are the following patentees, some of whom are also entrepreneurs: Virgie M. Ammons of Eglon, West Virginia (removable fireplace damper tool that can be wedged into position to lock the damper closed; #3,908,633: 1975); Beatrice Kenner of Washington, DC, (completely adjustable sanitary belt with front opening and an adhesive means for securing the ends of a sanitary napkin; #2,745,406: 1956); Virginia Scharschmidt of Harlem (a safe window-washing device usable from inside: 1930); Mrs. Mabel Williams of Chicago (Quick Buttons, a device that attaches buttons in seconds without needle or thread: 1957); and Mrs. Jessie T. Pope of Detroit (a thermostatically-controlled electric curling iron patented with the aid of Eleanor Roosevelt: 1946).

It has been common to dismiss many of the kinds of inventions listed just above as insignificant. Certainly none of them has ever appeared in a history of U.S. inventions. However, as the more perceptive observers of patents and inventive history have often noted, it is often a seemingly small idea that makes the most money. Moreover, under any proper definition of significance, an invention that could, like Beatrice Kenner's sanitary belt, increase the comfort of half the developed world's population during their menstrual periods should certainly be entitled to as much consideration as a new kind of gun.

Because of their traditional roles as nurses and caretakers, women often invented devices used in health and medicine. Two notable black women in this category are Bessie J. (Griffin) Blount, and Reatha Wiggins. Blount, a certified physiotherapist and teacher of educational therapy at Bronx Hospital in New York City, became so involved with her patients' problems and with their needs for independence that she resolved to invent something to help them in at least one area. The result was her invalid feeder, allowing a multiple amputee to eat without the aid of nurses or attendants. Blount spent five years and $3,000 of her own money developing the device. After trying repeatedly to interest the U.S. Veteran's Administration in the invention, she donated it to the French government, which willingly accepted it. Upon signing her agreement with the French, Blount commented, "A colored woman is capable of inventing something for the benefit of mankind." She added that she felt she had thereby made "a definite contribution to the progress of her people."

Reatha Wiggins, a technician at New York's Metropolitan Hospital, invented a multiple aspirator. Wiggins made many trips to children's wards, first as a volunteer and then as a hematological technician, where she observed that technicians often unexpectedly needed aspirators to clear children's throats of obstructions. In the early 1970s, with the aid of inventor Solomon Harper, she created a portable multiple aspirator to be carried by a nurse. As of 1972 she had been unable to interest any manufacturers in her device, but had already begun to see imitations of it on the hospital wards, and feared that companies would simply wait for her patent to run out and then manufacture their own versions.

Perhaps the most ingenious-looking invention on this twentieth century list is a home security system invented jointly by Marie Van Brittan Brown and Albert L. Brown of Jamaica, New York. The device, on which Marie's name comes first (Pat. #3,428,037: 1969), enables an occupant to use a television set to view a person knocking at her door and to hear the caller's voice, all without getting out of bed. This combined capacity, of course, involves both video and audio components and is an electronic application of some complexity. Brown's achievement is a reminder of something never hinted at in most histories of technology: that women can and will invent in whatever fields and roles they have access to. The only questions are which roles they shall have access to, and whether they get credit for what they have done.

Leonora Hafen's frustrations as a black female inventor — her lack of money, lack of education, need for a backer with marketing expertise or collaborator with technical skills — demonstrate the problem of "access."

Hafen, of Jackson Hole, Wyoming, was born in Cuba in 1941, and came to the United States at the age of five. Although she never finished high school and by 1969 she was a widow with four children to support, Hafen began to focus on her ideas for inventions. At first, luck seemed to be with her. A male backer had faith in her and paid for her first patent on a cleaning brush that can get into small corners, cracks, and crevices — "those places you usually end up using your fingernails for" — in tiled bathrooms. When her patent came through (Design Patent #235,942: 1975), Hafen was in the hospital. Visiting her there, her backer told her about the patent and urged her to get her other ideas ready. They planned to form their own company, but the next day he was dead.

Only temporarily daunted, Hafen knows she is a born inventor. She now has ideas for a toothpaste dispenser that will eliminate waste, for a rug shampooer that will eliminate splattering and clean within an inch of the wall, and for other kinds of brushes. Still looking for a backer, she works at two jobs in order to save money to market her first invention, just in case no backer appears.

Clearly, black women, like other women, have shown their creative and inventive abilities throughout the ages in any and all fields open to them, and even in some where they were forbidden to function. The stereotype that women of *any* color do not invent, persisting in the face of contradictory stereotypes of women as intuitive, creative, and intensely practical — the prime characteristics of an inventor — would be ridiculous if it had less tragic consequences. Its persistence is a far better reflection of *horror mulieris* — fear of women — than of historical accuracy. In other words, it is far easier for a camel to go through the eye of a needle than for a woman to pass into the kingdom of history. Doubly so if the woman is Black.

Notes

1. George P. Murdock and Caterina Provost, "Factors in the Division of Labor by Sex," *Ethnology* 12 (April 1973): 203-25.
2. H.J. Mozans, *Women in Science* (New York: Appleton, 1913, reprinted MIT Press, 1976).
3. Susan Feldmann, ed., *African Myths and Tales* (New York: Dell, 1963).
4. Geoffrey Parrinder, *African Mythology* (London: Paul Hamlyn, 1967).
5. Denise Paulme, ed., *Women of Tropical Africa* tr. H.M.Wright, (Berkeley: University of California Press, 1963).
6. Otis T. Mason, *Woman's Share in Primitive Culture* (New York: Appleton, 1894).
7. Elise Boulding, *The Underside of History* (Boulder, CO: Westview, 1976).
8. Nancy M. Tanner and Adrienne Zihlman, "Women in Evolution, Part I: Innovation and Selection in Human Origins," *Signs* 1 (Spring 1976): 585-608.
9. Barbara Seaman and Gideon Seaman, *Women and the Crisis in Sex Hormones* (New York: Bantam, 1978).
10. Norman E. Himes, *Medical History of Contraception* (New York: Schocken, 1936; Schocken paperback ed., 1970).
11. Dorothy Sterling, *Black Foremothers: Three Lives* (Old Westbury, NY: Feminist Press, 1979).
12. Deborah J. Warner, "Women Inventors at the Centennial," in *Dynamos and Virgins Revisited* ed. Martha Trescott (Metuchen, NJ: Scarecrow, 1979).
13. McKinley Burt, Jr., *Black Inventors of America* (Portland, OR: National Book, 1969).
14. United States Patent and Trademark Office, *Revolutionary Ideas: Patents and Progress in America* Washington, DC, 1976.)
15. Patricia Carter Ives, "Patent and Trademark Innovations of Black Americans and Women," *Journal of the Patent Office Society* 63 (February 1980): 108-26.

See also:
LWP: United States Patent Office, *Women Inventors to Whom Patents Have Been Granted by the United States Government, 1790 to July 1, 1888*, with Appendices (Washington, DC, 1888, 1892, 1895).
Notable American Women 1607-1950; A Biographical Dictionary, 3 volumes (Cambridge, MA: Harvard University Press, 1971).
Lois Decker O'Neill, *The Women's Book of World Records and Achievements* (Garden City, NY: Anchor, 1979).
Autumn Stanley, *Mothers of Invention* (Metuchen, NJ: Scarecrow Press, forthcoming).

A full list of sources is available by contacting the author through the publisher.

Chapter 8

Women and Appropriate Technology

A Feminist Assessment

by Judy Smith

As a feminist who has chosen to live in Missoula, Montana, where there is a lot of wilderness but not a lot of people, both women and nature are important to me. When I was a graduate student at the University of Texas in ustin in the late 1960s, I became involved in two social change movements. One was to empower women; the other was to stop the imminent ecological destruction of the earth. I now travel around the country talking about how these movements might work together, and involving more women in science and technological decision making. Although growing numbers of women I talk to say they are concerned about what technology is doing to the earth, many say, "I don't want to talk about technology. Technology isn't something we can control." Women who are math-anxious technophobes are not very interested in discussing the impact technology is having on them — even balancing their checkbook is just too much to handle. But to overcome a very basic socialization and psychological orientation in order to become confident in ecological and technological decision making is a prime priority for all of us.

There is no monolith called "technology." Technology is something we can indeed control — once we recognize that we live in an advanced technological age in which some people have power over techniques and inventions that affect other people. Developing a feminist assessment of technology will take a lot of work, but as a group of people with specific interests and desires, women can and must take some control over the technology confronting them in their daily lives.

Appropriate Technology

Before we determine why a feminist assessment of technology is so important, let's first define what "appropriate technology" is. An appropriate technology is one that is small scale rather than large scale, labor intensive rather than energy intensive, and decentralized rather than centralized, functioning on a human scale to meet human needs. Examples are solar and wind energy, gardening, aquaculture, and food preservation. Next let's ask ourselves, do any of the people doing the public debating over appropriate technology represent our interests as women? Does E. F. Schumacher, who wrote **Small is Beautiful**,[1] represent the interests of a feminist assessment of technology? Partly because we find so few allies in our struggle to develop such an assessment, and partly because different technologies affect women in different ways, assessment will be difficult. But it is urgent.

In 1978 I helped write a pamphlet for the National Center for Appropriate Technology called **Something Old, Something New, Something Borrowed, Something Due: Women and Appropriate Technology**.[2] In writing it, we looked at the literature of the appropriate technology movement and found a great deal of discussion of voluntary simplicity. We also found that the people who espoused those ideas and who led the movement were men, making decisions based on the same old values.

The inventions are made by men. At solar energy conferences, all the technical talks are still being given by men; however, all the education and public relations talks are given by women: sex role separation continues even within these "advanced" movements. The historical correlations are fascinating; men continue to the "hard work," while women do the "soft work," despite the fact that we are professing a "new technology." For example, one of women's traditional technological fields is agriculture. Time and time again, we find women in appropriate technology dealing with the construction of solar greenhouses, while the "important" projects, such as large-scale energy projects and solar collectors, are addressed by men. Technologies for preparing food and keeping the home are discussed by women and seldom, if ever, by men.

Thus, one of the basic problems we face in the appropriate technology and alternative energy movements is that adherents still reflect the value system we live in: men have the technical skills and make the technical decisions, their interests are self-assessed as more important.

That women's issues should be discussed within the context of appropriate technology is never even considered. For example, someone named Johnny Solarseed recently came to my campus, the University of Montana, as an advocate of appropriate technology. I should have known anyone traveling around the country calling himself Johnny Solarseed might have some problems! A friend tracked him down and asked, "What do you think the implications of appropriate technology are for women?" He paused and said, "Maybe it's sewing curtains so the heat loss out of houses won't be so bad." My friend asked him if he hadn't heard the discussion of how appropriate technology really affects women's roles: that if we use less energy, women might have to spend more time on home maintenance and wouldn't have time for other things. She asked him if he'd heard that men are controlling the appropriate technology movement. He became very defensive and responded, "I don't understand why feminists have to be so selfish. Why don't you want to stay home? I think the home is a really great place to be." Such conversations are disappointingly typical.

Being aware that alternative energy and appropriate technology people are not necessarily representing the interests of women who have questions about a sustainable society — one that is manageable now, yet capable of prolongation in the face of energy cutbacks — is very important. Proponents of these movements have internalized the very same values held by traditional technologists. Solar power, like nuclear power, has been discussed too long without consideration of its impact upon women. Until our basic interests as women are reflected in the decision-making process, the choice of high or low technology will not matter to us.

Can High Technology Be Appropriate?

Determining what would make a technology appropriate from a feminist perspective will be a complex task, for some technologies have actually expanded women's role options while others have restricted them; moreover, some technologies are so threatening to women that they should be completely eliminated.

Consider home maintenance technology. Appropriate technology people, down-playing the importance of women's time, say, "It's not a big problem if women have to spend more hours baking bread in a wood burning stove, or if they don't have as much leisure time because they have to raise a garden and do all the food processing too." But to me, that's a big problem. Studies have shown that when technology came into the home, women didn't really save a great deal of time because their standards for cleanliness went up. Technology only changed the type of labor that had to go into those housekeeping processes. Think of the amount of time and physical labor that used to go into home maintenance — would you be willing today to do what your grandmother did? Then ask yourself whether modern gadgets and appliances have really freed women's time, or have they just changed the way we allocate the time we have? Women must demand that more effort be made to create homes which truly require minimal maintenance.

One of the most heated debates in technology for the home involves the microwave oven. Personally, I think the microwave is appropriate, but most people in alternate energy see it as a symbol of everything wrong, saying, "It's dangerous. It's high technology. It will change the aesthetics of the food we eat." The image of the woman who uses a microwave is one of a selfish, flighty woman out doing something unimportant, who rushes home, puts her food in the microwave, sticks it in front of her husband and children, and who doesn't care about her family.

The other side of the argument is that microwaves do not use a great deal of energy and can be used safely. In addition, women who have two careers, one outside the home and one in, say the microwave is a significant help to them. So, as a feminist developing criteria for appropriate technology, I would say the microwave can be appropriate. In fact, a technology that saves women's time or expands their role options is almost by definition appropriate, unless it can be shown to be hazardous, or energy consuming.

Another example of how technology has expanded women's possibilities is in the area of physical strength. In Montana, where we still have the image of the rough, tough cowboy, biceps are important. People there and elsewhere say women can't do the forestry work men do; they say women shouldn't be out building highways. Women aren't strong enough, they say. But technology has eliminated the size of an employee's upper arm as a bona fide qualification for work. Nowadays, any woman can work a chain saw or run a fork lift, despite what the muscle-flexing cowboys think, and there are women in Montana, and elsewhere, doing these jobs and doing them as well as men. In these cases, technology has helped women.

Contraception has also been of technological benefit to women. But the kinds of contraceptive choices available are the result of high technology, and pose some distinct dangers we must be aware of. The question must be, is this technology appropriate? Granted that for the first time in history women can choose whether and when to have children. Is that a sufficient criterion? What about side effects? Are we willing to invest more time, more energy into research to develop even better methods? If not, why not?

Some technologies, on the other hand, restrict women's role options. How many of us work in offices that are going to be computerized? Or in automobile manufacturing plants that are going to be computerized? The people who market computers say one computer can take the role of 20 women in an office. When a machine enters a new field, it usually drives out female expertise, and women tend to be restricted: technology in these cases means jobs losses for women.

Childbirth is the perfect example of this progression. Since we're the ones who give birth, this is one area where women certainly should have expertise, yet men are the experts. Historically women have been denied access to medical technology. Midwives, therefore, were considered less well trained and thus less capable, even though statistics never proved it; finally, women were legislated out of involvement in childbirth.

The fetal monitor is a technology that is very dangerous to women although most of us are, unfortunately, exposed to it when we go through delivery. It was developed for a very good reason — to help with high risk pregnancies,'' but its prevalent use shows how the existence of a technology can, in and of itself, be a problem for women. Doctors or obstetrical nurses admit they routinely use the fetal monitor in almost every delivery; by using the machine, medical personnel can watch what's going on without having to rely on what women say. But the fetal monitor has a high rate of negative side effects and complications and is probably directly responsible for the increase in Caesarean sections, which themselves are much more dangerous to women than normal deliveries.

A Feminist Perspective

These examples illustrate my point that technologies can either expand or restrict women's role options; and, in some cases, can be very dangerous to women, especially if women themselves are not making the decisions about their use.

Who is deciding which technologies to use? This and other fundamental questions must be dealt with as we develop a truly feminist assessment. We are being told, for example, that to maintain the present level of growth in our society and to achieve equity for those of us who have been denied access to power, we are going to have to use up our resources. Is that true?

Nuclear power advocates are literally telling women that if we don't go nuclear, we will be back on our knees scrubbing floors. If that is true, what are we as women going to do about it? What are we women going to do in the sense of trade-offs between our power, our equity, and energy development?

If we go back to low technology alternatives, that is, labor-intensive rather than energy-intensive solutions, whose labor will we depend on? We're usually talking about women's labor making up the difference. In some cases that may be acceptable because a high energy-resource utilization society is not always going to be sustainable. That sometimes we may have to be willing to trade our time is a consideration we should be aware of as feminists, but, when we make that trade, we must always ask what our reward will be for putting our labor back into more traditional environments.

Another question is, do we need technological fixes for past oppressive roles? Is a technological solution appropriate? Do we need household technology, for example, or can we rely on a political social fix? To me, the answer is very clear, at least for the present. I have never seen a political social fix that works; I have never seen a piece of legislation that gets men to do half the housework, and it has been tried — Cuba actually passed a law requiring men to do 50 percent of the housework. Can you guess what happened?

Therefore, the most important task ahead is involving women in technological decision making. We have to educate ourselves, and all women, about the impact technology has on our lives, then we must apply what we learn. And that means we have to reach out to women who now feel totally unequipped to deal with technology, even the technology they use daily in their homes and at work. There are growing groups of women around the country who are trying to make that contact. For instance the American Association of University Women is addressing the whole issue of women taking hold of technology.

If we wish to live in a sustainable, ecologically-sane, nonsexist society where women are equal and have power, women as a group must be involved in the decisions that affect their lives, decisions which are now being made without them. Feminist involvement is essential today, tomorrow, and always. For if we do not figure out how we can develop and maintain such a society, all of us, woman, man, and child, will lose not only the benefits of the present but the promise of the future.

Notes

1. E. F. Schumacher, *Small Is Beautiful: Economics As If People Mattered* (New York: Harper and Row, 1973).
2. Judy Smith, *Something Old, Something New, Something Borrowed, Something Due: Women in Appropriate Technology*, second printing (Missoula, MT: Women and Technology Project, 1978).

See also:

Judy Smith, et al., *Women In Technology: Deciding What's Appropriate* (Missoula, Mt: Women and Technology Project, 1979).

For further information, contact: Women and Technology Network, 315 South 4th East, Missoula, MT 59801, (406) 728-3041.

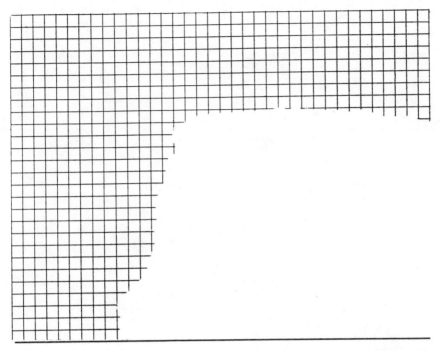

Part II

Ladies' Home Technology

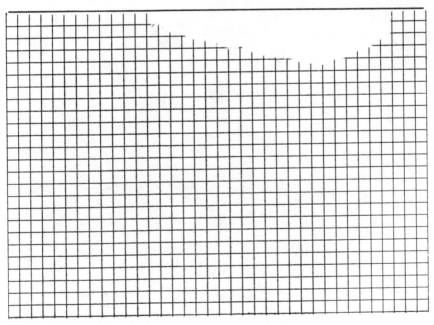

For much of their history, women have been confined to roles in the private sphere. This restriction has not only limited their role options in the public sphere, but has resulted in a general devaluation of the (unpaid) work done within the home and an almost guaranteed anonymity for those who do it. Yet within this assigned context of home and hearth, women have not only controlled and improved numerous technologies, but have invented both basic processes and various devices to sustain daily life.

As Autumn Stanley showed in the previous section, women were responsible across many cultures for the development of horticulture, housing, and healing. From Native American women who constructed the tipi and the travois for transporting it, to Shaker women who designed revolving ovens and cut nails, women historically have used their ingenuity to invent the tools needed to function effectively in their environment. This tradition is carried on by Frances GABe, a 67-year old artist and inventor who has been building a Self-Cleaning House (SCH) for the past 20 years. "I don't see why women have to do their work either on their knees or with their head hanging in a hole," she explains.

Other women, as Kristin Luker and Katherine Jensen show, also have technical skills that are displayed in a domestic setting. Consistent with their historical knowledge of fertility, contraception, and healing, women managed abortion as a domestic technology, prior to the growth of a powerful medical profession in the twentieth century. And rural women have longed played a critical part in managing family ranches and farms, acquiring a degree of technical competence that puts their urban sisters to shame. Not included here but obviously important would be the numerous lesbian collectives and other all-female communities that have supported women's efforts to learn nontraditional skills and develop technical mastery. In all these cases women have or had the knowledge and opportunity to cope with the material world around them. Most women, however, somewhere along the way to the "all-electric" home with two cars in the garage have — through no fault of their own — been deprived of a sense of self-sufficiency even in the private sphere.

Now many of us are vulnerable to the poor quality and planned obsolescence of modern appliances. Over our lifetimes, we probably spend several months waiting for other people to repair the cars, telephones, stereos, washing machines, digital clocks, dishwashers, TV sets — and soon computers — that frame our lives. The schedule of our day-to-day lives, particularly in a complex urban network, has become the aspect of our lives that appears to be the least under our control. Whether it is a matter of matching public transit schedules or allowing the time needed to commute to work by car, of driving children to after-school activities in three different directions, or of taking sick leave in order to wait for a repair service, our feet are stuck in the gooey mud of daily life.

To be sure, much of this is due to women's double burden of jobs both inside and outside the home. And to be sure, social changes that would more equitably distribute the responsibilities of a household among all its members would help. But as many authors cite in these pages, neither social change nor technology has been enough. The Women's Movement and home appliances notwithstanding, women still do over 90 percent of the household chores and the time they spend on housework has either remained the same or increased since their grandmothers' day. The reasons for women's lack of status or pay for their work in the home are too lengthy for full exploration in this section, but the lack of validation for homework as *real* work certainly has contributed to women's burden.

Four of the authors in this section explain how technology has conspired to increase, rather than decrease that burden. Household technologies, urban planning, transportation systems, and energy production are the types of technologies we tend to take for granted. These systems, along with the water that comes from the faucet and the highways we ride on are part of the invisible technical infrastructure that defines our lifestyles. Christine Bose and Philip Bereano take a critical look at the popular myth that utilities, appliances, convenience foods, and purchased services have improved the housewife's lot, while Ann Markusen explores the problems of architecture and urban planning from the microscale of the kitchen to the macroscale of the city.

Complementing this study of urban space, Genevieve Giuliano analyzes why transit alternatives from the car to the subway fail to help women get around it adequately. And Irmgard Hunt approaches an alternative energy future by showing how women's power as consumers can alter patterns of both energy consumption and production. Finally, Jaime Horwitz and I consider the consequences of a "terminal future" in which many activities, from shopping to work, are carried out on home computers. In this "domesticated city," women may have little reason or opportunity to leave their homes.

Thus this section is part celebration of women's technological competence, part exposition of how this competence has been eroded by large-scale technical systems, and part concern about the future of the private sphere. All of it is about the ways that *material* reality — the man-made, man-built world — affects women's lives, choices, and options. By extension, then, it also points to ways that feminist concerns and values could be embedded into alternative material constructs.

Chapter 9

The GABe Self-Cleaning House

by Frances GABe

I am often asked why I invented the Self-Cleaning House (the SCH), what it was that got me started doing it in the first place, and why I felt it was important enough for me to be willing to spend 27 years of my life doing it. These questions always amaze me because to me the answers are obvious — *there had to be a better way* .

Necessary as it is to civilized living to have clean surroundings, if there is a family whose members have ever appreciated their mother's efforts enough to have so much as told her "thank you" for having spent hours on end doing one repugnant household cleaning job after another for them, I've never met them.

Men decided a few centuries ago that any job they found repulsive was women's work. *They* didn't want to clean up someone else's dirt either, and who can blame them? How clever it was of them to find a way to make someone else do it instead. But in all fairness, why me instead of you? Why you instead of me? Housework is a thankless, unending job — a nerve-twanging bore. Who wants it? Nobody. With my jaw set hard I was determined that *there had to be a better way* ! Some way, somewhere, I would find it.

But the above is only part of the reason. I saw old people being shipped off to rest homes because they could no longer take care of the homes they had worked for all their lives. I was outraged that now, when they needed the familiar, the personal, more than at any time in their lives, their so-called "golden years," they had to put up with just the opposite — a foreign, shrunken environment, without privacy, among strangers. *There had to be a better way* !

I remember with bitterness the years that my children were growing up. I never had a quarter enough personal time for them. Try however hard I might, I was always forced to work like a slave instead of care for their physical needs, with little time left over for their emotional and mental needs. I did not enjoy my children; I didn't have time! I resent this bitterly. For that matter, so do they. *There had to be a better way* !

Since the media has been publicizing the Self-Cleaning House, I have been in contact continually with women the world over. Of all of them, only three either didn't care how dirty their environment became or would actually miss cleaning their houses. The rest of the ladies loathed housework with a rabidity that surprised me greatly. I wonder why I was surprised, since I, too, resent the wasted years of my life that were used so much against my will merely to throw dirt out of our home faster than the family could bring it back in again. There's got to be something better in life than that. Seeing women working a regular eight-hour day, then going home to put in a second shift to take care of their houses and families — moonlighting in their own homes — did nothing whatever for my sense of justice, either. *There had to be a better way* ! The Self-Cleaning House *is* that better way.

Understandably, the cost of building a Self-Cleaning House (SCH) is of primary importance to most people. They think the electrical and plumbing expense alone will be prohibitive. But not so! For instance, the entire self-cleaning functions of the average SCH home, or their equivalent in a business building, including the clothes-freshener and dishwasher cupboard, will be automatically operated with the use of *one* rotary contact switch, either triggered manually or by an electrical triggering device. Other costs connected with the SCH are similarly measured. The SCH system was not planned as a luxury item for the wealthy only, but as something most average people could afford to buy and operate.

There have been many preliminary tests and modifications made on the first concepts of the SCH, but the basics have changed little. To date, as intended, all the inventions used in the full-scale house are functioning perfectly. This past and present success promotes faith in the inventions yet to be installed to complete the house. Great care has been taken to keep this house the home we have been accustomed to, and still have it function perfectly. This is a much *better* home, not just a different one. It is a much better office or business building, a truly sanitary hospital, rest home, restaurant, bakery, bank, or pharmacy. My **Top Security** window-walls are designed for mental hospitals, banks, warehouses, or drugstores. It would be virtually impossible for anyone to fall out of an upper-story window if GABe **Top Security** windows were installed, whether the windows were open or closed. Owners of public restrooms will glory in the SCH system.

During the early days of the SCH, there was the expected ridicule for trying to do something impossible. When I finally proved the SCH was not only possible but practical, the howl changed to "if you can do something as difficult and unheard of as cleaning a whole house or other building economically and efficiently, why can't you also invent something to pick up a house before the apparatus is turned on? Like kids' toys and clothes. When everything is picked up, half the work of cleaning a house is already done."

The answer is "why pick things up at all?" Why not leave out everything but clothing to be cleaned along with the house itself? *Everything* gets dirty, toys especially. Most of them are already washable. And that's the way the whole concept of the SCH was worked out.

One does not cover up hi fis, desks, TVs, or pianos. There is a way of protecting and washing them with the SCH system. Beds are not stripped before the cleaning system is activated. Pictures and wall decorations are left in place on the walls. There is no word in the dictionary for the way the water is used so it must be explained. It is warm mist under controlled pressure. One can't drench one's home, office, or restaurant with water, certainly not a hospital or school building. Many people have deduced that that is the way it would necessarily have to be done. Not so; every drop of water has to earn its way in cleaning power.

The SCH was never intended to clean a dirty house or building, but to keep a clean house or building clean. (If people won't even punch a button to clean their quarters, one can only deduce that they like them dirty.)

The **General Room-Washing Apparatus** is connected to the feeder pipe. The feeder pipe is used to bring the water to the cleaning apparatuses, to blow warm pressurized air for drying the room after cleaning, to dispense warm air for heating the building in winter and cool air for cooling it in summer, to eject a fine mist of germicide into a room where there has been a communicable disease, and to dispense bug repellent or killer, in case of infestations of termites, carpenter ants, bedbugs, cockroaches, fleas, or stinging or biting insects.

The half of the apparatus that is in the ceiling is only ten inches long, about four inches wide and extends into the room less than four inches. Each apparatus promises to clean and dry a 45-foot by 50-foot area. A little more time for experimentation is needed to determine this fact conclusively. So far it has been lab-tested. Since the apparatus revolves when in action, there will be no stale, hot, or cold spots in a room where the SCH apparatus is used. The ceiling part of the apparatus is not exposed to view. It has an ornate grillwork housing that looks very much like a ceiling light fixture. These cleaning apparatuses are not electrically powered. *The cleaning water also serves to power the apparatus* .

The second half of the room-cleaning apparatus is located at the junction between the wall and floor and looks like a slightly larger-than-average baseboard. It will do everything that the ceiling half of the cleaning apparatus does, except revolve. It will wash the floor and blow all the collected water from the rest of the room toward the floor drain located in one corner of the room.

The SCH **Spot Cleaner** is for cleaning spills or small areas that need really heavy cleaning. This auxiliary cleaner employs a hose with a modified nozzle. With this cleaner one has a choice of hot or cold water, the choice of using soap or not, and forced air for drying. Once again, it is not the amount of water used that does the cleaning, but the manner in which a very small amount of water is used.

Dishwasher Cupboards and **Cupboard Dusters**, use the same type of cleaning apparatus as the room washers. There are modifications to suit each usage, but basically they are the same. Present dishwashers require taking dishes off the table, putting them in the dishwasher, taking them out of the dishwasher, putting them in the cupboard, taking them out of the cupboard, and putting them back on the table. What a dreary merry-go-round! The lucky owner of an SCH **Dishwasher Cupboard** will take the soiled dishes off the table and put them in the cupboard, where they will be washed and dried and ready to be put back on the table.

SCH dishwashers come in several sizes and can be mounted below or above the counter. I recommend that a family choose one approximately the right size for the dishes for one meal only; this one would be used every day. Then there would be a larger one for company dishes, which would also serve as the storage cupboard for those dishes. This minimum handling of dishes will cut down radically on breakage. Because of the arrangement of these **Dishwasher Cupboards**, there is no dish in front of, in back of, on top of, or under any other dish. There are no stacks of dishes anywhere. There is no stack of saucers to remove from the middle of a stack of plates before one plate can be taken out. The arrangement of the **Cupboard Duster** cabinets also makes it possible to dust the cabinets and their contents without removing anything from the cabinets. One merely presses a button, counts to 50, and the job is done.

The **Dry Cupboard** in every room is for the few things that must be protected from moisture. In the bathroom the dry cabinet will house toilet tissue, bath towels, medicines, electric shavers, and bathroom scales — they won't require a very large cabinet. These dry cabinets sport rubber gaskets on their doors and the same dust-expelling construction that all the cabinets, shelves, and drawers in the SCH have. It is virtually impossible for dust and lint to collect in them. In the kitchen the **Dry Cupboard** will hold packaged and canned foods, dishtowels, paper towels — what else? Is there anything else that cannot benefit from a warm mist-washing? No, because there is also a water protector for the cookbooks. They can be left anywhere they have always been left — on the counter, in a cupboard, or drawer.

Kitchen canisters can be as cheap as the give-away glass jars that nondairy creamer once came in, or as lush as some of the GABe hand-carved, sculptured bowls and boxes with built-in, water-guard lids. Canisters should be nonmetal, if they have to be left standing on countertops, to prevent rust and stains on the counters. There are hundreds of nonmetal containers that will serve very well.

GABe SCH Furniture includes GABe desk and dressing table designs with **No-Bother** tops that seal themselves from moisture before the apparatus is activated. All wooden furniture is glued with resin glue and finished with high grade spar (marine) varnish. Often it is necessary to leave items out on top of a dressing table or desk. There are GABe designs for flat boxes with **No-Bother** lids in which to store all the papers on the desk; put the lid down and forget them. These container lids are hinged in such a way that when a box is opened, the lid folds out of the way. These covered boxes are most desirable because papers would otherwise collect dust. These boxes are made of a rigid, transparent material so that one can see through them and know without lifting the lid what papers are inside. They can be stacked on tables or desks as high as one chooses and forgotten indefinitely, if the lids are on. One small **No-Bother** container at the side of the typewriter, using dust-expelling construction, protects papers, pencils, erasers, and other small items.

Dressing tables are handled in much the same way. Nonwashable items are stored in dust-expelling drawers or, if left on top of the dressing table, in see-through **No-Bother** containers. Items kept in the dust-expelling drawers need no other containers, unless they need confinement because of their small size. Most things, however, would benefit from a good washing and drying — combs, brushes, lipstick cases, powder boxes, soaps — all with waterproof lids.

Books can be left anywhere as long as **GABe Shields** are used on them. These covers fit over books, come together in the center of the pages, and are sealed around the back upon the closure of the book. They are very easy to open and close. Pictures have their own protective covers that can easily be removed with no ill effect to the pictures whatever. They are invisible. Paintings and pictures can be slipped into these shields, then put into the frame they came out of.

The GABe **Clothes-Freshener** is a unique way of washing clothes. Hang the soiled clothing in the closet, press a button, and in approximately an hour the clothes are washed, dried, and hanging in the closet, ready to wear again. This takes place without affecting the rest of the contents of the closet in any way whatever. It is the arrangement of the closet that does the trick. The **Clothes Freshener** has been lab-tested and promises near-miracles in clothes washing and drying. At this time a full-scale model is being installed in my experimental studio addition. I originally thought that it would freshen clothing worn once that was mussed and sweaty. Lab tests have indicated, however, that it will likely do much, much more. Experiments will continue on the full-scale model until it becomes a true washing machine and dryer.

The closet proper is also self-cleaning. Dripping raincoats, umbrellas, muddy shoes can all be put in the closet. They will leave no puddles. The floor will not get dirty. The same water that washes the clothes in the freshener also washes and rinses clean the closet floor, without in any way affecting anything on the floor of the closet. Again, it is the arrangement of the closet that does the trick. The same apparatus that dries the clothes in the freshener will also dry the closet floor.

GABe Beds are not stripped before the room cleaning apparatus is turned on. They are fully made up. The springs are protected from moisture by putting a waterproof mattress cover on the *underside* of the springs, and leaving it there permanently. This keeps the moisture from the floor away from the springs on the bed. The mattress and bedding are protected during the washing cycle by a sheet of plastic that is pulled window-shade fashion from a roller at the head of the bed, down over the foot end. The pillows at the head create enough slope to serve as a drain for the water during cleaning. After the room is cleaned and dried, the plastic cover is released from the foot end and rolled up into a small bolster above the pillows at the head of the bed. The bedstead itself is cleaned with the rest of the room. The bedding is the only item of the Self-Cleaning House that is covered during the cleaning cycles.

The only thing, at this stage, that we are accustomed to having in our homes for which a solution has not been found, is wall-to-wall carpeting, which is one of the things I feel needs to be eliminated. For the life of me I can't see why we need carpeting under heavy pieces of furniture, furniture that has to be painfully dragged away before the carpet can be cleaned by vacuuming, and then struggled back into position once again. Wall-to-wall carpeting came into vogue when it was discovered that carpeting is much cheaper than a good floor.

For an SCH I recommend old-fashioned hall runners to eliminate noise in the traffic lanes and area rugs elsewhere. These can be rolled up and taken out before the washing cycle begins. The SCH can survive without wall-to-wall carpeting, but it cannot survive without the **General Room-Washing Apparatus**. At this time the two are not compatible.

The SCH plumbing fixtures consist of a self-cleaning washbasin, shower, a self-cleaning therapeutic bathtub, and a waterless, organic composting toilet that is truly beautiful. The porcelain toilet has no base to collect spatters and dust. One cannot see down through the toilet bowl to the pit below. This toilet has either a side or back discharge orifice. The pit can be either outside of the building or in the basement. The toilet "flushes" automatically when the lid is closed, and it does so without a drop of water. It is less bulky than our present toilets and very sanitary; it is completely silent.

The **GABe Bathtub** is never cold because its base is made in such a way that it serves as the furnace outlet for the bathroom. The same outlet on the tub serves as a body-drier. The tub is slip-proof; its inside is made of a soft material. The foot end of the inside of the tub is higher than the hip section, raising the knees and feet for maximum therapeutic benefit. The head end is much higher than in conventional tubs and becomes a very comfortable head rest. The water can be continually circulated if one wishes, merely by pressing a button on the control panel located at the side of the tub. The tub, like the rest of the fixtures, is self-cleaning. All of the bathroom fixtures are readily adaptable to any architectural and decorative design.

An SCH can use any building material that can be made waterproof — glass, wood, cement, frame, stone, or brick. It can be any size from a one-room cabin to a 100-room resort hotel. The **Window-Wall Building Blocks** come in a number of designs — **Blushing Splendor** is one of the loveliest; **Wasp Waist** is also beautiful. **Top Security** blocks stand alone in the category their name implies; they are designed for security for banks, hospitals, warehouses, mental institutions, prisons, drugstores, and upstairs bedrooms — especially for children. They can also be used behind cupboards, closets, and otherwise dark stairwells. Even if vandals broke out every window pane in the SCH, they could not get inside to do further damage or thievery. They would have to use a jackhammer to tear away the cement wall first. This could be done, of course, but the cement would certainly be a deterrent. All GABe windows are made of building blocks that can be stacked or interlocked. There is a full 7¼ inches of dead air insulation in each **Window-Wall Block** because there is a window pane both on the outside and the inside of the window opening. For those windows that open, there is a pair of small glides (or guns) that opens the outside and inside window panes at the same time. This operation is activated by pulling on a pair of small handles on either side of the window. Between the two panes of glass in the opening windows is a window screen. This screen is permanently protected from the weather and therefore will resist rust and corrosion indefinitely. However, replacing them is a simple matter.

The **Self-Cleaning Fireplace** is a fact. The days are over when, just because you cleaned out the fireplace, you also had to dust the whole house to remove the ash dust. The SCH fireplace removes the ashes by washing them down a drain at the back of the fire pit. No dust. No muss.

SCH floors have no visible floor drains. The floor itself serves as the drain. Therefore it must have a controlled slope. A local official, some builders, and several architects asked me what I was going to do when the house settles, after it has been built a while, and it loses its carefully engineered drainage system. "People are going to be damned mad when they find puddles of dirty water here and there on the floors of their new home!" "All buildings settle some! How are you going to know what the right floor slope is in the first place on any building? Nobody knows that!" "Floors are all a bit irregular and nobody worries about that, but builders never expect to control their slope exactly!" "Hope you're rich enough to afford to tear the damned things up 50 times and do them over!"

Granted, floor joists in an SCH do have to be adjustable to insure a constant, properly-engineered slope. They are. This solution doesn't add a single cent to the cost of the construction.

Eventually I showed one of the gents my SCH **Floor Joists**. He looked and gulped as though he'd swallowed a bug. He stared at me for some unbelieving seconds, then shook his head to clear it. He cracked up, guffawing loudly, and said at last, "Well . . . why in the hell not?!!!!" What could he say? It *is* good construction. And like all the SCH, the floor is built according to code.

Another time an official visited the SCH and walked around and around the studio addition. He reported, "No wonder you can't get a man to work for you; you're sure par-tic-lur." (I hadn't been trying to get a man to work for me. I couldn't afford one.) I answered, "Sure. Do you leave me any choice? I have to prove myself over and over and over . . .!" We stood there grinning at each other, both of us enjoying the contest. He could give me a very bad time, but he hasn't. It's been my experience that it is only the insecure, petty, "little" men who feel compelled to be antagonistic and even vicious to me. This man is not petty or little, even though he is no taller than my 5 feet 4 inches. He is convinced that I know what I am doing, and how to do it.

When people see the SCH for the first time, they are surprised that it is not straight out of Fantasyland. Instead, the building is attractive and functional. The type of windows used throughout, for example, are windows as we know windows. Before seeing it, some people have asked, "What is it? A cement culvert down which one plays a fire hose to clean it? I suppose the furniture is plastic and chrome steel bolted to the floor."

That would have been easy. But to come up with upholstery that can take rugged living, that can stand the day-to-day cleaning system and still be good looking — *that* was hard. All of the SCH was hard work. There are many, many things about it that are brand new and that have never been done before, although few of them are visible. I have worked very hard to preserve our homes as they are, even though they are self-cleaning — I've been successful.

Notes

For more information about the Self-Cleaning House, contact: Frances GABe, c/o F. GABe Studio, Route 5, Box 695, Newberg, OR 97132, (503) 538-4946.

Chapter 10

Household Technologies:

Burden or Blessing?

by Christine E. Bose and Philip L. Bereano

Both the general public and many academics assume that technology, broadly defined, has "freed" women for other, nonhousework tasks, in particular for employment in the paid labor market. These assumptions are reflected in the popular names of several of the products: "fast foods" to save time, "convenience foods" to increase ease, and "labor-saving devices" to lighten the work load. This imagery has such power that much traditional research assumes these effects occur and rarely bothers to test these assumptions. Yet even with the unprecedented growth of the market sector and the almost universal availability of certain items of household equipment and goods, recent studies show that labor in the home today still accounts for approximately half of this country's total work time.[1] Thus nothing appears to have freed women from their household burdens, even though increasing numbers of women are working for pay as well. Our goal in this paper is to investigate technology's role in the development of this apparently contradictory situation.

Technology is widely, and largely incorrectly, believed to have increased the convenience or efficiency of performing housework. Internal household efficiency (and certainly equity) might be affected if technology could change the household specialization of labor, or the way in which household maintenance tasks are divided among members of the household. But the practice in North American households today is for women to do the largest proportion of these tasks, and there has been relatively little change in this over the last 15 years.[2] Further, the total time spent on housework either increased or remained stable between 1930 and the 1950s.[3] Technology certainly has the potential to alter household labor demands so that housework would absorb a smaller percentage of women's total available work time; and some of the work that is performed in the home could be accomplished by provision of equivalent market services, such as domestic help, fast foods, laundries, and daycare.

Historically, however, technology has done none of these things: it has *not* reallocated more tasks to other members of the household, it has *not* reduced the actual demands on women, and it has *not* provided many services outside the home. The past holds some lessons on these issues for the future.

Prior to the Industrial Revolution the household was a center of both production and consumption for all its members. As industrialization began, the household retained its dual character, producing goods both for home consumption and for the market economy under the cottage system. The latter function diminished rapidly as centralized factories developed, leaving the home solely as a center for consumption and socialization. The market economy produced goods for use in the home, rather than developing food, laundry, or childcare services to take more functions outside of it. It has been suggested that this path was foreordained between 1907 and 1916, when large capital investors chose the automobile as a profitable outlet.[4] The resulting residential sprawl made many group services unprofitable, compared to technologies such as appliances and convenience foods, which fit the atomized pattern.

Although production moved out of the home, housework did not decrease. If anything, standards of output rose. Once the industrial ethic of efficiency and labor savings (known as rationalization) developed in the outside workplace, the home became the next logical site to apply these values. The declining number of available servants early in this century (due in part to immigration restrictions), was seen as a "crisis," increasing the pressures for efficiency and higher standards in the home.

Market services probably had the greatest chance to redefine the household specialization of labor, taking a burden off women. Historically, households were becoming smaller by 1900 due to the reduction of the extended family and the decline in boarders and servants. In theory, this change in household composition could have been handled either by applying technological solutions in the home or by bringing household functions into labor force production modes outside the home. In practice, the former prevailed and technology was brought into the home where women could now perform all the work previously done by other family members or servants. Technology kept women in the home at this point, rather than liberating them from it.

Two social trends in the early twentieth century make this connection explicit. The first was the "domestic science movement" of the 1920s, which attempted to make housework more like industrial management and the second was the "new home economics," based on the early works of Margaret Reid, who sought to apply microeconomic theory to household production. These movements used the technical and theoretical principles of scientific management, originated by Frederick W. Taylor for factories and extended to the home by writers such as Christine Frederick and Lillian Gilbreth.

By now technologies cumulatively have made a reallocation of household labor difficult to accomplish. They have been used to privatize work and thereby increase the work load on many individual women.

Housework remains within decentralized, inefficient units. In fact, it may now be difficult to move some housework tasks out of the home because the small scale of household work and technology is labor intensive. Second, the work has become so emotion-laden that moving it into a more communalized form may be impossible. Finally, since women's labor at home is unpaid and thus seen as "cheap," it can be used indefinitely for these tasks, retaining the specialization of labor within the home and keeping housework structurally separate from the paid-work system.

Keeping these factors in mind, it is now possible to look at the impacts of specific technologies that can reasonably be said to have changed household work structure. It is clear that different technologies such as utilities, appliances, foods, and services have varying impacts. For example, how can we compare plumbing, the vacuum cleaner, and the wire whisk? They are developed, marketed, paid for, and used differently. The task is easier if the impacts of these four types of household technologies, divided according to their purpose and place in the economic system, are defined and examined separately:

- *Utilities* (running water, electricity, gas, sewage) are the technological infrastructure of the household. They operate continuously, hook up virtually all households to the system, and are provided under special legal and regulatory schemes.
- *Appliances* are the actual small or large machines or objects used in performing housework.
- *"Convenience" and prepackaged foods* are brought into the home to replace growing, preserving, preparing, and even many cooking chores.
- Private sector *market services* (private garbage service to replace household burning of trash; fast food restaurants; diaper services) are found outside the home and can be chosen to replace household functions with the labor of others.

This model allows a test of the traditional idea that changes in technologies for the household have brought benefits previously unavailable to household members, particularly to women. Utilities, appliances, foods, and services are assumed to have reduced the *time* and *cost* necessary to perform housework, to have increased the *ease* with which household tasks are performed, and to have decreased the *share* of housework allotted to adult women; our examination contradicts these assertions.

If Not Less Time, More Ease or Interest?

The term "ease" of housework includes the reduction of physical fatigue, increased pleasantness of tasks, improved task variety to stimulate interest, protection against boredom, and increased feelings of self-worth. Thus, ease of housework is not identical to a reduction in time.

Although waxing a kitchen floor may seem to be an odious task under any condition, the traditional image of technology and housework insists that the new household technologies are adding interest to the job and creating a more cheerful attitude in the houseworker. If we believe advertising in women's magazines and on television, it would appear that technology makes work easier and more pleasant, and therefore makes the housewife happier. Yet, insofar as household technologies were designed to reinforce the home system and thereby keep women economically marginal to the larger society, they may actually decrease satisfaction with housework. Several studies have documented women's actual preference for paid employment.[5]

Housework, like other alienating work, is basically manual; mechanization of tasks does not change this. It only means the worker must now tend machines, while remaining socially isolated, monitoring several activities at once, and having no one with whom to share the emotional burdens of housework.[6] Therefore, there are inherent limits to the degree that technology may ease the homemaker's lot.

Impact of Utilities

Although it is difficult to prove, utilities probably changed household work more than any other technical improvement because they eliminated several truly burdensome tasks. Hot and cold running water ended pumping, carrying, and heating water; electricity and gas eliminated chopping wood, carrying coal, and continually stoking and cleaning stoves. The actual impact is hard to measure for several reasons.

First, prior to 1910 there are few data on total time and effort expended on housework before and after the installation of utility systems. Second, it is not clear how to define housework for pre-industrial periods. Much of the household work now done by utilities (water, electricity, oil, and gas) and paid for monthly, was once done by the labor of individuals pumping water, chopping wood, or hauling coal. Thus, if housework is anything done *in* the home, then chopping wood and felling trees for heating might not previously have been considered as housework; but, if housework is defined as unpaid work or work necessary to maintain the home, then the installation of centralized heating can certainly be counted as having *eased* housework. The *cost* of this labor will still be hard to measure and compare to current dollar outlays for utilities. It is easier to make cost measurements and studies of changes over time since public utilities began their operations. For example, no one can ignore the increase in cost of home heating in the last few years and the need for other home technologies, such as insulation and wood-burning stoves, to offset these costs. Undoubtedly some of these costs are being met with the labor of family members who install insulation themselves and who once again chop, split, and carry wood.

Third, evidence indicating that the total volume of housework has not declined remains consistent with utilities having a profound impact on the nature of labor within households. It is likely that effort saved on some tasks was merely passed to other activities carried on by women. Rural/urban time budget studies from later periods all show a reallocation of wives' labor from meal preparation to childcare, purchasing, and management.[7] These trends do not change who does housework, but rather its content. Some of these changes over time may be due to appliances rather than utilities, but it is likely that utilities eliminated some tasks to make room for others. Furthermore, utilities such as gas and electricity undoubtedly fostered second-level effects by facilitating the development of many small and large appliances. In household production, as elsewhere, there is a tendency to use the time provided by technological change to produce more goods and services or meet rising standards, rather than to enjoy more leisure time. Utilities undoubtedly *allowed* for the possibility of women entering the paid labor force or for changing household separation of labor, but they certainly did not *cause* such a change.

Impact of Appliances

How do small- and medium-sized appliances make tasks more difficult instead of easier? Often such technological innovations require considerably more complex and tiring work than did their preceding hand tools. Even **Fortune** magazine has cited the fact that many separate appliances require a great deal of time and work to take out of the cabinet, put together, use, and clean up. Cleaning kitchen appliances can become a major project for the conscientious housewife, since their plastic moldings and ridges, chrome trim, and doodads all seem designed to harbor dirt. Appliance repair has become more difficult and mysterious, often costing almost as much as replacement. With the increased specialization of household machinery, the difficulty of understanding the actual mechanical and/or electrical operation has increased, so that someone who is knowledgeable about how a certain type of appliance operates may not be able to understand another, much less fix it. Further, much of our equipment is designed in a faulty manner that embodies planned obsolescence to sustain demand. Appliance operation also increases the amount of noise in the house, decreasing work pleasantness. These factors all argue against the view that household appliances necessarily *ease* the performance of housework. "Labor-saving devices" may actually create new forms of labor and increase job fatigue.

Time spent on appliances is easier to measure than fatigue, but virtually the only machine that has been studied in detail is the mechanical/electrical dishwasher. Most studies do show a reduction in dishwashing time by using appliances; however, the figures for time saved vary from 12 to 37 minutes per day among different studies conducted over a 40-year time span.

There are few other individual studies of appliances. We do know that in some middle class families an increased number of appliances results in a small *increase* in household work time. Apparently large numbers of appliances create more work and/or women use the time saved elsewhere to keep up with rising standards.

It is also possible that some household appliances have been used as a substitute for more equal allocation of household labor. Husbands do little housework, spending an average of 1.6 hours a day on all household work, whether or not wives are employed. Studies of this question control only for age, class, and number of children, and not for equipment. Task-specific technologies may develop so that women can take over tasks previously done by other family members rather than vice versa. For example, when families have garbage disposals, wives are more likely to take care of the garbage than in those with no disposal; the pattern is similar with dishwashers. In other words, new technologies may reduce the amount of time men engage in housework, and increase that of women, a finding which contradicts conventional wisdom.

One way to save that time is to eat out. The appliance industry has felt threatened by the increased trend of families to do so, cutting into the demand for small kitchen appliances. As a result, the industry recently has been tailoring its wares to compete with fast food outlets. Small deep-fat fryers, single and double hamburger makers, and electric hot dog cookers are being marketed in an effort to bring the fast food taste into the home. For the affluent consumer, the single professional, and the full-time homemaker, another line of goods has been developed, including sophisticated multipurpose food processors, crepe makers, electric cookie and canape makers, electric woks, and crock pots; apparently higher income groups are combining eating in expensive restaurants with more elaborate cooking at home. For others who spend full time in the home, cooking has become a creative outlet or a chance to improve the nutritional content of family members' food intake.

As usual, there are few crossethnic or racial data. What little evidence exists concerns black families. Blacks have been found to purchase appliances or convenience foods at a slower rate than whites of the same income level, preferring to spend money in other ways.[8]

So who buys all these appliances that do not appear to save time, even though they are normally quite expensive? White households of higher income and/or those with a full-time homemaker. Why? First, people believe that appliances save time. Second, appliances have symbolic value for men and women which overrides an "efficiency and rationality" approach. If a woman believes that the latest equipment increases the quality of her work and in turn the quality of home life, she has a powerful incentive to want a well-equipped home. As for men, their household domination rests on an ability to provide a comfortable standard of living (or even luxury items) for their families. We know that much household technology is bought by men for women, sometimes as gifts for holidays, and that Mother's Day is the busiest one all year for housewares departments. Thus men, too, see the value in household technology. The purchase of these appliances is symbolic of patriarchal power relations.

Impact of Convenience Foods

Most studies of convenience foods focus on *time* saved, rather than on savings of effort and ease. Since these tests of "starting from scratch" versus convenience foods have not compared shopping, planning, and management time, or meal types, they report only small time differences regarding part of the meal-preparation process. To the extent that convenience foods require fewer operations from refrigerator to table, and necessitate having fewer ingredients on hand, they may save some effort; but to the extent that they impose different planning, shopping, and storage activities, they may require *more* exertion.

The time involved in raising food is also usually ignored in the studies of prepared, packaged, meal-sized goods. A hundred years ago most North Americans raised their own food, or relied on local markets for those things they did not grow themselves (consequently there was less variety than today). Moreover, most food was bought in bulk, so that shopping was likely to be a less frequent venture. Today, while we may have the convenience of saving time and effort with prepared foods as opposed to "starting from scratch," this convenience is severely undercut at the door of the supermarket. There we find aisle after aisle of food choices afforded by a national marketing system and the wonder of food technologies. The sheer number of choices available, together with the need to serve nutritious, attractive, and tasty meals, can make meal-planning and food-selection time lengthy. Shopping two or three times a week, each time going to a centralized shopping center, making selections with care, loading the goods into the car, unloading them at home, and putting them away — all of this amounts to a considerable expenditure of time. In this light, the tendency for black women to shop less frequently than white women and to buy basic ingredients in large quantities may be most sensible for all householders to follow.

One might argue that the smaller meals served today compared to the meals served 50 years ago have surely decreased the time spent in meal preparation. Before World War I the average family in the United States ate three gigantic meals. Breakfast, lunch, and dinner consisted of steak or roast, fried potatoes, cakes or pies, starchy vegetables, hot cakes, and relishes. Today, meals are smaller. Volume alone would seem to suggest less time in the kitchen, irrespective of technologies. On the other hand, the larger meals of past eras were made up of similar foods: roast or steak and potatoes were common at all three meals, and the breakfast roast probably was reheated and served at lunch or dinner. Modern meals, in contrast, are clearly differentiated by food type, making three separate preparations common. Thus urbanization and declining family size may have made meals smaller, while new technologies complicated and gave variety to the cooking process. Certain food-related technologies, for example, do try to make formerly elegant or exotic experiences readily available to the masses, just as the prosaic tin can and refrigerated railroad car once revolutionized eating by bringing out-of-season foods to those who could not travel to far-away places.

Such convenience foods are costly. The U.S. Department of Agriculture found that 64 percent of the processed foods it studied were priced higher than the equivalent amount of homemade food. Until recently, however, consumers assumed that convenience foods were "convenient" and were willing to pay the extra costs. Now shoppers are much more wary of the extra costs of convenience. Increases in food prices have led to the replacement of the canned soups, frozen entrees, and prepared desserts in the normal market basket with fresh fruits, vegetables, and cheeses. The consumption of canned fruits and vegetables also declined between 1972 and 1977, in spite of efforts to stimulate demand.

There are yet other reasons that convenience foods may be spurned. Capitalism has fostered a mass market which tends to eliminate ethnic differences in cuisine,[9] although there now are *ersatz* ethnic convenience foods. Anthropological studies have shown the importance of food in maintaining ethnic identity. However, researchers do not know how rapidly or in what manner majority-culture food preferences in the United States affect subculture eating patterns or ethnic identification. Today, the re-emerging sense of cultural heritage among many ethnic and racial groups probably has contributed to the recent trend away from convenience foods.

Impact of Market Services

Private market services represent the alternative of moving housework outside of the home, performed by others, instead of having each household performing every task. In the post-World War II period, the combination of women's labor at home and commodities produced outside the home prevented the growth of labor market services relevant to housework in the larger economy. As a general pattern, this may still hold true, although the number of services provided varies with the household task. Laundry services and home food delivery appear to have declined, while eating out appears to be a long-run trend that became necessary and acceptable during World War II with the mass entry of women into the labor force.

This trend is supported by several factors. First, there is a continued increase in the rate of married women's labor force participation. Second, there is real convenience to eating out. This ease, combined with the fact that between 1972 and 1975 the cost of eating at home rose faster than that of eating out, has made restaurant sales soar. Third, although the relative cost advantage of eating out was reversed in 1976, most women value their own time and effort. When Mrs. Average Housewife tells us on a national commercial that she likes her chicken "finger lickin' good" because her time is valuable, we can suspect that she knows a bargain when she sees one. After 50 years of "convenience foods" and "labor-saving devices," women have come to realize what the fast food industry has been aware of: *true convenience only comes when someone else does the work* .

However, there are also limitations on the ability of market services to replace home food preparation. Massive advertising campaigns by supermarkets and appliance industry representatives, both facing a major threat to their profits, point out that it is now cheaper to eat at home — if the cook's time is not counted. In addition, overall quality and nutrition remain more controllable with home cooking. Inflation also cuts back on the ability of middle- and low-income groups to eat out. As real income declines, more families may be forced to eat at home. Among higher income groups, the trend may be different, with women combining meals in better restaurants with gourmet cooking at home. Certainly eating out is a long-run trend, with one meal in three eaten away from home and some experts predicting one in two in the near future. Fast foods are seeing the most rapid growth, but it seems unlikely that market services will entirely replace home food preparation within our current economic system.

The long-term cost advantage of food services and restaurants probably will depend upon how women's time is valued. As women's participation in the paid labor force increases, their time becomes scarce and of potentially greater value. Professionally-employed women will tend to pay for outside help, while those with lower paying jobs will get more unpaid labor from themselves and family members.[10] Thus class differences might be expected in response to market food services.

The use of market services seems to be related not to their technological convenience *per se* , but rather to the employment of women outside the home, together with diminishing family size. We would speculate that the availability of market services has facilitated a decline in time spent on some forms of household production (for example, laundry or cooking), a decline that was initially made possible by utilities and some large appliances and by the lack of availability of a full-time homemaker. However, centralized market services have also meant an increasing percentage of housework time is spent on consumption tasks such as buying groceries.

Technology: A Burden

Thus when we finally sum up who has benefited from technological applications to the home, the prime gains do not appear to go to women. While technologies may have decreased the physical effort of housework, they have not reduced the time involved, lowered the psychic burdens on women, changed the allocation of labor by gender, or released women to enter the paid labor force. Household technologies themselves are purchased primarily for reasons related to one's stage in the life cycle and economic means -- not to enable women's entry into the paid workforce. It is likely that the purchasers believe that the appliances and foods do save time, effort, or costs. Often they are purchased for symbolic reasons as well. However, many of these outcomes are not achieved, and overall, household technologies have led to less satisfaction with the work environment and to the proletarianization of housework.

The greatest impacts on housework have come from nontechnological changes — increased labor force demand for women, reduced household size, home monotony, aspects of contemporary feminist thought, and the pressures of inflation drawing women to paid work. These in turn, have decreased the time available for housework. Technology has fostered the redefinition of housework away from production and toward consumption, transportation, and childcare. This redefinition may have facilitated, but has not caused, the current distribution of women's time and effort between paid and unpaid labor. Technology itself does not determine outcomes; the impact is determined by society's use of it. Thus, technology is not an independent variable, but an intervening one that facilitates change processes. Technology allowed individual women's labor to substitute for loss of servants and other primarily female family members' aid; to raise the standard of living; and to reduce the necessary hours of housework. But its goal was never to decrease male power in the home.

Thus we cannot rely solely on technology to liberate women. In the future, public and market services have the potential to replace home food production and other work, finally lightening women's burdens in the home. An even more equitable, and hence preferable, solution would have men assume increased responsibility for the necessary life support and sustenance activities that comprise housework. Other forms of political intervention will be needed as well to challenge the "naturalness" of the nuclear family and housewife role. Since consumption and childcare are now major housework tasks, community or home-based, client-controlled childcare centers and decentralization of stores would help alleviate this responsibility. Neighborhood houses can supervise children after school; work can be restructured (shorter hours, flextime, job sharing, for example) to allow shared parental responsibility; housing can be redesigned to facilitate many family forms other than the nuclear one. All of these would help challenge the conventional attitudes about technology in the home.

Notes

The authors wish to thank Mary Malloy for her contributions as a research assistant in the early stages of this project.

1. Ismail Sirageldin, *Non-Market Components of National Income* (Ann Arbor, MI: University of Michigan Survey Research Center, 1969).
2. Catherine W. Berheide, Sarah F. Berk, and Richard A. Berk, "Household Work in the Suburbs: The Job and Its Participants," *Pacific Sociological Review* 19 (1976): 491-518.
3. Joann Vanek, "Time Spent on Housework," *Scientific American* 231 (1974): 116-120.
4. Susan Strasser, *Never Done: A History of American Housework* (New York: Pantheon, 1982).
5. Myra Max Ferree, "Working-Class Jobs: Housework and Paid Work as Sources of Satisfaction," *Social Problems* 23 (April 1976): 431-441.
6. Allison Ravetz, "Modern Technology and an Ancient Occupation: Housework in Present Day Society," *Technology and Culture* 6 (1965): 256-60.
7. W. F. Ogburn and M. F. Nimkoff, *Technology and the Changing Family* (Westport, CT: Greenwood Press, 1955).
8. Raymond Bauer and Scott Cunningham, *Studies in the Negro Market* (Cambridge, MA: Harvard Graduate School of Business Administration, Marketing Science Institute, 1970).
9. Stuart Ewen, *Captains of Consciousness: Advertising and the Social Roots of the Consumer Culture* (New York: McGraw-Hill, 1976).
10. S. S. Angrist, "Socio-Economic Differences in How Working Mothers Manage Work, Childcare and Household Tasks," *Social Science Quarterly* 56 (1976): 631-637.

See Also:
   Ruth Cowan, "A Case Study of Technology and Social Change: The Washing Machine and the Working Wife," *Clio's Consciousness Raised: New Perspectives on the History of Women*, eds. Mary Hartmann and Lois Banner (New York: Harper & Row, 1974), pp. 245-253.
   Lenore Davidoff, "The Rationalization of Housework," in *Dependence and Exploitation in Work and Marriage*, ed. D. L. Barker and S. Allen (New York: Longman, 1976), pp. 121-151.
   Barbara Ehrenreich and Dierdre English, *For Her Own Good: 150 Years of the Experts' Advice to Women* (Garden City, NY: Doubleday, 1978).
   John Galbraith, "The Economics of the American Housewife," *The Atlantic Monthly* 233 (August 1973).
   Dolores Hayden, *The Grand Domestic Revolution* (Cambridge, MA: MIT Press, 1981).
   Myra Strober, "Wives' Labor Force Behavior and Family Consumption Habits," *American Economic Review* (February 1977): 410-417.
   Martha Moore Trescott, editor, *Dynamos and Virgins Revisited: Women and Technological Change in History* (Metuchen, NJ: Scarecrow Press, 1979).

A full list of sources is available by contacting the authors through the publisher.

Chapter 11

The Lonely Squandering

Of Urban Time

by Ann R. Markusen

I want to start with a story. Some 15 years ago, a woman who is now an assistant professor of city and regional planning went to a medium-sized urban university in the east where she lived with three other women: Ellen McPeake, who grew up in a rural county near Philadelphia; Sarah Schumacher, from a suburb of Dayton, Ohio; and Drusilla Aileen Bachman, who hailed from a suburb of Beaumont, Texas.

In the years they lived together in the eastern city, each one of these women swore that she would never find herself,later in life, living in the same situations in which she had grown up. Their determination reflected their fear of the dullness of the places in which they had been raised, and the grueling pace at which their mothers had lived their lives. It is now 15 years later, and Ellen McPeake is living in a rural county in Pennsylvania, not far from Philadelphia — not the same county in which she grew up, but nearby. Sarah Schumacher is living in a suburb of New York City on Long Island. Drusilla Bachman is now living in a suburb of Dallas, Texas, not that far from Beaumont. And yours truly is living in a suburb of San Francisco.

Talking about cities as existing and alternative technologies can explain why the results are the way they are. In general, social sciences and humanities people are not supposed to know anything about technology, and if we do we are considered to be "soft." The language, incidentally, of "soft" and "hard" has sexist connotations to which we should be sensitive. Technologies are not simply innocent accidents with unattended consequences about which we complain. Rather, they are intentionally constructed with an eye toward serving some groups and not others. In considering cities as built environments, as technologies within which we live, I am going to talk about them both on the microscale, that is, in terms of the household, all the way up to the macroscale, meaning the cities and the suburbs and the real spaces that we move around in.

Clearly urban technology affects women's lives. The cliche here is the automobile, and the way in which it has restructured the lives that we live. Southern California is everybody's favorite example of just how important the automobile has been. What is less clear is that urban technology itself is the product of elements of the social system. It is not just an accident. It is not an unforeseen consequence that women have difficulties using urban space the way it is structured. I am going to suggest that cities are built in a gender-based manner, built for men, and that they function to preserve men's privileges and power over women. Changing technology first requires changing social relationships that have begotten the old technology. Perhaps in thinking about changing technology, we need more than visions: we need a strategy that changes relationships as well as changes the urban built environment. Such changes are going to be difficult but not impossible.

Now another story. I calculated how much time I spent yesterday moving around the urban space in which I live. In the morning I spent 15 minutes taking my child to childcare. I spent 15 more minutes driving to work. At noon I spent 10 minutes driving to the "Pay and Save" to get diapers. I spent 5 minutes driving to the travel agent to buy my tickets to go to a conference, and I spent another 10 minutes driving back to work. At 5:00 I spent 15 minutes in heavy traffic to pick up my child from childcare, and 15 more minutes getting home. At 7:30, after dinner, I spent 10 minutes driving to the grocery store, another 10 minutes driving to the liquor store, and another 10 minutes driving home. Now, if you add up the travel time, it comes to one hour and 55 minutes. That does not count the time I spent at each of the places I went — that is just the time I spent in my automobile. I would like to point out, too, that I live four blocks from where I work!

This illustration points out at least some things about the personal nature of urban space, and the ways in which it absorbs tremendous amounts of time, particularly from women who must negotiate it. My story is somewhat apocryphal, because in my household my child's father participates fully in housework and childcare. So the truth is, I did not spend two hours driving around Berkeley yesterday. I only spent one hour, because he picked up the baby from childcare, and he did the errands in the evening.

However, most studies show that women do over 95 percent of the housework, childcare, errands, and shopping in this society. Not only has that pattern been consistent over the years, but recent studies show that as women begin to work in the labor force in increasing numbers, men have stopped working overtime, without increasing the amount of work they do around the household. Instead, they spend more time in front of the television. Thus, the realm of women's household work is an extremely important aspect of urban structure, one that is largely ignored in planning, and certainly in any analysis of urban spatial structure.

My illustration is designed to suggest that contemporary city structure impedes efficiency in women's household work and on related urban journeys, especially in auto-intensive suburbia.

The Housewife Is a Working Woman

In addition to wage labor that women perform in the economy, women are responsible for direct provision of the conditions of physical and mental health for themselves and their families. This includes tasks such as cooking meals, running personal delivery services and errands, caring for and educating children, purchasing inputs for the household, scheduling and managing household tasks, maintaining the housing, maintaining clothing, providing therapy, nursing, nutrition, and first aid services for family members, accounting, and a number of other functions, such as gardening, being a maid, and all of the rest. These are extremely time-consuming tasks and very labor intensive. Studies have shown that full-time housewives spend as much as 90 hours per week at such work.

Although these activities occur at home, they are not consumption activities. The models developed in economics and in urban studies organize what goes on in cities into production and consumption activities. Production is what happens in work places; what occurs in households is indiscriminately called consumption. The image is of a passive, wasteful family unit simply sucking in goods and services from the larger economy without any productive activity going on inside the household. Yet a tremendous number of actual work tasks that require labor go on within the household, demanding a great deal of skill and organization to do them successfully.

This means that the relationship of people within the household constitutes a work relationship as well as a family relationship. This work relationship is very different from the one we contract for as workers when we go out and work for a wage. First of all, the only agreement we ever make to provide these services, as women in charge of household work, is the agreement we make at the time of marriage (or an agreement to share a household with somebody). Essentially, what we are doing when we "sign" the marriage contract is promising to provide household services for a lifetime period, during which the wage is unspecified. As opposed to being a worker in the labor force, where we have a right to quit our job, it is very difficult in society to quit working in the household. The sanctions surrounding divorce and separation make them very painful experiences socially and psychologically.

A woman receives no wage or salary for performing household services. Instead, the return for her labor, which is a very real return, goes to the wage earner in the household (if there is only one), as a return for his services in the labor market. Recently women political economists have been working out a notion called the "family wage." This concept is designed to show that amount of money a man makes in the labor force covers the labor expended by himself on the job, as well as the labor expended by his wife and other family members at home. Therefore, it should be seen historically as a return to all forms of labor expended. However, the traditional arrangement has resulted in men having power over all income that comes into the household. Women must rely upon the largess of the man concerned, or on a very complicated implicit bargaining process between them as to how that wage will be expended within the household.

The upshot of all this is that a housewife is a working woman. The notion that women are only beginning to work (meaning finding a paid job) is a real misconception. It obscures the fact that for many, many years, for centuries, women have been working in the home.

Finally, contrary to the total idea of women being dependent on men, men are very dependent on women's labor in this process. If you stop and think about it, very few men stay out of marriage for the major portion of their lives. The reason for this is that there are very real privileges and services provided to men by women through this arrangement, in which a woman's work is obscured by an ideology that views her services as consumption and not production.

Urban Form and Function

Let us further consider the way that urban technology shapes women's household work, and ask whether or not it is structured in a way that really enhances, makes efficient, and provides for quality working conditions, starting with the house itself.

Housing, as a number of women architects have begun to point out, is not particularly structured to make housework very efficient. One of the most interesting studies shows how kitchens in particular have been structured in ways that deprive women of enough space to work, and which segregate kitchen work from the rest of the household. Housing built since World War II offers living rooms and dining rooms that go virtually unused, while tiny kitchens are crowded with activity. Almost all women, when surveyed, complain that their kitchens are too small — too small for visiting, too small for cooperative cooking. The innovation of the family room is also very telling, as it suggests that there should be a room in which families get together (usually to watch television), but that kitchens are really just women's, not family, space.

Touching on the spatial array of housing, we note that the detached, single-family structure of housing in this country, which has been the norm since World War I, makes the sharing of household work very difficult. It involves the replication of household appliances and service functions in every single house, and means that women tend to work in isolation without much intimacy, sharing, or camaraderie on the job. It makes cleaning much more difficult. Consider the popularity of neighborhood barbecues: they move cooking out of the kitchen, make eating communal again, and prompt Dad to get into the act. You cannot pack neighbors into your house, it is too small. They mess up your kitchen, and you're stuck cleaning up after them. I suspect the informal popularity of the barbecue has a great deal to do with trying to restructure the way that meals are prepared in detached single-family space.

The same thing goes for laundry and other household tasks. I steadfastly refuse to purchase a washer and dryer for our rented house because the laundromat offers me an opportunity to participate in a kind of spontaneous community venture with other people. I enjoy it. I take my mate with me, we bring our child, and we have a wonderful time, even though it is not always convenient.

Moving up to the macroscale, we can next consider the decentralized location of housing in the society. Clearly, an automobile is a must for most people living in the cities and suburbs today because of the arrangement of residential space. There is little spontaneous or unplanned community. In Jane Jacobs' **Death and Life of Great American Cities**, written in 1961, she spoke about how city streets in urban areas provide for public surveillance of children, so that women are much freer to go about their household work, shopping, and other tasks. People working on the street, including barbers and shopkeepers, helped watch after the children, and disciplined them.[1] This is public childcare of a spontaneous nature.

One remarkable fact about the structure of our private housing is that when we look for housing we consider the price, the value, the schools, the tax rates, and even the journey to work. But we never consider neighbors. We do not interview our neighbors when we move into a neighborhood; yet the microlevel neighborhood into which we move is really our society. It is going to be our society for some time to come. Housing as an asset and as a public service takes precedence over housing as a community decision. Older forms of community that helped with women's childcare responsibilities and household tasks have fallen away. Women's work has become increasingly individualized.

In addition to housing, there are other aspects of women's work that involve work outside of the household, but are connected to the reproduction of social life in the household. Purchasing activities, for instance, require a great deal of quality and skill. They also demand, in this society, owning and ceaselessly operating an automobile. As illustrated with my own urban travels, going from workplace to drug store to grocery store to "Pay and Save" to shopping mall to health clinic amounts to many little trips; this absorbs time in traveling to different locations.

Childcare is much more onerous when combined with this extensive short trip sequence. The decentralized single family tract pattern is an incredibly inefficient design for trundling children from place to place. We had to purchase a $60 child seat because it was the only brand that was safe to put in different kinds of cars, to take out of one and put in another. Trying to tote a child to these different locations — stores, schools, clinics — taking her out, putting her in a backpack or a stroller, getting the stroller in and out of buildings, is a very complicated process.

Needless to say, the places we shop do not have childcare. Can you imagine childcare in supermarkets? Wouldn't that be a fantastic idea? In museums, in health clubs, in theaters, in all the places we would really like to go, but which aren't built for doing two things at once — childcare plus recreation. And the streets are not safe for our children. We do not feel safe leaving our child in front of the store we're going into because we are afraid somebody might run over or kidnap our kid.

In addition to shopping, childcare, and household work, more and more women work for wages, meaning that in addition to doing all these things in our "spare time," we also have the problem of moving back and forth from our household location to our workplace activities. The trip from home to childcare to work and back is a growing burden on women, particularly because childcare is not generally available either in neighborhoods or at the workplace activities. Homes that were once peopled with children during the day now lie idle while their adult occupants work for wages, yet childcare centers have trouble finding space.

Moreover, transportation options are very poor for most women. At a women's conference I heard a very interesting discussion of Latina women who do piecework in their homes. One of the major incentives is the time and cost saved on transportation to any workplace. This is extremely time consuming in the Los Angeles transportation system if you do not have a car. If you work out of your home, you can take care of your children at the same time; you can even have them help you with your work. The result is extremely low wages and exploitative working conditions, yet some groups of women prefer these conditions to traveling to work and finding childcare. Time-consuming commutes discourage women from working and perpetuate the cycle of women having the major responsibility for housework and childcare and being forced to work for low wages.

Alternative Spaces

There are ways we can change this. Let us examine the way in which we shop for housing and neighborhoods, and the demands we can make on developers, real estate people, planning departments, and zoning boards. First, we need bigger kitchens, with space within them to sit and chat, as well as room to cook together. Second, housing needs to be restructured so there will be more communal space in neighborhoods. Dolores Hayden at the University of California at Los Angeles has taken an average suburban block and redesigned it so that garages and other spaces are restructured as childcare centers, as communal laundries, as soup kitchens; very visionary, very utopian, but very interesting.

Another possibility is to increase density in living areas so there are more people available to help do childcare, so journeys to the various places in which we work and shop are not as long and hassled. A study done a couple of years ago of women in the San Jose area showed that if they could *find* housing, they would prefer it closer to the city center than in the detached single-family areas in which they lived.

We need better transportation. We need child- and senior-designed environments which make it easier for integrated family units to live with or near each other. Many seniors have been forced to move to other neighborhoods and even regions because they can no longer afford the high price of housing in the neighborhoods where they reared their children.

The banks and the real estate, building, and development industries are partly responsible, as their capitalist concerns supersede a consideration of housing design geared to meet women's needs. Employers find it useful to have women work at home. Further, men also benefit from the situation as it is: the arrangement of housing really reflects the idealized nuclear family relationship between men and women, which guarantees men's privileges in receiving household services over time.

People on their own are beginning to challenge the suburban model by moving away from it. The fact that gay people, especially gay men, choose to live in inner cities like San Francisco shows that if you are not leaning on women too heavily to do the work for you, you must live in a high density, mixed-use city location because it is the only way you can efficiently get your clothes cleaned and take care of your household chores. The fact that most single-parent families tend to live in inner cities is another illustration of the same thing. Gentrification, the increasing tendency for two-wage earner families (if they can afford it — which means mostly professional and managerial-class families) to live in central cities, shows again that if you have two people working, the only possible efficient place to live is where services and work places are more compactly located. The growth of medium- and small-sized towns is also a response to the increasing difficulties of congestion, traffic, and the time costs of living in decentralized, urban locations. Finally, the movement of retired people to the sun belt and other rural areas is another indication of the disfunctionality of suburban places for meaningful family life. These movements reflect the breakdown of patriarchal relationships between men and women, and a recognition of the inefficiency of suburban space.

There are some concrete examples of women organizing to change space. One is the tremendous example of Soho in New York City, where large numbers of women moved into lofts and old warehouses, which they restructured to provide selected childcare and living space. They fought an intense, protracted battle with the City of New York to change the zoning and permit them to live there. After all, it was not zoned for residential use and was not considered the kind of residential structure that people are supposed to want! But the women won.

Women have also done a lot of organizing around urban childcare collectives and networks. Tremendous strides are being made toward the provision of quality childcare, but the needs are growing faster than centers and family daycare homes. In trying to organize around these issues, we need to first start struggling in the household. The number one front is changing the relationships between men and women around household work. The more I see the man I live with struggling with childcare, laundry, cooking, and shopping, the more I see him appreciate the difficulties that women have always faced. It helps for him to see the neighborhoods and spatial structure the way they are, as handicaps to home life. We need to start by having all family members in society experience difficulties and dissatisfaction with things as they are.

When we look for housing, we ought to be vocal with real estate agents and builders about the ways in which we would like to see housing structured. Moreover, every time a public building is built, it to have childcare space. It has parking spaces, why doesn't it have childcare space? We need improved transportation. This is a desperate issue now. Mass transit is being cut by the Reagan administration, while we need increasing amounts of decent transportation for young children, for seniors, for women, for all people who cannot afford that extra automobile.

Think about the urban space and the housing that you live in as a technology. Look at the ways in which it is difficult and time consuming for you. Look for what the constructive things around that space are, and the things that are helpful to you in doing your household and childcare work as well as your work as women wage earners. Is it efficient? How could it be changed?

The issue of urban women's space is an issue of alternative urban technology just like anything else. Urban technology as built now is technology that serves employers and men in a male-dominated system. We have a long way to go in creating even better visions of how urban space could be restructured.

Maybe 20 years from now we could get together and talk about our successes in restructuring our workplace environments, household environments, and our play spaces to serve women's needs for intimacy, decent childcare conditions, and pleasant and intimate household social life.

Notes

1. Jane Jacobs, *Death and Life of Great American Cities* (New York: Random House, 1961).

Chapter 12

Getting There:

Women and Transportation

by Genevieve Giuliano

Travel is one of the most common activities of daily life. With the exception of those who are infirm, incarcerated, or otherwise physically unable to journey from one place to another, traveling is an integral part of everyone's schedule of activities. The transportation facilities available for daily travel — local streets and roads, highways and expressways, railroads, and mass transit systems — are provided and maintained primarily by the public sector. (The major private contribution is, of course, the private automobile.) These facilities have been built with billions of tax dollars, and they require billions more each year for operation and maintenance. The transportation system as it exists today is thus the result of public policy decisions about the expenditure of public resources. It is therefore quite appropriate and important to evaluate the present system from women's perspective; to understand how traveling affects everyday decisions, and to determine how the existing system can be improved to better suit the travel needs of women in the future.

The Role of Transportation in Daily Activities

Transportation is consumed because it enables the individual to participate in activities which are spatially separate. Trips are made to work, to shop, to obtain medical care, or to engage in social or recreational activities; rarely are they made for the sheer joy of traveling. To participate in an activity, an individual must have both the desire or need for that activity and the willingness or ability to pay for it, including travel costs in money and time. Thus, an individual's choice of activities is affected by location, by the transportation alternatives available, and by time and budget constraints.

The daily activity pattern of each person is the outcome of both long-run and short-run decisions. Long-run decisions include the selection of a place of residence, the choice of a job and its location, and automobile ownership. Once these basic decisions are made, short-run decisions can be made about the schedule and sequence of daily activities.

Activity schedules, and therefore travel patterns, are affected by several factors. First, the geographic or spatial structure of the area — the location of residences, employment sites, and commercial activities — is important. A compact or dense spatial structure is one in which different activities are located within close proximity, as in older small- and medium-sized cities. Dispersed spatial structures where activities are widely separated characterize most suburban and rural areas. As activities become more distant from one another, more money and time (ignoring for the moment the effect of congestion) is required to get from one to another. Consequently, people with severe time or financial constraints, including the poor, the elderly, single parents, and two-career couples, frequently live in higher density areas.

The second factor affecting activity and travel patterns is the socioeconomic profile of the individual's household. This profile includes the level of household income, the number of automobiles available, size of household, number of workers within the household, and such family characteristics of the household as marital status and the number and age of family members. As income level rises, so do the ability and desire to travel. Higher income households travel greater distances and engage in more discretionary travel, such as trips to restaurants and weekend vacations. Similarly, as auto availability increases, resources for travel are increased. Conversely, travel options — and therefore activity options — are constrained for low-income households. Discretionary trips may be nonexistent, and the fulfillment of basic household needs may be limited to locations accessible by foot or bus. Income level constraints on activity patterns are common and frequently severe for female heads of households.

A third important factor for the determination of activity and travel patterns is the socioeconomic profile of the individual, including age and sex, employment status, stage in the life cycle, and nonwork responsibilities. Sex is particularly important because household roles and responsibilities continue to be determined largely by gender, despite the efforts of the last ten years to equalize women's and men's roles both in the home and in the workplace. In most households the division of labor within the home continues to be determined by gender: males take care of cars and yards; females take care of everything else. Even when female household members are employed outside the home, these patterns persist.

Women's Activity and Travel Patterns

These three factors combine to affect women's activity and travel patterns in significant ways. A woman's "gender-determined" responsibilities as wife, mother, or partner require that she participate in many activities — housecleaning, meal preparation, shopping, childcare, medical and dental care, and family social activities — in *addition* to full or part-time employment. Because these activities generally take place in the context of other household members' schedules, there are many limitations on women's activity choices. This problem is most severe in households with young children, because activities must take place around the children's school and activity schedules.

Although women generally have more responsibilities and more constraints on their time than men, their position within the household is such that their resources for carrying out these activities are limited as well. As mentioned earlier, female-headed households tend to have lower incomes than male-headed households and thus less money available to finance activities and travel. Moreover, when transportation resources are limited, the male usually has first choice on the options available. For example, in one-car, two-worker families it is usually the man who drives to work and the woman who takes the bus.[1]

Within this context of limited time, many responsibilities, and limited resources, it is easy to imagine that the impact of geography on women's activity patterns is quite substantial. As Ann Markusen aptly points out, spatially separated shopping, work, childcare, and medical facilities are the bane of the working mother's life. The travel time involved in performing routine chores under these circumstances adds up to hours, even for women who have access to an automobile.

Characteristics of Women's Travel Behavior

What is known about women's travel behavior? First, women use the automobile less than men do. According to a 1977 federal survey, 89 percent of all males 16 years or older hold driver's licenses, while 73.4 percent of females in the same age category do. Not surprisingly, about 73 percent of the total miles driven annually in the United States are driven by males; male drivers average 13,563 miles per driver per year, but female drivers average only 5,943 miles per driver per year. Furthermore, while males make 60 percent of all trips undertaken by *any* mode of transportation as an auto driver and 22 percent as an auto passenger, females make 41 percent of all trips as an auto driver and 47 percent as an auto passenger.

Conversely, women use public transportation more than men. Nationwide, about 5 percent of all trips are made by public transit. Among transit users, women outnumber men by about two to one. That is, women make up between 60 and 70 percent of all transit passengers, depending on the urban area. For the work trip, Table 12.1 shows that women rideshare (carpool) and use transit more frequently than men, while more men drive alone. Moreover, although women's work trips are shorter than men's, women's work trip travel time may be longer due to the slower speed of public transit.

Second, the trips women make differ from men's in several ways. The number of daily trips seems to depend on access to an automobile. For example, one study indicates that in a two-car family with children, in which both husband and wife are employed, each makes an average of 3.2

one-way trips per day. In a similar family with one car, the daily trip rate is 3.0 and 2.5 for husband and wife respectively.[2] Women also tend to travel shorter distances than men. This is particularly true for the work trip, but holds true for most other types of trips as well. In addition, the purpose of trips made by women differs from that of men. Since the employment participation rate for men is higher than for women, a higher proportion of men's trips are work trips. In contrast, a higher proportion of women's trips are made for purposes of shopping, social activities, and providing chauffeur service for other family members.[3]

Table 12.1
Work Trip Mode Choice Percentage by Sex

Sex	Drive Alone	Ride Share	Public Transit	Walk	Other
Female	60.46	22.93	6.38	5.73	4.50
Male	68.08	18.42	3.54	3.75	6.21

Source : Adapted from William Rohe, Michael Stokes, Kenneth Zatarian, and Leland Barbour, *Travel to Work Patterns: A Preliminary Analysis of Selected Data from the Annual Housing Survey Travel to Work File* , Final Report, UMTA-NC-11-0009-81-1, (Chapel Hill, NC, January 1981): PB-81-181513.

These characteristics of women's travel patterns result from women's roles both in the home and in the workplace, and these roles clearly place women in a disadvantaged position. In terms of travel options, women are disadvantaged by virtue of being more dependent on public transportation than men. Public transit users make fewer trips than nonusers. This recurring finding in transportation studies can be explained in a number of ways. For example, transit users have such low incomes that transit fares are relatively expensive and consequently, frequently unaffordable. Another, perhaps more reasonable explanation is that the mobility provided by public transit is so inferior to that of the automobile that many trips by transit are not made because of the inconvenience of the long waits and transfers involved in making them.

Recent research has shown that public transit users not only travel less frequently and make shorter trips, but also incur higher time costs when they do travel. Furthermore, the differential between the mobility of transit users and automobile users has increased over time. That is, while automobile travelers have enjoyed increased levels of mobility over the years, bus travelers have suffered a loss of mobility.

Table 12.2 presents daily travel information for Washington, DC, for the years 1955 and 1968. It shows that public transit does not provide a level of service comparable to that of the automobile, and that its relative service quality has declined over the years. Given an individual's set of alternative opportunities, distributed throughout the area in which she/he

lives, then to the degree the ability to reach these opportunities is constrained, the set of opportunities is constrained. Quite simply, job
possibilities are not possibilities at all unless one can get to them, and the
same is true for choices of medical care, social activities, or shopping. As
demonstrated here, women face these problems more frequently than
men.

Table 12.2
Daily Travel Characteristics: Washington, DC

	Car Users			Bus Users		
	1955	1968	% Change	1955	1968	% Change
Total Distance (km)	20.48	25.91	+26.5	13.60	14.35	+5.5
Speed (km/hr)	18.83	23.33	+23.9	10.70	10.04	-6.2
Trip distance (km)	6.68	8.21	+22.9	5.89	6.77	+14.9
Trip rate/traveler	3.07	3.16	+2.9	2.31	2.12	-8.2
Trip time (hr)	0.35	0.35	0.0	0.55	0.67	+21.8

Source: Adapted from Gabriel Roth, "Improving the Mobility of the Urban Poor," paper
presented at the summer meeting of the Planning and Transport Research and Computation Conference (Geneva, Switzerland, June 1977).

Why Women Are Disadvantaged

The reasons for women's greater dependence on public transportation
may be traced to women's roles. In the workplace, it is a well-known fact
that women, on the average, do not yet receive equal pay for equal work.
In addition, women tend to work in lower paying occupations than men
and more frequently work part-time than men. Because women earn less
than men, the presence of an employed male in the household largely
determines the relative affluence of the household unit. When the male is
unemployed, or when there is no male household head, household income
is significantly smaller. Thus, as pointed out earlier, female-headed
households are frequently low-income households and are much more
dependent on public transportation.

In addition to the wage discrimination that exists for employed women,
women's household-related responsibilities also contribute to their lower
earning potential. Employment opportunities for women, particularly
mothers of dependent children, are often limited by the availability and
location of childcare services, by the need to be close to home for
emergencies, by dependence on public transit or other household
members for transportation, and by the volume of home-related responsibilities. As a result, women frequently "choose" jobs which don't pay
much, but which fit within these household-related limitations.

An extreme example of how such limitations affect women's earning potential is the existence of female at-home workers. In some cases, women simply cannot leave the home because of the lack of affordable transportation and childcare services. In order to support themselves, these women may work at home on a piecework basis for clothing manufacturers or electronics firms under circumstances that promote exploitation.

Because of the rigid constraints built into many women's daily lives, institutional changes that are expected to be beneficial to women may not be. For example, provision of flexible work hours (flex-time) is often heralded as beneficial to women. Flexible work hours allow the employee to set her own daily or monthly work schedule, usually within certain bounds of "core time" when all employees must be present. Since women must conform to childcare and other schedules, it was argued that flex-time would allow women to shift to more convenient work schedules, and that consequently women would be the major beneficiaries of flex-time programs.

Several flex-time experiments were carried out in various areas of the United States during the 1970s. The primary purpose of these demonstrations was traffic management; flexible work schedules would spread out the peak traffic period, since arrivals and departures would be distributed over a greater length of time, and thus reduce traffic congestion and work travel times. In fact, those expectations were fulfilled. Employees who shifted their work schedule did experience travel time savings. In the majority of cases, workers chose to work an earlier schedule in order to travel before the worst congestion period. For transit users, flex-time provided the opportunity to adapt the work schedule to the transit schedule and to avoid the "crush" of the peak hour. However, those who shifted were predominantly male. Although no research has been conducted as to why this happened, there is a plausible explanation. In the short run, women are frequently locked into their existing schedule and cannot take advantage of flex-time. Conforming to one's schedule limitations is a prerequisite for taking a job; consequently women had already self-selected jobs with acceptable hours. Options such as flex-time can only be beneficial in the long run by providing women with more employment opportunities which fit within schedule limitations.

Future Travel Trends

So far, this chapter has discussed women's travel behavior as it exists today. But the subject of this book is tomorrow. Let us therefore turn now to the future — to some of the social trends which may shape women's activity patterns in the future, and to some public policy changes which might improve women's travel and activity opportunities.

There are three future trends which are particularly important for women's travel behavior. First, the pattern of increasing workforce participation by women will continue. The participation rate for women 16 years or older increased from 43 percent in 1970 to 50 percent in 1978. The largest increase took place among women between the ages of 25 and 34. For this age group, the change in participation was from 45 percent to 62 percent. It is expected that future increases in workforce participation will come primarily from women with school age and younger children who either remain in the workforce through childbearing or return to work after relatively short absences.[4] As a result of increasing numbers of women joining the workforce, the total demand for travel will increase. Studies show that when married women are employed, household trip rates increase. Rather than reducing the number of nonwork trips, the work trip is added on to all the others. Moreover, since mothers with young children have so many responsibilities, there will be a greater need for *efficient* transportation options.

Second, it is expected that the proportion of female-headed households will continue to increase. This reflects not only the anticipated increase in the number of people (both male and female) living alone, but also a rising number of single mothers living with their children. These families will continue to be disproportionately represented in the lower income categories. If the increase in two-worker households continues, median household income will rise, and thus the relative position of one-worker households will drop. In addition, there is no reason to expect that women's wages will reach those of men's in the near future. Thus, on the average, single women will continue to have lower incomes than single men. This means that while these women will have a great need for access to high quality transportation services, they will have fewer resources (in a relative sense) with which to pay for them.

The third trend relates directly to transportation. Quite simply, the cost of travel is going to increase for everyone. For automobile travel, the rising cost of energy is the driving force behind the expected increases. According to a relatively recent estimate, the real cost (taking into account inflation) of gasoline by the year 1990 is predicted to be at least 1.5 times its current price. Although forecasters assume that this price increase will be offset by rising real (again, controlled for inflation) disposable income and continued improvements in auto fuel efficiency, this will quite likely not be the case. The expectation of higher disposable incomes is based on the assumption of a 3 to 4 percent per annum growth in gross national product (GNP), something which this country has not consistently experienced during the past decade. Furthermore additional gains in auto fuel efficiency are progressively more difficult to achieve.

In addition to anticipated increases in the gasoline price, the gasoline gallonage tax is expected to increase as well. Because of the rising cost of maintaining the existing road and highway system, and because total consumption of gasoline has actually fallen slightly since 1979, the revenues generated by the gas tax are no longer sufficient even to maintain the system at its current level of disrepair. By one estimate the gas tax would have to be doubled immediately simply to prevent further deterioration.

The future for public transportation is also one of rising costs. In the older cities of the northeast, a primary problem is deterioration. In Chicago, New York, and Boston, for example, portions of the subways and rail systems are literally on the verge of collapse, the result of several years of delayed maintenance. Large sums of money will be required to reconstruct these systems if they are to continue to operate in future decades. More generally, the problem is one of deficits. The cost of operating and maintaining the nation's public transportation system has steadily increased over the past decade, while fares (in real terms) and patronage have declined. The revenue shortfall up to now has been made up with government subsidies, but these subsidies are expected to be drastically reduced over the next few years. In order to cut costs and increase revenues, many public transportation systems will be forced to cut back services and raise fares. Consequently, the public transit user of the future will most likely be paying more but getting less.

Taken together, these three trends of more women working, more female-headed households, and rising transportation costs indicate a growing need for quality transportation options. However, more costly, and possibly inferior transportation may be available in the future. It remains now to discuss some options for better meeting women's transportation needs in the future.

Transportation Options for Women

When considering changes in the transportation system which might better meet the needs of women, the underlying mechanisms that shape travel behavior must be kept in mind. Women's transportation needs must be evaluated in the larger context of activity patterns and the forces which affect them. Improving the transportation system in isolation is equivalent to attacking the symptoms rather than the disease. In this case, it is women's role in the home and in society that has created women's transportation problems, and it is changes in women's role that in the long run must solve mobility problems for women. The suggestions here are short-run solutions; solutions that can help women perform daily tasks more efficiently and that can provide women with more travel options.

The anticipated cost increase of private transportation is unavoidable. No form of public transportation can replace the comfort and convenience of the private auto for most daily trips. Consequently, the automobile will be with us, essentially in the same form as today, for many years to come. Today, the purchase and maintenance of autos are major problems for women. Equal access to credit for auto purchase must be established for women. In addition, basic auto repair and maintenance, as well as driver education, should be taught in high school so that the next generation of women will be both more capable of handling roadside emergencies and less vulnerable to exploitative auto repair shops.

The impact of cost increases also can be somewhat ameliorated by utilizing the automobile more efficiently. It is not the auto itself which is particularly inefficient; it is the single passenger auto trip. Thus, carpooling, sharing grocery and shopping trips with neighbors, and encouraging older children to ride bikes or use public transit for their social activities can all help increase auto efficiency and reduce individual trip costs.

Workplace-centered transportation programs have a potential for providing efficient group transportation services that is only beginning to be realized. Throughout the country the number of ridesharing programs sponsored, organized, or supported by employers is increasing. These programs support and sometimes subsidize employee vanpools, provide assistance for carpool organization, and in some cases include subsidized public transit use as well. Employer-organized transportation services can be tailored to the need of employees, providing them with a convenient, available, and economical alternative to driving alone. This represents a substantial travel cost savings for those participating and demonstrates the potential for reducing reliance on the single passenger automobile. Interestingly, existing evidence shows that women and men are equally represented in employer-sponsored ridesharing programs.

The challenge for public transportation, on the other hand, is to provide services which suit the particular needs of different user groups in a cost-effective manner. Up to now, public transit has not been successful in meeting this challenge. For the purpose of this discussion, trips can be roughly divided into two categories: work trips and nonwork trips. Public transit historically has been more competitive for work trips because of peak hour congestion, which slows down the private auto and makes driving more stressful. The most competitive forms of public transportation are commuter rail systems. By nature of their exclusive right of way, rail systems are not affected by rush hour traffic congestion. However, rail systems are very expensive. Massive subsidies, provided by tax dollars, are required for their construction and operation.

For most areas around the country, a more economical option is to provide an exclusive right of way on existing freeways for buses and other high-occupancy vehicles (HOV), thus giving these vehicles the same advantage as rail systems. Commuter buses collect passengers at suburban stations (most of which offer free parking for those who drive to the station) and then transport them to downtown destinations. The HOV lane allows cruise speeds of 50-55 miles per hour during peak hours, so the total transit trip time is competitive with that of the automobile. The HOV lane concept is more flexible than a rail system because the same vehicle (a bus or van) can be used for collection and distribution of passengers at both ends of the trip. In areas where HOV facilities are not appropriate, bus service can be improved by traffic management techniques such as pre-emptive signaling, in which buses are able to maintain the green light at signaled intersections.

For local or nonwork trips, there is a need for better neighborhood public transportation. What is needed is a door-to-door, taxi-type service.

For mothers of young children, such a service avoids the necessity of hauling children, strollers, and packages to and from a bus stop. For older women, the safety and convenience of such a service are primary considerations. The major problem with door-to-door or demand-responsive transit (DRT) is its prohibitive cost. In recent years, costs have been reduced by contracting with local taxi operators to provide services. However, even the most efficient DRT systems cost from two to three times as much per passenger as regular fixed-route service; thus when funding problems exist, DRT services may be the first to be eliminated. If neighborhood demand-responsive transit services are to be maintained (and hopefully expanded) with reasonable fares, a public commitment to support these services will have to be made.

Looking Further Ahead

As mentioned earlier, flex-time is a long-run strategy for reducing work trip travel times and promoting ridesharing. By allowing work schedules to be more flexible, employees can choose to travel at more convenient times and can adapt their working hours to public transit schedules. Flex-time also provides added flexibility in scheduling nonwork activities.

Another way to attack transportation problems is to reduce the need for travel. In order to do so, a basic change in geography is necessary; activities and residences should be located in close proximity. Not only the liquor store and the dry cleaner, but also medical and childcare facilities should be located in the neighborhood. As pointed out above, only older cities are likely to have this compact pattern of spatial structure. In suburban areas the pattern of development is dispersed, and more travel is required to move from one activity to another. In some areas zoning restrictions add to the problem by prohibiting certain types of commercial activities, such as childcare, in residential areas.

The needs of women must be taken into account as new residential areas are developed and older areas redeveloped. These areas should be developed as communities, not simply as groups of homes, and the geography of these communities should complement rather than conflict with daily activity patterns. In a sense, time spent traveling is time wasted. When home, job, and services are conveniently located, less time is spent in travel. For working women, such savings may be truly precious, as this time can be put to many better uses.

Ultimately, the source of women's travel behavior can be traced back to the roles of women in the household and in the workplace. The suggestions presented here can improve the quality of travel alternatives available to women in the future, but they cannot change women's roles. In contrast, however, equalization of women's position can have a marked effect on travel behavior. As women approach an equal position in society, the uniqueness of women's travel needs will disappear; women's travel needs will become people's travel needs, and transportation policy can be developed on that basis.

Notes

1. Cambridge Systematics, *Assessment of National Use, Choice and Future Preference Toward the Automobile and Other Modes of Transportation*, Executive Summary, Final Report, NSF/PRA-7716108/4 (February 1980).
2. R. McGinnis, "Influence of Employment and Children on Intra-Household Travel Behavior," in *Women's Travel Issues: Research Needs and Priorities*, ed. Sandra Rosenbloom (Washington, DC: U.S. Department of Transportation, 1978).
3. David Hartgen, "Can Current Transportation Planning Methods Analyze Women's Travel Issues?" in *Women's Travel Issues: Research Needs and Priorities*, ed. Sandra Rosenbloom, (Washington, DC: U.S. Department of Transportation, 1978).
4. Frank Spielberg, Edward Werner, and Ulrich Ernst, "The Shape of the 80's, Demographic, Economic and Travel Characteristics," (paper presented at TRB, January 1981).

See Also:
Tommy Carlstein et. al., eds., *Timing Space and Spacing Time* Vol. 2: *Human Activity and Time Geography* (New York: Halsted Press, 1979).
Genevieve Giuliano, "Public Transportation and the Travel Needs of Women," *Traffic Quarterly* 33 (October 1979): 607-616.
David T. Jones, Jr. et al., *Flexible Work Hours: Implications for Travel Behavior and Transport Investment Policy* (Berkeley, CA: University of California, Institute of Transportation Studies, December 1977).
Risa Palm and Alan Pred, "A Time-Geographic Perspective on Problems of Inequality for Women," working paper no. 236 (Berkeley, CA: University of California, Institute of Urban and Regional Development, 1974).
Sandra Rosenbloom, ed., *Women's Travel Issues: Research Needs and Priorities*, Proceedings of the Conference on Women's Travel Issues, sponsored by the U.S. Department of Transportation, Washington, DC, September 17-20, 1978 (Washington, DC: Department of Transportation, Research and Special Programs Administration, 1978).

Statistics were also gathered from:
Federal Highway Administration, "Characteristics of 1977 Licensed Drivers and their Travel," *Nationwide Personal Transportation Study*, Report no. 1 (October 1980).
Federal Highway Administration, "Mode of Transportation and Personal Characteristics of Tripmakers," *Nationwide Personal Transportation Study*, Report no. 9 (November 1977): 9.

Chapter 13

Living Better Vicariously?

by Jan Zimmerman and Jaime Horwitz

Having rubbed the electronic genii twice before to control telephone and television, large corporations are now experimenting with ways to rub the genii once again, combining video and computer technologies to produce potentially lucrative home-based information services: shopping, banking, news delivery, library research, fire and burglar alarms, energy monitoring, appliance control, travel arrangements, entertainment schedules, ticket reservations, electronic mail, and targeted advertising.

While companies seeking to cash in on the gold at the end of the electromagnetic rainbow are busy exploring service delivery through every possible combination of telephone, computer, cable television, and broadcast TV, a video-glazed public remains foggy about the social implications of these systems for privacy, health, gender-based division of labor, and power.

Under The Looking Glass

Some of the consequences of interactive home information services are nonsexist: they will affect everyone. For example, any computerized system that enables people to gather information electronically, simultaneously enables others to gather information *about them* . Patterns of energy usage, selections of programs from a cable station, lists of requested news articles, electronic purchase receipts, billing and banking records, tallies of votes on electronic referenda — a collection of this information provides a nearly complete picture of daily life. Already a theater exhibitor on trial for showing an X-rated film sought to subpoena records of subscribers who saw the same film on cable. (The judge allowed access only to the numbers of viewers, not the names).

The ability of an interactive system to pinpoint the precise audience for a product — or for a political pitch or a particularly slanted news article — may be good for an advertiser, but bad in terms of further fragmenting an already divided populace. In several markets, companies are now assessing the effectiveness of commercials by correlating the ads shown to a particular target audience with records of purchases as revealed by Zebra code scanners at grocery check-out counters.

The long-term effects of low-level radiation from the video display terminals (VDTs) that will present all this electronic information are still in dispute. Long hours sitting in front of a video screen may be harmful to anyone's vision, muscles, back, or psychological well-being, let alone of particular harm to women's reproductive organs. Current approval from the Occupational Safety and Health Administration is not considered acceptable by unions of clerical workers.

In a world in which "information is power," and that information is privatized though home computers, not being able to "hook in" may become a permanent handicap. Since these systems are not thought of as *services* like a laundromat, but as products like a washing machine or television set, they may well become one of the most expensive items on a household budget. Low-income families may find themselves living in a state of information poverty that both results from and reinforces their class status. An increasing division of society into information "haves" and "have-nots" may follow, based not only on income, but on age as well, since younger generations will have greater familiarity with technological systems.

Equally frightening in its sociological confusion is Alvin Toffler's prediction that the pro-family movement may embrace the concept of a video-serviced community of tele-workers as a means of bringing the family together at home once again.[1] This prophecy has been echoed by a National Science Foundation report on video services which sees electronic homework as a means of re-creating the extended family by making the elderly self-supporting and "more desirable to have around."[2]

The computerization of homes and offices is particularly critical for women, who are likely to absorb the social costs of the new information systems and products through re-isolation in the home, increased household labor, and loss of jobs. Before considering the contradictory implications of home information systems for women, let's take a closer look at how these services work.

Electronic Service Delivery

Home information services are categorized in terms of the type of signal delivered to the home. While the French and the British already have such systems in use, these services are still experimental in the United States.

Teletext is *broadcast* in the black bar called the vertical interval at the bottom of a television picture. The signal can either replace the regular broadcast picture or be superimposed over it using a special decoding device. Two-way or interactive services for teletext generally involve the use of a special keypad which allows limited forms of response (yes, no, numerical values) or the use of the numbers on a touch-tone phone.

Videotex information, on the other hand, is delivered by a *wire* — a telephone line or cable television — for display on either a regular television set or on a video monitor connected to a home computer terminal. Interactive response is handled by keyboard entry from a computer or, once again, by the ubiquitous touch-tone phone. Both types of information delivery are expected to be used for shopping, reservations, entertainment and travel schedules, and news reports.

Some automated services just rely on the use of a telephone to call a computer. This category ranges from the rapidly proliferating bank-by-phone operations to a voice-synthesized shopping service called PAL in San Diego County, California. Naturally, Ma Bell plans to offer some of everything, from medical monitoring to utility management, according to its advertisements.[3] Many businesses already use the telephone lines — or their satellite and microwave adjuncts — for communication between computers at various sites. The rapid expansion of low-cost personal computers, even ones that fit into a briefcase for use "on the road," will permit an ever-increasing number of people to work from their homes or from decentralized computer facilities, connected to the main office only through the umbilical cord of a telephone.

Computer utility management, using existing household wiring to monitor home appliances, with or without remote telephone control, is the last, but not least, of the home information services. These systems simply "mind the store," automatically turning on and off anything that lights, tunes, warms, cools, alarms, rings, or records. By using an existing home wiring network, such computers are able to control all the basic household functions for convenience, security, or energy saving purposes.

The Domesticated City

When futurists envision the home of tomorrow in the year 1998 they see some strange images in their crystal balls:

> Family life is not limited to meals, weekend outings, and once a year vacations. Instead of being the glue that holds things together so that family members can do all those things they're expected to do — like work, school, and community gatherings — the family is the unit that does those things and the home is the place where they get done.[4]

For whom has family life ever been limited to meals, weekend outings, and vacations? Not even a part-time parent or mate has such a limited participation in the sustenance of human lives. The electronic image of family life here is being grafted by futurists onto a home that no one ever lived in, and is suggesting a home, that by the year 1998, no one will be able to get away from.

An assessment of video services must carefully and critically separate out assumptions about "the family" from assumptions about "the household" in a discussion of the absorption of new technologies. Why should any technical invention dictate some particular form of family life? Why should the households of 1998 be composed differently from those of 1980, only 7 percent of which corresponded to an idealized version of homemaker Mom, breadwinner Dad, two kids, and a dog? The danger lies in viewing technological change as a sole *cause* of social change, rather than understanding that there is a shared but unstated social vision (not a conspiracy), involving political and economic forces, which shapes new technologies into a particular pattern of product development, use, and accessibility. This form of "technological determinism" also camouflages the cultural and ideological values that are implicitly embedded in technical development.

It would be a serious error, for example, to blame the "penetration" of videotex and teletext services into the home for the increasing privatization of women's lives, without recognizing the many ways in which overwhelming social problems, like caring for the elderly and educating children, are currently being recast as private, family responsibilities through massive cutbacks in federal social programs. The development of videotex and teletext services is reinforcing, not creating, an increasingly privatized, socially-isolating domestic life. It is thus highly conservative in nature, not revolutionary. An examination of the consequences of electronically-mediated reality bears this out.

The Limitations of Electronic Reality

First of all, when Alice's adventures are restricted to the video glass through all these home information services, she will pay dearly for them in the loss of human contact. As mundane as trips to the market and the bank may be, such excursions often include surprises and informal social contacts, and can establish a basic framework for people who don't regularly go "out" to work. They create opportunities to compare notes on world news, local events, personal troubles, and in large and small ways become a check on one's sense of reality.

Women, much more than men, risk imprisonment in the singular soul and the privatized household, since the female experience finds no accurate images in the public media, no expression in history, and no easy participation in the public life of traditionally male-dominated parts of neighborhoods, such as bars. Women break the shackles of silence with spoken contact — gossiping, consoling, and helping each other in the places they meet, such as worksites, churches, schools, markets, laundromats, and playgrounds. A home information service may reduce the comfort of shared reality that has held women together in the past because it will reduce the reasons for leaving the house.

At the same time opportunities for "getting out" are being reduced. Federal cutbacks that shift more caretaking responsibilities onto individual households are only compounded by video services that enable women to work and shop from home. Tomorrow's homebound house-and-office worker may not only spend half a day or more working at a terminal in her bedroom or dining room, but may simultaneously care for young children and infants, an elderly parent, or a disabled family member. Home video services will thus make it *more* feasible to consign additional responsibilities to the family bungalow, turning it into a little, electronically self-sufficient, domesticated city.

Lastly, the imposition of these technologies may bury this century's renewed feminist vision of women united by common interests — a vision that has grown along with women's expanded communication networks. Because of the fragmentation of the women's community into individual units as a result of video services, it will become even more difficult and expensive to identify and reach a women's audience. The development of a mass movement demands communication networks far different from those narrow demographic categories that will be encouraged by advertising on video service channels.[5] In contrast, feminist organizing relies on posted notices, hand-distributed flyers, newspapers picked up at various community sites, and other forms of unexpected, inexpensive, and face-to-face communication.

Women's attempts to organize by video are already frustrated by the costs of distributing information to home receivers, minimal access to production equipment, the inadequacy of database systems for information about women, and the limited availability of information terminals for low-income women. These factors will only be aggravated by electronic information services that consume ever more "tube-time" at a high cost per selected user. In addition, such services may not generate more and better choices of information for women, but rather may define some arbitrary set of preselected, retrievable data. The determination of which information should be stored and how it should be categorized is in the hands of system owners, not users. Witness the fact that no computerized database exists for feminist publications. Need it then be noted that women, whom Beverly Jones called the "neglected orphans of the technological age," will be the last to control the flow of information over home delivery services?

Thus, women may lose not only opportunities to reflect about their own life experiences, but they may also lose access to essential political information about the Women's Movement. As public work and private consumption tasks move from outside the home to inside it, women may find their feet bound once again, but this time with optical fiber, coaxial copper cable, and the invisible chains of electromagnetic waves.

Video Homemakers

What will women be doing inside the "high-tech" house? They will be shopping and checking out their groceries, paying bills and maintaining bank accounts, keeping household records and inventories, storing utility meter readings, booking travel tickets, reserving seats for sporting events or theaters, handling correspondence, searching through databases for information, writing books and letters, studying, and very probably doing paid work as tele-commuters.

In fact, new information management chores are likely to *expand* the housewife's role to counter any potential savings in her travel time, contrary to recent speculations.[6] Feminist scholars have noted a similar phenomenon in the history of household labor after the introduction of home appliances.[7] The dishwasher, vacuum cleaner, and washer and dryer may have changed the nature of housework, but they certainly didn't decrease the hours it took to do it.

Standards of cleanliness rose with the availability of technology, while additional chores in the form of management, scheduling, repair, and consumerism quickly filled the void left by the end of the rug beater. During the 1950s, a period of enforced female presence in the home, increased expectations for entertaining, gourmet cooking, chauffeuring children, and fashionable dressing even *extended* the duties of a wife into domains that previously had been reserved for upper-income women with domestic servants.

The assumption that history will repeat itself need not be left to innuendo. The run-away success of cable television's "*hot*, new advertising tool," The Home Shopping Show, proves that audiences can be convinced to "save" shopping time by watching a weekly, half-hour program that consists of nothing but "infomercials" — "nonstop commercials in a talk show format."

Whether or not consumer demand exists, argue media critics like Dallas Smythe and Martin Koughan, these services will be of such great value to their corporate sponsors that video services will overwhelm any resistance to the technology.[8,9] Taking into account advertisers' needs for demographically-pinpointed audiences, the enormous amount of capital already invested in an extensive communication infrastructure, and business' desire to reduce the size of the labor force, the momentum of the present may well determine the inevitability of home information services in the future.

Equally discouraging is the seeming inevitability of these services falling into women's traditional domain. As disheartening as it is to feminists, the division of labor within the household has resisted change in spite of the rapid rise of two-income families. It is sadly reasonable to assume that any new tele-duties will become women's work as well.

An expansion of demands on the female homemaker, without meeting any of her existing *real* needs, is explicitly acknowledged in a radio commercial for Atari Computers that ran frequently in 1982. Responding to a female voice asking what she could possibly do with a computer, a male voice recited a sing-song litany of household management and educational activities. In what the sponsor clearly intended as a joke, the woman asked at the end, "But can it cook dinner?"

Taking from Petra to Pay Pauline

One of the most ignored implications of home information services is the fate of those who provided services before a consumer could "dial direct" from home. Unfortunately, in each case, *unpaid* female labor will replace *paid* female labor. Already live female voices have been replaced by telephone company speech synthesizers for forwarding numbers and directory assistance. Airplane reservations and ticket purchases are about to go the same way. And those bank tellers who haven't already lost their jobs to automatic teller machines will lose them to bank-by-touchtone services, while grocery check-out clerks will forfeit jobs to the housekeeper checking out food on her (or his) television set.

Almost all of the job positions that will be supplanted by unpaid labor from the home are now overwhelmingly held by females: retail sales clerks 70 percent, librarians 81 percent, billing clerks 87 percent, cashiers 87 percent, bank tellers 91 percent, telephone operators 93 percent, receptionists 97 percent.

In contrast, males hold the overwhelming percentage of jobs that will increase as home information services expand: shipping clerks 83 percent, electronic technicians 94 percent, delivery services and route workers 95 percent, TV and computer repairers 98 percent, home appliance repair and installation technicians 99 percent.

Thus, even in the unlikely event that childcare and housework become distributed more evenly among household members, women will still suffer disproportionate job loss as home information services proliferate. And even if housework becomes a highly technical, skilled task, it will remain unpaid, underestimated, undervalued, and privatized labor.

The other common assumption about home-based information services is that purchasing costs to the consumer will decline because advertisers will pick up most of the expense. Lower expenditures on gasoline, public transit, postage, and paper are cited to offset the cost of equipment, charge per transaction, and increased use of telephone lines. Detailed economic studies need to be done before this assumption could be considered anywhere near realistic. Such studies might very well demonstrate that the real cost savings will accrue to the corporate suppliers (utilities, banks, retailers) whose savings in labor, energy, office rent, postage, and paper will be far greater than consumers'. Assumptions about consumer savings also ignore the cost of information transmission over local telephone lines. The divestiture of local telephone companies from the AT&T corporate umbrella may ultimately raise local calling rates and connection charges. If this does occur, then home information services could quickly become the most expensive of all home utilities.

Calculating Trade-offs

Yet, given the reality of many women's lives, there may not even be much resistance to home information services. Indeed there may be benefits for a woman who carries the double burden of jobs both inside and outside the home. Chronically short of both time and energy, physically constrained to be in only one place at a time, many women would welcome the possibility of handling daily transactions from home. Since public transit only rarely serves women's needs and daycare options are limited, working from home appears attractive. Alvin Toffler even goes so far as to suggest in *The Third Wave* that computer information services will allow "married secretaries caring for small children at home to continue to work."[10]

To avoid typing the annual report while jiggling crying babies on their laps, women will need to define clearly for themselves what needs *they* want home information services to fill, and to what extent they will allow video services into their homes.

Assuming that information technology becomes a fixture of the American household, it is possible that men would work at home and share in childcare. And the Women's Movement could establish video or computer bulletin boards to protect and enhance networking among women and organizational communication. If information utilities become the linchpin of knowledge and power, women must demand that utility or video service companies provide terminals as cheap as the telephone, or that terminals be easily available for "common use" in other settings like laundromats, women's centers, and neighborhood libraries.

Information equipment and services could increase household self-reliance and reduce dependence on the mother as the household beast of burden, as long as they are accessible, serve the real needs of family members, and are accompanied by new forms of face-to-face social life. For instance, neighborhood or apartment house dining facilities, as well as work or recreation areas could provide social occasions for all the people who work and live at home. We need to imagine and strategize — personally and collectively — our demands for accessible, home computers, demands that go beyond boxes that are "painted pink," as one manufacturer not so facetiously remarked.

While it may be too late to stop the invasion of the video-snatchers, it is not too late to try to assert some control over what services will be provided in and out of the home. Since women do not have sufficient access to capital to control the ownership of such systems, we must concentrate our efforts on maintaining contact with a network of women to resist fragmentation and isolation; on sharing home maintenance tasks with other members of the household; on creating more community-based and communally-organized services; on assuring access to information services through the development of municipal information utilities; and on educating ourselves and our daughters for the information age.

Otherwise, women may find themselves in the year 2001 living in something like a space shuttle grounded on the earth — a private, electronic, home/work capsule — viewing the world through a rose-colored video screen.

Notes

1. Alvin Toffler, *The Third Wave*, (New York: William Morrow, 1980), p. 219.
2. Robert Rheinhold, "Study Says Technology Could Transform Society," New York *Times* (June 14, 1982): A16.
3. AT&T Advertisement, "Restructuring the Bell System Will Open a Whole New World of Communications," New York *Times* (January 14, 1982): B20.
4. Rheinhold, *Op. Cit.*
5. Sandra Salmans, "Scanners Monitor Buying," New York *Times* (August 17, 1981): D8.
6. Jack Niles, "Teleworking — Working Closer to Home," *Technology Review* (April 1982): 58-62.
7. See, for example, Christine Bose, "Technology and Changes in the American Home," *Women's Studies International Quarterly* 2, (Fall 1979): 295-305; Ann Oakley, *Woman's Work: The Housewife, Past and Present* (New York: Vintage Books, 1974); Susan Strasser, *Never Done — History of American Housework* (New York: Pantheon Books, 1982).
8. Dallas W. Smythe, "Communications: Blind Spot of Western Marxism," circulated paper, available from the author, Department of Communications, Temple University, Philadelphia.
9. Martin Koughan, "The State of the Revolution 1982," *Channels* (December 81/January 82): 22-29,70.
10. Toffler, *Op. Cit.*, p. 215.

Chapter 14

Putting Women in

The Energy Picture

by Irmgard Hunt

Men make energy decisions, women live with them. This is a reality which we must strive to change. There is no other single issue more important for the future quality of our lives than the energy path we take. The options are many but conservation and solar energy are viable and economical right now; they should play an increasingly important role as energy sources. Women, who traditionally have been excluded from scientific and technical areas, are uniquely qualified to participate actively in the transition to a society based on clean, renewable resources and energy-efficient life styles. To assure that the transition is indeed beneficial to women, we must be aware of the danger of continued discrimination and sex role stereotyping even in a solar society.

If women are to become an effective pressure group and part of the energy decision-making process, they need to understand some basic concepts and know about the main technologies gathered under the catch word "solar." They also need to become familiar with the economic implications of energy choices and how these could affect their lives and careers. Since educational programs to assist women have been eliminated from the federal budget, these goals will be more difficult to reach. It is beyond the scope of this paper to deal in depth with all these issues, but I hope to provide an overview that will stimulate thought and discussion about women and energy.

Women and the Energy Industry

Women make over 80 percent of consumer purchases in this country; they manage family budgets and control energy use in the home. Over 17 million American families are headed by single mothers and over 50 percent of all women hold jobs, not to indulge in luxury, but to make ends meet or for personal fulfillment. Because women traditionally have been excluded from higher paying jobs, many are hard hit by constantly rising fuel costs. Yet few women understand the economic impact energy has on the cost of living and many still believe that energy and other "technical" issues belong in the "masculine" domain.

Hence, women generally remain outside the network of both public and private energy decisions. Very few targeted educational programs are specifically suited to bring women into the energy picture. But if women are to play a major role, they need assistance to overcome many traditional handicaps and to break out of those stereotyped roles which have excluded them from technical, scientific, and blue collar fields, and rendered them ineligible for many professional and skilled jobs. Barriers of stereotyping and sex discrimination are as strong in the energy field as in any other.

An article in the New York **Times** in 1982 stated that taxpayers spent $3.6 billion during 1980 for installing conservation measures and solar devices in their homes. How many women were able to partake in the jobs implied by this figure alone? How many women were instrumental in the purchase decisions? The fact is that thousands of energy decisions had been made and thousands of conservation and solar jobs were held by somebody: very few of them by women.

Of course, it is traditionally the man who installs, who builds, who wields the tools. Consumer Action Now (CAN) recently published a book called the **Energy Tool Kit for Women**.[1] At the same time, Al Ubell's **Energy Saving Guide for Homeowners** was published.[2] Ubell's guide may be very good, but it does not show a single woman engaged in any of the procedures. In fact the only picture of a woman in the whole book is that of a cave woman holding a baby by a camp fire to demonstrate use of radiant heat. This book, which was a Book of the Month Club gift, is an example of how stereotypes are perpetuated. Yet hundreds of people want to know *why* a book geared specifically towards women is necessary.

The list of obstacles to women's involvement in energy decision making on a managerial level is long. Women do not have an established "old sister" network; they are not automatically appointed to a position because they went to the same school or belong to the same club. Female schoolmates may be at home, perhaps unemployed, or even more likely underpaid, pink-collar workers. Thanks to the Women's Movement, however, women are making changes. They may have the courage to break into the male-dominated world, for by now 18 percent of blue collar workers are women. As women learn about energy, they are building their own solar greenhouses, heading solar franchises, or writing on energy issues.

Most women are unaware that they have considerable economic power as consumers. Since they control energy use in the residential sector to a large degree, women who know the energy implications of their buying decisions can have an enormous impact on energy consumption. If women buy fuel-efficient cars or opt for mass transit for their travel, if they buy a solar home or insulate the one they have, or if they select energy-efficient appliances, they exert a major influence on the market and on manufacturers. In the early 1970s it was women, after all, who

turned around the entire detergent industry when they started demanding low-phosphate detergents to reduce water pollution.

Some feminists are alarmed at the possible exploitation of the very control women have in the domestic sector. Will women be blamed for high
energy consumption and turned into scapegoats? Will they be expected to
stay home once again to guard over family resources, caring, preserving,
recycling? Or, as we move towards a society with less growth — usually
associated with conservation of energy and resources — will women be
the first to suffer from any ensuing economic depression or unemployment? The argument of increased unemployment can be countered
because jobs will increase in a more service-oriented, energy-efficient
society. The question is, will these service-oriented jobs be paid on an
equal footing with other technical and nontraditional, that is men's jobs,
or will they be labeled "satisfying" or "improving the quality of our
lives," and use women as "morally superior" but cheap labor? A recent
analysis of the potential of energy conservation undertaken by the Solar
Energy Research Institute concluded that by adhering to strict economic
principles and assuming a strong growth-oriented, full-employment
economy, the United States could cut its current energy consumption by
over 20 percent by the year 2000 without sacrificing any of its productivity
goals.

This scenario does assume growth and full employment. The question
still remains, what kind of jobs and what pay will women command?
There are other facets to be considered. What will be the impact on
women of increased gasoline prices or of reduction in highway construction? Since women now suffer from lack of access to automobiles, as
Rebecca Peterson points out, increased mass transit will eventually
benefit women and should draw the attention of feminist decision
makers.[3]

An energy-efficient society must pay particular attention to housing
and neighborhood design. The present one-family house does not meet the
needs of either the conservationist or the feminist. Energy-efficient or
solar homes designed for single heads of households, working mothers, or
participatory, nonstereotyped families need to reflect and accommodate
new life styles. The danger in this time of transition is that women will not
be able to move rapidly enough into the decision-making process;
technological fixes will be used to fix present inequalities. Feminists and
conservationists must become aware of the interdependence of these
issues and realize that socioeconomic, as well as philosophical and
technical questions must be addressed simultaneously to result in a just,
safe, and renewable society.

Alternate Energy Technologies

Women need to acquire a knowledge of the solar option, learn about
energy efficiency, and recognize the implications of the options they

choose. For that reason I wish to quickly summarize various solar terms and applications.

According to Daniel Yergin's study in **The Energy Future**, conservation is the most cost-effective way to reduce energy consumption.[4] In the private sector it is the number one option, even before investigating any kind of solar system. At present, only 5 percent of our energy needs are met by clean, renewable resources, for which solar is usually the catch word. Actually, 3 percent is hydropower, 2 percent is wood, and a small fraction consists of active and passive solar sources and other sources, such as wind, biomass, and solar cells.

Active solar means using a mechanical device or solar collector for water and space heating, while *passive solar* is nothing but energy-efficient design. Earth berms, wind sheltering, large sun-facing windows, and shading through trees are examples of passive solar approaches. About 7,000 companies are already involved in the fast-growing solar industry. Over $150 million worth of collectors were sold in 1980, and between 1978 and 1982 the industry grew about 40 percent annually.

Other common or exotic renewable energy sources include photovoltaic cells, which convert sunlight directly to electricity, wind power, hydropower, cogeneration, tidal power, biomass conversion, ocean thermal differential, and wood power.

By the year 2000 the morning chill may well be broken in millions of homes by the heat captured by sunlight the day before, while early risers make their coffee with electricity generated from solar cells. This is not just wishful thinking. California already has established a goal that 10 percent of the state's electricity will be wind generated by the year 2000, while New York State has assessed the generating potential of its small dams at 3000 megawatts of electricity. This compares to the average output of a nuclear power plant of about 800 megawatts and could thus replace three to four major nuclear power plants.

As the solar and conservation industry grows, there will be a whole range of job openings in the field from well-paying blue collar positions to professional and management positions. For women, this is a chance to get in on the ground floor, create training programs, become entrepreneurs, participate in shaping a new world based on a renewable energy supply. However, special programs and special attention are needed to give women a fair chance to make up for lost time.

Energy Education

Targeted education programs are crucial. When CAN reached out to women of the Stamford, Connecticut, community through a home heating and weatherization pilot project, it found that the average woman's knowledge of energy implications was minimal. Rising fuel bills sent up warning signs, but homeowners did not always make the connection between those bills and the energy wasted by a brightly-lit garden path or a drafty crack around a window frame. Few considered the possibility of going to the hardware store for a caulking gun or the right kind of weatherstripping to reduce those costs. But when 5,000 women participated in the Women's Energy Fair in Stamford, their interest in learning and the potential to apply what was learned was palpable.

But there are far too few sources of information. How can the average woman or consumer exercise her freedom of choice if the information that is available to her is at best skimpy, often locally irrelevant, and at times biased and inaccurate? Since the government shows no interest in providing the consumer with any information about solar energy and conservation, who is going to tell a woman that the replacement of an updated boiler system may result in 15 percent energy savings? Who is telling her what the trade-offs are between double-glazed windows and additional attic insulation? Who will enforce energy efficiency labels on appliances? The educational programs that would help consumers make the right decisions are being dismantled just when price policy makes them most necessary. It is as if one promoted travel but hid all the maps.

At this time many citizens of this country can no longer afford to live in comfort; over the past year 1,000 elderly died of hypothermia or froze to death, retired homeowners can no longer hold onto moderate homes because their heating bills are larger than their mortgages. "The elderly poor are faced with the cruel choice of 'heat or eat' during cold weather since most of them must spend 20 percent or more of their income on fuel, according to a study conducted with federal support by the National Council of Senior Citizens."[5] And because women outlive men, a large percentage of these elderly is *female* .

Yet the federal government is calling for a reduction of 97 percent in conservation and 88 percent in solar programs. The funds for the solar and conservation bank, which were to provide subsidized loans to low- and moderate-income people for energy efficiency improvement, were illegally impounded in 1981. The Reagan White House has tried to eliminate the solar and conservation tax credit, the weatherization program, and appliance-efficiency standards. The impact of such cuts can be severe. For exampl, the State and Local Programs Office, whose budget has been eliminated, had by 1982 helped weatherize more than 750,000 homes occupied by the poor, the elderly, or handicapped, saving roughly 3 million barrels of oil and making possible much larger accrued savings over a period of time. It had helped 125,000 schools, hospitals, and public institutions to conduct energy audits and another 25,000 to install conservation measures, saving the estimated equivalent of 18 million barrels of oil.

These and other programs have created jobs, stimulated private investment in conservation, and cut loss of life from hypothermia and the ills of winter. While some federal programs were inefficient and cumbersome, many served a real and urgent need and were instrumental in decreasing national energy consumption and protecting the environment, as well as providing a safety net for the poor. It is critical to recall the ongoing "feminization of poverty." Currently, two out of three adults who fall within the poverty classification are women. And the National Advisory Council on Economic Opportunity has predicted that by the year 2000 all of the nation's poor will be women and their children. Thus, any cutbacks in energy assistance for low-income families are disproportionately borne by women.[6]

To counteract these disastrous trends, women, who throughout history have organized to bring about social change through peace, environmental, consumer, and equal rights movements, must continue to insist on social justice, economic equality, and a sustainable energy future. As women become more technically skilled and willing to cross traditional barriers, and as energy decisions are based increasingly on social sciences and politics, women's social consciousness, their ability to negotiate, to adapt, to cooperate, to see a broad rather than a single-track picture are invaluable for achieving the transition from our present energy supply system to a renewable one. If women continue to be excluded from energy policy-setting and energy decision making, as well as from education and assistance programs, they will be blocked from moving themselves and this society towards an acceptable and sustainable standard of living in an environment that nurtures healthy minds and bodies.

Notes

1. Joan Byalin, *Women's Energy Tool Kit* (New York: Consumer Action Now, 1980).
2. Al Ubell, *Energy Saving Guide for Homeowners* (New York: Warner, 1980).
3. Rebecca Peterson, "Impacts of the Conserver Society on Women" *Conserver Society Notes* (Spring/Summer 1979).
4. Daniel Yergin and Roger Stobaugh, editors, *The Energy Future: The Report of the Harvard Business School Energy Project* (New York: Random House, 1979).
5. Los Angeles *Times*, September 8, 1982, Part I, p. 2.
6. Barbara Ehrenreich and Karin Stallard, "The Nouveau Poor," *Ms.* 11 (August 1982): 217-224.

Since 1970 Consumer Action Now (CAN), a pioneer in energy conservation training, has been providing consumers with the skills required to develop self-reliance in the face of energy shortages. CAN's successful efforts have included the organization of the widely publicized Sun Day in New York City, the creation of the popular **Women's Energy Tool Kit**, leadership training for women, and the establishment of a national energy seminar program, including consumer panels and community workshops.

For more information contact: Consumer Action Now, 110 West 34th Street, New York, NY 10001, (212) 736-8170.

Chapter 15

Abortion:

A Domestic Technology

by Kristin Luker

In the late 1960s women, as well as some men, began to organize for more liberalized abortion. What is interesting about these women in the light of more recent developments on abortion, is that they represented a broad spectrum of political persuasions — from Republican women's groups and the American Association of University Women to the Redstockings, a radical feminist group. A rallying cry common to all these organizations, however, was that abortion was a private, personal decision, to be made "between a woman and her doctor." To be sure, different women had different interpretations of what this phrase actually meant: conservative women tended to assume that physicians would exercise some control over the abortion decision; more radical women assumed that abortion would be like any other elective medical procedure. But from the most conservative to the most radical, it was rare to find women who questioned the fact that abortion should be a medical decision.

It was on these grounds that the United States Supreme Court found all existing state laws on abortion to be unconstitutional. Physicians, argued the Court, had the right to practice medicine as they saw fit, free from vaguely worded laws which sought to introduce philosophical dilemmas into a practical, technical world. For over a century physicians in the United States, had been legally permitted to perform some abortions (those necessary to "save the life of the woman"); now they were entitled to do whatever abortions they felt to be "medically necessary."

We have come to take for granted the assumption that abortion and contraception are medical matters. But surprisingly, abortion, and for that matter contraception, came under the control of physicians only within the recent past. For most of U.S. history, abortion was decidedly domestic.

Medicine: A Domestic Art

In order to have a clear sense of the domesticity of abortion during the eighteenth and nineteenth centuries, it is important to realize that medicine itself was primarily domestic during that period. Until quite recently, consulting a physician was a rare event, limited to the very wealthy or the very ill. This was due to a number of factors. In England (and most other European countries) there was an active guild tradition in the healing arts, which limited the right to practice to those who were bona fide members of the guild. And guilds, like unions today, tended to limit their membership to the sons of those already in the guild. (I use the term deliberately: women were not typically permitted to be guild members).

But medicine in the colonies lacked this guild tradition. In part because the colonies represented a bleak and uncivilized prospect to well-established physicians, pharmacists and surgeons — the three traditional guilds of England — few of them chose to emigrate. Thus healers in the colonial American setting tended to be people who were recognized in their communities as being skillful, rather than those who were officially recognized by a guild. And women were often among those recognized as successful healers.

In the early nineteenth century, Jacksonian democracy enhanced this tradition. It was an era which was openly anti-elitist, and whatever minimal laws had existed to regulate medical practice were eliminated. People who felt themselves to be gifted at the medical arts and/or those who were recognized by their neighbors as such, were often the only healers to which the typical family might have access. Some of these self-recruited healers, however, in an attempt to professionalize, did call themselves "doctors" and "doctoresses."[1]

Thus for most Americans, except the well-to-do and urban, medical treatment was something that happened in the home, usually performed by the women of the household. Women were helped by home medical books and their own family remedies, handed down from mothers to daughters. In extreme cases, a doctor or doctoress might be sent for, but this person, despite the title, might very well be nothing more than a highly skillful neighbor with some community reputation in hopeless cases.

Perhaps the closest thing to eighteenth and nineteenth century medicine which modern-day Americans can imagine would be sex therapy. The options available for people dealing with sexual problems are exactly those that earlier Americans had available: they can read books about it, they can talk to their mothers (or their mothers-in-law) about it, or they can talk it over with their friends. If things are seriously wrong, they may consult their minister or their physician, neither of whom is very likely to know anything more than they do. If they get desperate enough, they may seek help through the Yellow Pages or the newspaper, but the person they find will be regulated by no state or federal agency that insures that the practitioners are honest, ethical, or effective. With the exception of the Yellow Pages, this entire process in seeking help for a medical problem would have seemed very familiar to our ancestors.

"Female" Problems

True as these comments are about the general state of medicine in U.S. history, they are even more true of women's medical problems. To an even greater extent than for other medical problems, medical treatment surrounding women's reproductive systems stayed domestic, familial, and female-controlled until almost the beginning of the twentieth century. Control of childbirth by male physicians rather than female midwives was a relatively late (and very contested) event. And even when male physicians did control childbirth, they did so in the women's home for a considerable period of time: as late as 1930, an estimated 75 percent of all American babies were still being born at home.[2]

It is in this context that abortion remained a domestic practice for so long. Official, "professional," medical care was a rarity, and doctors and doctoresses were rarely the technical experts we now think of them being. Then, as now, women were the primary medical caretakers of their families, and when it was the woman herself who needed medical care for her "female frame," as it was called, she was often likely to turn to family, more experienced female friends, and female healers such as midwives and doctoresses.

During much of that historical period, a dominant model of the human body was that of a system which could get "blocked." People could get constipated, they could stop sweating, or, most importantly for our purposes, they could find their menstrual periods "stopped." All these event were thought to be harmful to health. Thus women with "blocked menstruation" faced a medical problem, and since the primary cause of absent periods in a healthy, sexually active woman is pregnancy, at times she faced a social and psychological problem as well.[3]

Limited Resources

Women in these eras had a limited variety of places to turn to for advice about their "blocked" menstruation. First, they could turn to written material. Many women had "home recipe" books which contained not only recipes for cooking, but also helpful hints and medical remedies, including directions for bringing on blocked menses. These home recipe books could be either a hand-written compendium of information handed down from mother to daughter or volumes that were professionally printed and sold. Similarly, there were home medical books available, useful because doctors were so rare and so expensive. Books like Brevitt's **Female Medical Repository**, published in 1810, or Thomas Ewell's **Letters to Ladies**, published in 1817, contained a number of remedies for "bringing down the courses."

Dr. William Buchan's **Domestic Medicine**, first published in the United States in 1782, was that era's most frequently reprinted medical book. It contains a number of home remedies for starting "blocked" menstruation. (In later editions, a footnote was appended denouncing induced abortion. It argued that women did it at the risk of their lives, and that it was most appalling when committed by the "respectable matron.")[4]

Despite this condemnation, during the latter half of the nineteenth century, women whose home remedies had failed could turn to advertisements in their daily newspapers, including, according to some sources, their church newspapers for patent medicines to bring on "suppressed menses." Also common were discreet advertisements for "clinics for ladies" where menstrual irregularities "from whatever cause" could be treated. These clinics often made a point of noting that they practiced confidentiality and that private, off-street entrances were available. A typical example is this 1873 San Francisco advertisement for a doctoress specializing in "female irregularities."

> Doctoress A. M. Hoffman, 4422 Folsom St. between 10th and 11th, 30 years experience; has her diploma of the highest school of Germany, will thoroughly treat all Diseases of Women and Children; She would intimate to Ladies suffering from Uterine Disorders that she has a sure specific for female irregularities. All communications strictly confidential. She has lately added a first-class Lying-In Hospital where patients can receive the best of medical attendance. Terms moderate.

Finally, women could turn to other women. It is one of the facts of history that professionals, usually men, are more likely to have passed on their views and attitudes to posterity, because they have commanded the printed page. Thus we know very little about what women of the time thought and felt about abortion. However, the picture that emerges through the lines of how physicians viewed women is clear: from Buchan's book of 1782 until the late 1950s doctors made two recurring complaints about women and abortion.

First, they complained that women did not think that abortion was morally wrong. Despite laws passed by physicians in the middle of the nineteenth century which outlawed abortions unless a physician deemed it necessary to "preserve the woman's life," women continued to seek (and have) abortions. And not only did they have abortions, they did it with no sense they were doing anything wrong. Second, doctors claimed that women passed on abortion technology among themselves. There was a "female network," according to physicians, whereby women would teach one another how to "avoid the duties of motherhood," as one disgruntled physician put it. How little guilt women felt about abortion, they argued, was demonstrated by the fact that this female information was often passed down from mother to daughter. Since physicians argued that abortion was "antenatal infanticide," their inability to convert women to such a view both baffled and angered them.[5]

Abortion Technologies

What were the abortion technologies available at that time? For most of that period, herbal remedies were the most common abortifacients. Black hellebore, tansy, oil of savin, rue, and black cohash were all listed in the home recipe and medical books for bringing on blocked menstruation. Since many of these recipes and remedies stress that women who think they are pregnant should not use them, as they will cause a miscarriage, the alternative use of these herbs was undoubtedly quite clear. Typically these herbs were brewed into a tea, which was then consumed. More rarely, these herbs were used as vaginal douches. And although they may also have been used as intrauterine douches (which probably would have increased their effectiveness), there is no clear evidence that women were willing to inject these plant materials into the womb itself before the first half of the nineteenth century.

Most of the herbs used for abortion are cathartics and/or laxatives. They may have stimulated abortion indirectly by means of gastric upset. At least a few of them may have been able to cause abortion more directly, by working on uterine muscles. There are no large-scale studies of the effectiveness of these drugs, but small-scale studies indicate that they may have had some abortifacient activity, although they were probably less than 100 percent effective. Problems in using these herbs include the fact that it is difficult to get reliable dosages from plant material; many of these herbs are poisonous in large doses, so that determining an effective but not lethal dose may have been quite difficult.

Starting around 1860, medical practice and medical models of the human body changed, and both of these changes affected the practice of abortion. In part because of the Civil War, where surgeons were called on to do many more amputations and major surgeries, physicians in general became more willing to enter the body surgically. In turn, physicians began to do surgical abortions: they began to dilate the cervix and actually enter the uterus. (Until this period, there seems to have been very little attempt to work on the uterine cavity directly.) Once physicians began to dilate the uterus, the medical practice of abortion began to include a willingness to clear the pregnant womb by the use of fingers, various kinds of curettes, and by "lavaging" (washing out) the uterus with various fluids squirted through the cervix by a rubber syringe. Perhaps the most interesting "medical advance" of the last half of the nineteenth century was the use of slippery elm tents to dilate the cervix and bring on labor. Like today's "laminaria tents," these small bundles of dry plant materials, inserted in the cervix, swelled when exposed to body fluids. None of these medical methods used sterile technique, however, and the consequence of this oversight — puerperal fever — often led to death.

The new "medical" techniques that physicians began to use to produce abortions after 1860 are clearly not so complicated as to be beyond the use of a reasonably determined woman, particularly if a body of information was shared among a group of women. Which way the technology moved will probably never be known. Whether women adapted these techniques from doctors, or whether as was so often the case, these new "medical" techniques were merely professional adaptations of home remedies, cannot be answered at this point. What is clear, judging from medical journals, however, is that the appearance of these "medical" techniques among physicians was followed in short order by reports of women using many of these same techniques for self-abortion.

Rubber syringes, for example, were available "over the counter" by the middle of the last century, and it would have been relatively easy for a woman, especially if aided by a female friend or relative, to inject a fluid — water, warm saline solution, or one of the earlier abortifacients such as rue or tansy — into her uterus. Similarly, since doctors did not control pharmaceutical practice as they do now, a woman could easily buy slippery elm tents (as well as other "over-the-counter" abortifacients) from her local pharmacy.

From the modern point of view, however, the most critical, and perhaps most lethal, change in the accounts of self-abortion that were published in nineteenth century medical journals was the increasing frequency with which women began to probe their own uteruses with whatever tools were at hand. For example, women wore high-button shoes, and buttoned those shoes with a button hook — a long, slender hook curved at the end. The button hook appears to have been the nineteenth century equivalent of the coat hanger. From the 1860s onward, medical journals contain accounts of fatal and near-fatal perforations of the uterus with buttonhooks. Women also used whalebone stays from their corsets, and there is at least one account of a woman who perforated both her uterus and her lung with an umbrella rib.[6]

By the second half of the nineteenth century, abortion began to emerge for the first time as a social problem. Newspapers began to run stores of women who had died from "criminal abortions," although whether this reflects more abortions, more lethal abortion techniques, or simply more awareness of abortion is not clear. Most centrally, physicians began to get involved in the issue, arguing that abortion was both dangerous to women and morally wrong. A number of prominent physicians began to lobby state legislatures to pass laws banning abortions, and they also began to write books and pamphlets for the larger public, endeavoring to convince them, too, that abortion was both medically and morally dangerous.

How did abortion move, in the middle of the nineteenth century, from a domestic, familial, and female pursuit, to a medical and moral dilemma? The answer is an enormously complex one: the period that saw abortion move from a domestic to a medical technology was a period of rapid social change. The birth rates of native-born women in the United States dropped in half, from an average of seven children per women in 1800, to an average of slightly over three in 1900. It was also a period of massive immigration, and many observers became concerned that as a result of the low birth rates of native "Yankees," the more fertile European immigrants would crowd them out, a situation that nineteenth century alarmists called "race suicide." The nineteenth century was also a period of change in the relationships between men and women, as this period saw the first wave of American feminism. Then, as now, the control of fertility, and whether or not women should control their own reproductive capacities, was a threatening political issue.[7]

Most clearly, abortion became a medical issue because of the efforts of physicians. Prior to the late nineteenth century, there was little legal punishment of either early or late abortion. Abortion before "quickening" (that period when a woman feels the embryo move within her) was not a crime at common law, and many observers argue that punishment even of late abortion (after quickening) was uncommon.[8]

Starting in the late 1850s, physicians began to argue that they had new scientific evidence which showed pregnancy to be a biologically continuous process, thus discrediting the laws which ignored abortions that occurred before quickening. (While varying from woman to woman and even from pregnancy to pregnancy in the same woman, quickening usually occurs in either the fifth or sixth month of pregnancy). Physicians were thus able to portray themselves as substantially more scientifically knowledgeable about pregnancy than laypeople (women). They were able to lay claim to a relatively esoteric and "technical" body of knowledge. Simultaneously, by defining the embryo as legally, morally, and most importantly, biologically "alive" at all stages of pregnancy, physicians were able to argue that they were protectors both of women (since abortion was argued to be so dangerous) and babies (as the embryo was now defined to be).

A Century of Silence

It may very well have been the case that abortions were not very closely regulated in the early part of the nineteenth century because they were not very common. A rural, agricultural country with a great deal of cheap land may very well have had a citizenry with little interest in abortion.

In fact, U.S. birth rates in the nineteenth century were among the highest in the world, and were much like birth rates in Third World countries today. But as the century progressed, and Americans became more urban and industrial, birth rates fell dramatically. At least some observers argue that the very rapid decline in U.S. birth rates (as noted, they were halved in a century) simply could not have been accomplished without the use of abortion. Neither abstinence nor the kinds of birth control then available either alone or in combination could have produced such a dramatic decline in births.

Women's bodies, therefore, became a matter of interest to those who were concerned about what seemed to be the relative depopulation of native-born Americans, as well as those who wished to continue traditional, God-fearing, rural ways of life untouched by the "modern ways" of the city and industry. Medical control of abortion met a number of social needs. It allowed physicians, who were then a weak, struggling, and disorganized profession, to claim both moral and technical expertise in the case of abortion. Simultaneously, it allowed those concerned with women's fertility the assurance that a profession which was rapidly becoming more white, more male, and more elite, would make "proper" decisions with respect to abortion. "Not one abortion too many, nor one too few," claimed an early twentieth century physician. The bid by physicians to regulate abortions, and its acceptance (or at least lack of protest) by the general public, may have represented a compromise between the twin dilemmas of outlawing abortion entirely, or leaving it completely in the hands of women. As a result, abortion as a major social, ethical, and political dilemma would disappear beneath the cloak of an emerging profession, there to rest quietly for over a century.

Notes

1. For the history of medicine in the United States, see Richard Harrison Shyrock, *Medicine and Society in America 1660-1860* (New York: New York University Press, 1971).
2. Dorothy and Richard Wertz, *Lying-In: A History of Childbirth in America* (New York: Free Press, 1977).
3. Charles Rosenberg, "The Therapeutic Revolution: Medicine, Meanings and Social Change in 19th Century America," *Perspectives in Medicine and Biology* (Summer 1977).
4. James Mohr, *Abortion in America: Origins and Evolution of National Policy* (New York: Oxford University Press, 1978).
5. Kristin Luker, *Abortion and the Politics of Motherhood* (Berkeley, CA: University of California Press, 1983).
6. For examples see T. A. Emmet, *The Principles and Practice of Gynecology* (Philadelphia: Henry C. Lea, 1879); and T. Gaillard Thomas, *Practical Treatise on the Diseases of Women* (Philadelphia: Henry C. Lea, 1876).
7. On the first wave of feminism, see Eleanor Flexner, *Century of Struggle: The Women's Rights Struggle in the United States* (Cambridge, MA: Harvard University Press, 1959).
8. Eugene Quay, "Justifiable Abortion: Medical and Legal Foundations," *The Georgetown Law Journal* 49 (Winter/Spring 1961).

Chapter 16

Mother Calls Herself a Housewife,

But She Buys Bulls

by Katherine Jensen

I have often been struck by the great gap between my unofficial existence as a woman made in rural America and my official training based on an urban perspective in sociology and women's studies. From my first days at college with housemates reared in New Jersey, Chicago, and Philadelphia, I knew that my life had been different. My classmates seemed not only urban, but urbane, better schooled, more sophisticated politically; these differences were not just ones of class. It was not until much later that I understood how much technical competence I had, as a rural woman born and bred, that was not only alien but terrifying to them, even though those skills seemed irrelevant to the mental exercises asked of me at the time.

True, most women in North American society are not rural women, even if many of us have a rural heritage. And many women who now "become" rural women may not share, or even really aspire to the contemporary rural subculture of the western United States that I want to analyze. It is a culture in which rural women's relation to economic production demands that they gain a higher level of skills and more diverse technological competence than is usually expected of urban women (and most urban men). I would argue that their competence and economic function give rural women greater authority and status within the family than they might have as urban wage-earners. Thus rural women are important not only as American cultural myth, but also as an important measure of changing contemporary reality.

The issues I want to deal with here are technical competence and control over technology. Feminist anthropologists have begun not only to question the idea that technology generally has come from the male domain, but to prove that it has not. Many early inventions not specifically attributed to women obviously belong in the larger history of rural women. Certainly horticultural techniques, food preservation, and clothing construction have been women's inventions and responsibilities in many different cultures for most of human history.[1] This technological skill extends to rural women today.

Men's Work Is Women's Work

A number of recent works — mostly oral history projects on rural women — have documented, though usually not analyzed, the roles and duties of rural women.[2] Over and over these histories reflect the apparent contradiction between a cultural norm and the social reality of women's work. Most women will say that while there is a general definition of "women's work" and "men's work" on farms and ranches, women regularly do "men's work," but men much less often engage in female responsibilities. The official division of labor follows the norms of the larger society in assigning women domestic, indoor labor, while men engage in the instrumental functions which reside primarily outdoors. The social reality, however, reflects greater complexity in work responsibilities.

> In the spring, before the lambing you have to shear. And that was hard work, especially for me. There were about 12 to 15 shearers and they brought with them about three wranglers and a wool tromper, and so with our herders and us, we hardly ever had less than 20 to cook for and that's what I did. Sometimes Bob would come in and say, 'Stop your work in the house and go get your horse and help the herder bring in the sheep.' The sheep went to a sweat shed to stay warm for the shearers because that way they shear better. You always kept your sweat shed full of sheep, especially if it looked like it was going to storm. You just can't shear sheep that are wet, and if the herder couldn't get the sheep in, I had to go and help him, and I'd be late with my evening meal. Bob'd get excited during shearing, because it is a precision-like deal, and it has to go right.[3]

> You wasn't in bed at five in the morning. And when we trailed cattle, you'd get up at two-thirty in the morning. I helped trail the cattle. We trailed from our place over to the Laramie Plains. We started in trailing right after the drought, well, you might say, in about 1933 and we trailed until in the '50s. We trailed cattle in the spring and fall. And you'd cook over a campfire and you get meals for the men as well as you help ride, too. But, if they needed me out in the hay field or on the horse, I was there. Wherever I was needed I would be there.[4]

There is a qualitative difference between these descriptions and those of the dual-career, urban, female wage-earner who must also do housework; this work is much more of a piece, partly because of the homestead-bounded enterprise.

Even household work is more clearly related to economic productivity than is usually the case in urban settings. A number of anthropologists

have posited that women's relationship to exchange economy is fairly
directly reflected by status within their families.[5] Several examples of
traditional farm women's work with important economic value illustrate
the point.

A woman who homesteaded in Wyoming with her husband in 1918 and
lived there until 1958 described her daily chores:

> Well, (you) always get the meals, and of course you scrub
> the floor. You always done the washing and ironing and you
> took care of the chickens and your turkeys and gathered the
> eggs. (You) took care of the milk and had to wash the
> separator and you churned, of course. You had to churn.
> Everybody churned, of course.

For most of U.S. history, women have sold eggs and butter or bartered
them for other goods and services. This exchange value certainly exceeded "pin money," as demonstrated by a former schoolteacher who earned
money from poultry after her marriage:

> I had a big incubator and I would hatch about 5,000 chickens
> every year and I kept a flock of about 300 hens and pretty
> much made a living for us for quite awhile, until we could
> get our farm paid for.

At the very least, women gathered, cleaned, packaged, and delivered the
eggs to stores or individual buyers in town. The steady cash income they
received was often very important to the family productive unit, which
might otherwise have had to rely on annual or semiannual sales of
agricultural products or livestock. But it was also cash to which women
had access and over which they had control. Thus the technology of egg
production and distribution was especially important to women and
clearly under their control. This particular economic function has been
largely eliminated in the last decade by large corporate egg factories of
several million hens, making local egg production uneconomical. But for
literally centuries, on both farms and ranches, poultry was a part of the
rural economy which belonged to women.

Contemporary rural women still do work which may have a more
direct economic import than appears on the surface. One example is the
function of the noon meal, appropriately called "dinner" by all the rural
people I know. Dinner is prepared by women, along with girls and young
children of both sexes, as one might expect. It is the most important meal
of the day; if the woman must be away from the household at noon or for
part of the morning, it will most likely be prepared ahead of time and left
waiting. Technological advances such as freezers, oven timers, and
microwave ovens make that easier now than in the past.

Dinner is not simply a symbolic ritual of dominant men who come home
to consume it; dinner is most literally a business lunch in which women
directly participate. As an important respite in a long work day, dinner

entails a full meal and perhaps a short midday nap afterward. It also typically includes reading the mail (mostly bills) and yesterday's just-arrived newspapers, hearing the news, weather, and market reports on the radio (all important factors in farm economics), and making several phone calls. Men and "men's work" are the focus of the meal, but women are included in the information, conversation, and usually the decision-making process. The movie image of a tableful of "hands" is often inac-curate. Meals produced for threshers and branders were important *annual* events, but hardly typical of daily routine. Indeed, the wife may be the only other adult present to hear about progress on the day's work: what machinery has broken down, the condition of the hay or grain, the health of the livestock.[6] In any case, she will be part of communication among workers who likely have been engaged in separate locations and activities during the morning.

That leads to a second important element of rural women's respon-sibility: going to town. Women very often go to town, because the men do not "have time." In fact, many women are skillful in finding reasons to have to go to town themselves.[7] Most trips are multifunctional, related not only to domestic consumption (buying groceries) and social roles (go-ing to meetings), but also to production demands (getting parts for machinery, doing bank business, buying feed or veterinary supplies, or taking a sick animal to the veterinarian). Rural women often go to social engagements in pick-up trucks or heavily-loaded station wagons.

The birthing and nurturing of young animals is another productive task in which women traditionally have been engaged. While pervasive Vic-torian ideas about female propriety and "the separation of the spheres" may have kept some women isolated from work such as breeding, bran-ding, and castrating livestock, these sanctions by no means affected all women. Technological change actually has increased their participation: more women are likely to have run squeeze chutes than have ever roped calves, or have prepared equipment for artificial insemination than have managed bulls.

The birthing process (here calving or lambing) is one area in which there has rarely been much doubt about the appropriateness of women's participation; changes in farm economics and technology may actually have intensified that role. Corporate agriculture has made far fewer in-roads in the "animal husbandry" area than in livestock feeding and feed grain production. Husbandry seems less amenable to large scale units, partly because it requires both intensive committed labor and sophisticated skills; it is ideal for a family enterprise. But technological change has meant a controlled breeding process in which more calves are born in fewer days, born larger, and born with more difficulty to younger mothers. Economic change means that survival rates must be higher for both the mothers, which are a major investment, and for the offspring, which keep production rates high.

Just as Eleanor Stewart helped "pull a calf" in the film **Heartland**, and the ranch wife in Theresa Jordan's book, **Cowgirls**, delivered a calf alone in the dead of night, many women continue to do this work in shifts alternating with their husbands.[7] Perhaps since birthing is a female process, and because women have most often gotten up in the night with small children, they are most likely to be the ones to make the late-night-to-early-morning rounds and vigils in the calving yards. Their knowledge of antiseptic techniques and birthing engineering can make hundreds or thousands of dollars difference with each difficult delivery.

Although large-scale poultry and egg production has had a negative effect on women's productive role on the farm, while new breeding techniques have increased their productive contribution, other technological changes have altered rural women's lives in mixed ways. The question is whether these changes help women participate more equally with their male partners, or whether they displace women from productive work because high technology is so frequently thought to belong to men. Paradoxically, technology seems to cut both ways.

Modern Times

Virtually all of the women interviewed in the Wyoming Heritage and Contemporary Values Project mentioned the importance of the telephone to put them in touch with family members, neighbors, and friends who might be several or hundreds of miles distant. The telephone ended the near-total isolation of rural women from each other, eliminating the reports so often found in pioneer diaries of months spent without ever hearing another woman's voice. The telephone also lessened the likelihood that other family members, including husbands, might be out of communication with each other for days at a time in dangerous weather and dangerous terrain. More recently, shortwave radio and citizen band radios (CBs) have made communication possible even with people working in pastures or fields. In Wyoming commercial radio stations still use regularly scheduled public service broadcasts to send personal messages for meeting arrangements between rural families. There is little doubt that the "isolation of the housewife" found its extreme in the sparsely populated rural west and that telephone contact has become an essential and often highly ritualized improvement.

Rural electrification provided more diffuse, though not necessarily more profound, changes. It often came later than dial telephones, finally replacing wind generators and carbide lighting.

> We had a 32-volt plant, they called it. And, if the wind blew enough, which in Wyoming usually has a way of happening, I could use my iron. We always had lights. You couldn't use your . . . I don't think we had toasters . . . I think we just had the iron and I could use it if the voltage was up real good. And that's why we didn't have any other appliances, like you'd have with electricity, because it would pull down too much. Most of the time, couldn't even use the iron. I'd have to use a gas iron and the iron on the stove. And then when, it

was about during the early '50s we got electricity out here. But we battled for it for a good many years before we got it.

Significant changes in household technology, including convection ovens, automatic washing machines, refrigerators, and freezers have had profound effects on the lives of rural women and men. While standards of housekeeping have escalated for rural as well as urban householders, women potentially have more freedom to engage in different forms of productive labor. Sociologists differ whether this is the case.

Corlann Bush, argues, for example, that the introduction of household technology eliminated women's traditional work as critical to the economic function of the family at the same time that new agricultural technology enhanced the importance of men's activities. Thereby men's roles became more crucial and women's roles less crucial on the family farm, at least in the Palouse River region of eastern Washington and northern Idaho.[8]

Some of this differential may have been more marked in large-scale farming than it was in ranching.

Bush makes a strong and convincing argument that cash income, the availability of fresh produce and inexpensive clothing, plus good roads and fast vehicles, have removed the economic necessity for a farm woman to do anything but shop. The farm woman's contributions, she contends, have become invisible and her function has shifted from production to consumption. However, this argument rests on the assumption not only of the separation of gender roles, but also on viewing traditional work in traditional ways. Bush acknowledges that women often drive huge grain trucks both in the fields and to the elevators in town during combining (grain harvesting) season, but she takes literally the frequently-used term "helping out" to mean that work to be exceptional, rather than integral to the female role.

Farm technology, like other technological advances, has to a large extent eliminated the muscular advantage men have had in engaging in productive physical labor. Women, girls, and boys can all drive tractors, trucks, or self-propelled machinery. That fact does not preclude the existence of a status hierarchy of machine operators, often based on the relative cost of the implement matched to the age (older is better) and sex (males are more competent) of the driver. When, as a 17-year old daughter, I was allowed to drive the most expensive new piece of haying equipment, I felt clearly to be a trusted member of the family enterprise. But I think I also understood that my brothers ran the somewhat less expensive baler because it was more complex and more likely to break down.

Evidence from Third World developing countries demonstrates that as more complicated machinery is introduced, men are more likely to be its exclusive proprietors. In part this tendency can be explained by recognizing that mechanized agriculture is somewhat less labor intensive, making the labor of both women and children less necessary.[9] So, at the same time they are more able, females are needed less in the fields and pastures. Or, in reverse causality, machinery might be purchased to compensate for lost labor. My siblings and I noted that when all the children left home to go away to school, more equipment was purchased to handle the work we had done with our backs and arms. It also became apparent that when our mother spent less time parenting, she participated in new ways in the exchange economics and technology entailed in livestock purchasing, breeding programs, and fieldwork. (She still retained much of the bookkeeping responsibility she had always shared with my father.)

Seena Kohl shows that in Saskatchewan farm families, as in most of rural North America, women's educational level surpasses that of men in any cohort. Because of that difference women not only take care of the books and breeding records, but also write important letters to businesses and government agencies. She asserts that control of information is a source of power, particularly when the information is directly connected to the economic productivity of an enterprise. The capital investment needed for technological farming and the cash flow resulting from large-scale operation both require extensive bookkeeping and business skills, for which women have more formal training. Moreover, household technology has freed women from continuous cooking, cleaning, food production, and preservation burdens, making it *possible* for them to function in this new or expanded economic capacity. But the participation is by no means automatic. Even if the technology is benign, the institutions which promote new technology are hardly nonsexist.

Perhaps the greatest test of women's continued authority in farm families will lie in their competence with computer technology. As capital investment requirements increase and margins of profit tighten, precise data on such variables as optimal feed grain prices and nutritional levels, feeding rations and weaning times, crop fertilization schedules, machine time utilization, storage loss, and breeding stock productivity must all inevitably be computerized. Many farmers and ranchers have for years sent production records to state universities for computer analysis. But as production costs rise in relation to wholesale prices, more variables must be closely monitored. Family farms and ranches will need their own software and data storage in order to survive. If women have been part of both the decision-making and the record-keeping functions in the past, they may now be in a particularly good position to step into this important technological change. That will depend on a recognition and continuation of the family, including women, as a unit of production.

Growing Up Rural

Even though it appears to me that the soundest explanation for women's place in rural families is their economic role rather than the socialization process, I want to return briefly to the theme of growing up rural. I believe that the socialization rural girls receive allows them to approach technology differently from the way many urban girls perceive it. The literature on child socialization generally suggests that the experiences of girls are more circumscribed; girls are protected from many experiences that boys have because girls grow up in more highly supervised and structured, usually indoor, environments.[10] In the country, even given the normative distinctions between "women's work" and "men's work," girls have responsibility for complicated technology that has an *economically productive* purpose.

An example from the early twentieth century describes expectations for children similar to my own experience.

> We leased (another ranch) so we could put up hay there and also we had our own place. . . .. I mowed every bit of hay on all those places. I had a bronc and Harv hooked up the bronc with a mare we had. He made five or six rounds, and then turned them over to me. Our daughter . . . did all the raking and (our son) had the sweep. (My husband) used to stack and the neighbors were all so worried for fear they'd have to help us out. But we beat them by three days. I didn't lose any time mowing, I can tell you. They would change my sickles or sharpen my sickles and I'd be off. (A man from town) cooked for us. . . .. Boy, he was a help because I didn't have to cook at noon. But he went home at night, and I had to cook and had all those cows to milk. Of course (my daughter) helped me milk, but we had maybe 16, 18, or 20 cows to milk by hand. I think it took me about ten minutes to a cow. The hardest thing to do was to carry it all in, and separate it, because we had a hand crank separator, and I'd have to stop and fill up the old bowl and go to her again — cranking.[11]

The point is not simply that girls are outdoors — as well as indoors — but that their chores, like their brothers', are directly connected to exchange productivity, rather than being artificial creations to "teach responsibility." In part, this means that girls as well as boys learn to hear when an engine or machine is malfunctioning, or to tell if a horse is lame, and to diagnose and repair the problem when possible. And they know the economic implications of failures in mechanical or physiological judgment. I would guess that most rural children still do not get "wages" in the form of an allowance in proportion to urban children. My siblings and I had the sense that during a "good year" we would share in the profits and that in a "bad one" we would do without, regardless of our personal merit, but still with the understanding that we could contribute or subtract in significant financial ways by our technological competence. We haven't forgotten those internalized lessons.

If that early experience makes females less technology-anxious, more confident of economic potential and responsibility, more assertive about power in family relationships, then there is something important to be studied further. Are there ways to maintain those socialization patterns in the face of less distinctively rural lifestyles and more corporate business styles? Are there ways of socializing our urban-reared daughters and sons with more egalitarian assumptions about technical competence and productive worth? My children are professors' kids, not ranchers' kids. I'd like to know.

Notes

1. Sally Slocum, "Woman the Gatherer: Male Bias in Anthropology" in *Toward an Anthropology of Women* , ed. Rayna Reiter (New York: Monthly Review Press, 1975).
2. Joan Jensen, *Women Working on the Land* (Old Westbury, NY: Feminist Press, 1981); Sherry Thomas, *We Didn't Have Much, but We Sure Had Plenty* (New York: Anchor/Doubleday, 1981); Linda Rasmussen, Candance Savage, Lorna Rasmussen, and Anne Wheeler, *A Harvest Yet to Reap* (Toronto: Women's Press, 1976).
3. Carol Rankin, "Spoken Words of Wyoming Ranch Women," a slide/tape presentation from a project sponsored by the Wyoming Council for the Humanities, 1979.
4. This and following first-person quotes are from interviews for the Wyoming Heritage and Contemporary Values Project, an oral history project sponsored by the Wyoming Council for the Humanities and staffed by Bernice Harris, Melanie Gustafson, Pat Hale, and the author, 1979-1980.
5. Peggy Sanday, "Female Status in the Public Domain," in *Woman, Culture and Society,* , eds. Michelle Rosaldo and Louise Lamphere (Palo Alto, CA: Stanford University, 1974).
6. Seena Kohl, "Women's Participation in the North American Family Farm," *Women's Studies International Quarterly* 1 (1977): 47-54.
7. Theresa Jordan, *Cowgirls* (New York: Doubleday, 1982).
8. Corlann Gee Bush, *The Barn Is His; The House Is Mine: The Impact of Technology on Sex Roles on the Family Farm* (New York: Sage, 1982).
9. Special issue on "Development and the Sexual Division of Labor," *Signs* 7 (Winter 1981).
10. Lenore Weitzman, "Sex Role Socialization," in *Women: A Feminist Perspective* , ed. Jo Freeman (Palo Alto, CA: Mayfield, 1979).
11. Rankin, *Op Cit.* .

Part III

A Living Wage

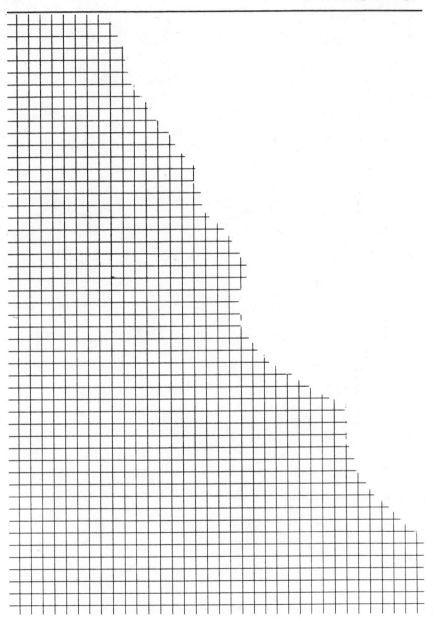

"A living wage" is perhaps a misnomer; in all too many instances women's wages are not sufficient for living. In spite of new technologies that open up new jobs, women still earn only 59 cents for every dollar men earn, and 80 percent of working women still remain occupationally segregated in only 20 of the 420 job categories recognized by the Department of Labor. (Those 20, not too surprisingly, include such low-wage titles as clerical, sales, light manufacturing, and service work.)

In a truly equitable society women would have the training and opportunity to take advantage of new job categories as they appear. Even so, it is not clear exactly what impact automation will have. In **Labor and Monopoly Capital** Harry Braverman suggests that under advanced automation, low-paid, low skilled jobs will proliferate while higher paid, skilled jobs (mostly middle management) will disappear. This will exacerbate the polarization between those (mostly women) occupying the increasing number of routine, poorly paid jobs at the bottom and those (mostly men) holding the upper management jobs at the top. The middle will simply fall through the floor.

Several contributions in this section seem to bear out Braverman's thesis. Sally Otos and Ellen Levy provide a sometimes hilarious, sometimes horrifying picture of their lives running word-processing equipment, while Barbara Gutek supplies essential background information on the "office of the future." Following up on Maria Patricia Fernandez Kelly's earlier description of women's role in Third World assembly lines, Rebecca Morales explores the role of Third World women here in the United States, particularly their participation in a system of piecework performed at home — a high tech, electronic sweatshop.

Two articles provide a more positive approach to women's occupational options in the technological hereafter. Mary Lindenstein Walshok reports on the challenges and job satisfaction cited by women now doing nontraditional work, showing that women, given access and information, have both the talent and the desire to undertake the blue collar jobs found in a burgeoning technical market. Diane Reynolds describes an especially successful apprenticeship program in California that opens up new job areas to women.

One aspect lacking here is an assessment of even newer forms of automation on women's job opportunities. Robots, computers that can listen and talk, and computer-aided design and machine tools promise with certainty only that change will continue beyond the current generation of technology. Will women be able to use these tools, rather than being used by them? Will new technology help or hinder women in their efforts to move beyond the confines of sex role stereotyping and job

147

segregation? Will there be new opportunities in technical fields for women re-entering the labor force, or will displaced homemakers be shunted into low-paying, increasingly rationalized, clerical tasks?

Since technical career possibilities span the job spectrum from electronics assembler to electrical engineer, two authors offer contrasting views on what happens to women at the often hostile, highly paid end of the spectrum. Natasha Josefowitz analyzes the ways in which she perceives technical positions to be similar to and different from other managerial positions for women. On the other hand, Sandra "Bambi" Emerson speaks with the voice of experience — and that of humor — about the life of women engineers. From her point of view, when it hurts too much to cry, you have to laugh.

There are some gaps, of course. Detailed breakdowns from the Bureau of Labor Statistics show that even those women who reach high technical positions still earn only 60 to 80 percent of equivalent male pay. Like female law and business graduates, women engineers find that wages offered at graduation, which are comparable to men's, quickly fall behind as men receive more rapid promotions in both pay and rank. And some job categories, like computer operator, that were once fairly well-paying niches occupied by men, have shown stagnating or even decreasing salaries as women move into them (see Chapter 6 by Margaret Benston for more about this issue).

While various chapters provide a good overview of health hazards associated with video display terminals and electronics assembly, severe health and safety hazards also accompany some of the nation's other highly technical industries: nuclear power, pesticides, and chemicals. Stories abound of women being forced to undergo sterilization to be allowed to work in certain chemical plants; and none of us should forget the "share-the-risk" philosophy of those who dump toxic and nuclear wastes into our oceans, air, and land. Such issues, which may at first seem to have no gender correlation, take on new meaning with the recognition that it is women, in their roles as mothers and nurses, who almost inevitably end up taking care of those whose health has been damaged.

This section, whatever its omissions, provokes the recognition that work opportunities in new technology are sex-, race-, and class-linked; that far from being neutral in its risks and benefits, technology (more accurately, those who control it) skews those factors in ways that have very different impacts on women than on men. Let's take a closer look.

Chapter 17

Word Processing:

"This Is Not a Final Draft"

by Sally Otos and Ellen Levy

Before we start we should explain what word processors are, though they're getting so common they probably outnumber bathtubs. They are a cross between a typewriter and a TV set, combining a keyboard and a screen. Word processors are also called "VDTs," which stands for Video Display Terminals, or sometimes "CRTs," which stands for Cathode Ray Tubes, because the words on the screen are created by a cathode ray shot out from inside the terminal, toward your face. The main advantage over a standard typewriter is that you can edit a document — fix typos, add new paragraphs — without having to retype any of the rest of it.

Despite their similar functions, word processors vary a lot in their designs. The size of the screen and of the letters on it, whether the screen and keyboard can be adjusted separately so that people of different heights can work on them comfortably, how much text is displayed at one time on the screen — all of these really make a difference when you're working on them.

Ellen: I went to look at word processors with my supervisor at the bank, and the salesmen were squirming. They had one pitch for supervisors and an exactly opposite pitch for potential operators; they didn't know how to talk to us together. To the operator they say, "This will make your work easier." They try to play up to your intelligence and pride in your work. "If you really know what you're doing, and if you're bright, as you obviously are, you can do a tremendous amount of work on this machine and make it look really nice." To the supervisor they say, "A cabbage can be fully productive in three hours."

Sally: When my bosses bought the word processor that I use, they made a big deal about getting the advice of those of us who had experience or were going to be working on them. We did a lot of investigation, but my recommendations got lost in the shuffle and they went out and bought the cheapest machines they could find. Which means that the keyboard is not detachable, though I felt strongly about having that, and the machine is very slow and clumsy, which makes the job aggravating.

Ellen: At the bank they always asked me and took me along; whatever I recommended, they invariably bought the other one. I've never seen the concerns of the operators taken into account, outside of a union situation. They want to buy what they think will maké us more productive.

Sally: We're looking for machines that will be easy on our eyes, flexible, and challenging to work on. But, the people who buy them and decide what they'll be used for often don't really understand their capacities. They see them from a very narrow point of view, as text editors or for letter production, and don't have a plan for setting them up that includes work flow, rational decisions about what should go on and what shouldn't, the physical layout, or worker comfort.

Ellen: Bosses get ridiculous expectations of increased productivity from the companies that sell the machines. The introduction of word processors automatically means a speed-up, because they expect major increases in output and put more pressure on you to produce; and also because they start to see you as an extension of the machine. They forget there's any operator skill involved. My bosses used to ask, "When can you do this?" Now they ask, "When can your machine do this?"

Sally: My bosses never ask whether I have time or if the machine is available; they just say they're catching a plane for a conference or have a publisher's deadline and need changes made immediately. They think it's like magic — any changes are instantaneous. They never acknowledge that other people are giving you work, too, and putting just as much pressure on you from other directions.

One thing I noticed soon after I started working on the Wang word processor was that my bosses' first drafts got real sloppy. When you're working on a regular typewriter, they take some care with what they give you, knowing that they can only expect two or three drafts. With the word processor, they give you any kind of garbage, knowing they can revise and revise — and you end up with maybe ten drafts. They get more perfectionist at the end, too. You want to ask them if they know how many trees they're wasting. I had a boss who sent back a page to change the word "showed" to "expressed." They'd never do that with a regular typewriter. Well, some would.

Ellen: As bosses make more and more use of word processing, they lose their ability to write English.

Sally: So do we. On a regular typewriter, you have an interest yourself in putting out a clean paper — you don't want to have to line it up later to correct grammar or typos. Now, I just bash out whatever they give me, and let them revise it.

Ellen: I don't do that. I hate so much staring into that screen to make corrections that I put a lot of effort into getting it right the first time. Not that that does much good, because even if you get it perfect, they're always going to make changes. There is *never* a final draft with a word processor.

Sally: That's one of the worst things about them, actually. You don't have the satisfaction of a finished, beautiful paper that you can look at, or feel that you have a completed project in your hands, and be proud of your work. I've done a dozen "final" versions of the same paper.

Ellen: It particularly affects your attitude on the early drafts. I get notes on old potato chips. There are half-sentences and uncompleted thoughts. Even if I don't make a single typo, it's so rough that a lot of work is just wasted time. It's going to be completely redone. I always feel a lot of resentment that no one takes the time to make it right, as though they think nobody else gives me work and I can spend all my time on their article.

Sally: That's why they get right down to the wire with deadlines, too — not that they didn't on regular typewriters. But they can come up with three more drafts during the last half hour before they have to leave with the paper.

I told one professor the other day, over and over, "I'm doing the best that I can. It will get done. Don't worry about it." When he kept expressing his anxiety, I calmly and firmly escalated, "I'm feeling very pressured. Please stop pressuring me. I'm doing the best that I can." What I *wanted* to say was "get the fuck off my back." He apologized for pressuring me — then went right on doing it. I finally said, "I feel like I'm getting an ulcer. I don't want you to keep telling me this. It will get done." I finally had to just walk away, which I should have done much sooner.

I've also noticed that bosses can be very nice to their peers, or even to you when you're not doing their work, and completely lose it when they want you to get something done. They can completely lose sight of you as a human being (a lot of bosses never do see you as one anyway), and they just see this machine; as if they can step on the gas and you go faster.

Ellen: Bosses make a big thing about how word processing is wonderful for us, but they can't hide the tremendous speed-up involved. For instance, at the bank when we got word-processing and computerized typesetting equipment, my boss always made a big thing of telling me when a crunch was coming. "In two days we'll have Project A and Project B and Project C and two Project Ds." I never understood why she said this — where did she think I was going to be? But I thought about it a lot, and I think it was the change in the structure of all our jobs. If you're backed up in a word-processing pool, there's no one to turn to — you can't ask the secretary down the hall to give you a hand, to help you so stuff gets done on time. What my boss was telling me was to get ready for the speed-up and that I was on my own — pre-ulcer week at the zoo.

Sally: Right. It does no good to inform you that you're going to be busy when there's nothing to be done about it. We used to send a lot of stuff out to free-lance typists, but now that everything goes on the VDT, we can't send it out. They're no longer saying, "Are you going to be overwhelmed? Do we need someone else?" It's harder on the free-lancers as well, since they're not getting the jobs. I know one who is thinking of buying her own word processor.

Ellen: Another aspect of the pressure you get from bosses is that they've spent all this money on machinery and have totally unrealistic expectations of productivity, so they expect your volume to go through the roof. When it doesn't, they accuse you of wasting time. They think, "The machine is doing the work. Why isn't it being done faster?" They ignore the skill that goes into, say, typing a table, which I think is harder on most word processors than on regular typewriters.

My boss's wife, when I was working at a place I called Psycho Type Shop, once saw me sitting in front of the screen waiting for a job to print out and said to her husband, "I thought we spent all that money on the machine because they said the operators never had to sit around and do nothing."

I've never seen people actually fired because machines were brought in, but my supervisor at the bank told me that they were not replacing people who left, so that the workforce was being reduced.

Sally: They expect to reduce staffs, and a lot of workers know that. I think there's a lot of anxiety when machines are being contemplated, because the staff isn't told what the situation will be. One office where I work had several VDTs installed, but no one is being trained. The workers — especially the older ones — are afraid they won't be trained; that they'll just fire them and bring in new people.

Training is a big issue all over. The manufacturers sell the machines, like you said, with the claim that domestic pets and garden vegetables can learn them, so they can't make a big deal about the amount of training needed. So people end up training themselves, or training each other. I know of some people who are being trained by their supervisor, which is even worse. In another instance, one person was sent to the manufacturer's training program and then expected to train 40 other people when she came back.

I know a lot of people who do look forward to word processing, who think it will make their jobs easier, and want to learn it (I do too — I'll get any skill I can). I think word processors *could* make our work easier, but not the way they're brought in. Like we said about buying the machines — we'd choose them and set them up in a different way than our bosses do. Their criteria are profit and productivity, and ours are making our jobs easier and more interesting. Those two desires are not compatible, as most workplaces are set up.

Ellen: Learning new skills is part of keeping your mind active, and not being bored to death at work. It could open up lots of areas — getting into the data processing end of things, really working on the copy editing, and working with the other people involved in a job.

If you had some say in how the work was set up, you could have a system where they couldn't just throw junky drafts at you, and where you could really have input about how to get the job done best and most comfortably for the people involved. As things are now, word processing is the most dead-end clerical job there is, except maybe for keypunching, because it's a very specific skill and there's no diversity in what you learn. As a secretary you have to be versatile; they care about how you look and whether you fit into an "office environment." With word processing they don't care about anything but your productivity, and they have no interest in increasing your skills in areas outside of word processing because they don't want to lose that.

Sally: I don't work in a pool — in fact, with the drastic workstudy cuts under Reagan, I'm now the only person where I work who knows how to use the word processor, except an editor who keeps being called on to do word processing in emergencies. The director said he didn't want me to spend more than three hours a day on the VDT, because I have other work to do and because he knew that that was the maximum I was willing to spend. But there's no choice with no one else knowing the machine; I've been on it almost full time for weeks now, and overtime as well. I appreciate his consideration in setting the limit, but we still have to figure out how to put it into practice.

I would love to have someone else in between me and the people who write the papers. Except I know if there were somebody there, her function wouldn't be to run interference for me, but rather to control and supervise me — I've worked under office managers, and I know what *that's* about. What I do now is tell the professors to talk to each other when they have rushes at the same time. I try to refuse to make decisions in that circumstance. But of course, just knowing they're there means I feel pressured.

Ellen: If word processing were set up for our advantage, you wouldn't do it all day long. You wouldn't have to just sit there under pressure all day, you'd have other parts of your job you could do. It makes such a difference when you only do it part time. For example, when the machines die, which they do all the time, instead of feeling even more anxious and having to work doubly hard to get that work done after it's fixed, you could go do other things, and get out from under it.

Sally: Just about the worst experience I ever had was when I was doing a book to meet a publisher's deadline; the machine was acting up, and I couldn't put off getting the job out until the service guy came. It kept turning documents into garbage, and I kept trying to salvage them, and having to re-do some. The anxiety of trying to finish the job, and having to keep trying to save them, and wondering when I was going to lose something else — I was just hoping I could get it done and printed out. The last page the guy gave me to type was the acknowledgments, and he thanked me on it. I wanted to leave my name off, I was so irritated, because he had *not* been pleasant about the problems I was having with the machine. If they appreciate my work, they should show it by laying off, not throwing me a sop when it's over!

Ellen: I am absolutely and totally physically exhausted at the end of the day.

Sally: My friends can always tell when I've spent several hours on the machine just from how I look — red, puffy eyes, and just real dragged out.

Ellen: It's especially bad during the summer, because the machines give off a lot of heat, and by the end of the day I feel like I'm slow-cooked. At the same time you're sitting under an air conditioning duct with your neck and shoulders craned so you can see the screen and your back just locks.

Sally: I have a permanent clenched muscle between my shoulder blades. My keyboard isn't detachable — the screen is too low but the keyboard is too high. There's no way to make it comfortable. If I cranked my chair up high enough to make the keyboard right — your forearms are supposed to be parallel to the floor — I'd be looking at the screen at a horrible angle, plus I'd have to find a footstool. I keep fooling around with heights and positions. I feel like I'm constantly fighting the tendency to slump, to keep my posture good. I sleep flat on my back with a pillow under my knees, to try to unroll my spine.

Ellen: I have a lot of trouble sleeping because my back hurts so much. I can tell how hard my day's been at work by the amount of pain in my neck and back. I edit in my sleep. Particularly if I've been working on a very difficult job where I really had to think bout the coding and the format, I dream about how to set it up.

We're supposed to get two 15-minute breaks per day — which is by no means enough, but at least it would be something — a rest period, when nobody could give you strange looks for sitting around or getting up or taking a walk outside. But I almost never take breaks, and neither do my coworkers. Try taking a 15-minute walk when a professor is having a nervous breakdown next to your terminal. Very messy.

Sally: Even when there's no hassle about taking breaks, I've seen a lot of people resist taking them. Your eyes are so focused on what you're doing, and it takes so much concentration, that it's hard to break away from it. It's like driving down a highway on a rainy, dark night, and telling yourself you'll make just one more exit before you pull off for coffee. Because it's hard, you want to keep plowing through it, to get it done (even though it's never done). You somehow get locked into your relationship with the machine. It's really insidious.

Ellen: That's exactly right.

Sally: There's also the problem of where to put your work — the damn thing is so big that it takes up all the space in front of me, so that I have to turn my head way over to the side to see what I'm typing from. And the problem of lighting — I turn off the overhead light and have a lamp to shine on the work, but I can't figure out how to keep it from also shining on the screen. My bosses are willing to get whatever attachments will help, but the problem is with the basic machine, and no attachments can really solve it. And it's up to me to experiment or guess what I need.

Ellen: On the machine I use now, the screen was designed for miniature people; it's a tiny little thing and the letters are real hard to see. So you're reading a hand-written draft that looks like a chicken walked on it, you're straining your eyes and your neck to see the letters on the screen, and you're working in lighting conditions that're not well-designed. We have no individual lamps, just overhead lights that are always on. The strain on your eyes is just terrible.

The last time I went for an eye exam, the optometrist told me that I have a lot of trouble focusing, that it takes me a lot longer than most people to get things clearly into my vision. He didn't know much about VDTs, but he said he had been getting a lot of complaints from patients who work on them. But I'm sure it's due to the machine that I have a lot more trouble focusing than I ever had before.

At a small press I worked at, we once worked overtime almost every night and usually on weekends for several months. My boss started to bitch about how big my paycheck was getting and he kept asking me what I was going to do with all that money. I told him I was saving up for a seeing eye dog.

Sally: Do you worry about radiation? The manufacturers keep insisting that the radiation isn't enough to hurt you because it's within government standards. But the government is always covering up gross accidents at nuclear power plants — they're not going to admit that a small dose of radiation can hurt you. I keep thinking about birth control pills, and the millions of women who were guinea pigs in *that* experiment — how many of us are going to have ill effects before they get recognized?

Ellen: A constant dose of low-level radiation hasn't been studied, only big, one-shot doses. They don't know. We'll find out the hard way.

Sally: I read an article that said there have been clusters of birth defects and miscarriages in VDT pools, but it's not clear whether it's coincidence or caused by the machines. At the Toronto **Star**, four out of seven infants born in one year had birth defects, and at Air Canada seven out of thirteen pregnant women in one pool miscarried. At the very least, pregnant women should be allowed to transfer immediately to another job, without loss of seniority, until they find out what the radiation is doing to *all* of us. God, let's talk about something else.

Sally: Working for a university department is a lot different from working for a corporation or a law firm the way I did before. In a law firm, the lawyers see every cent they spend on you coming right out of their pocket, as though your work wasn't making them money. They wouldn't hire you if they weren't making money off you, right? So the pressure is incredible, even aside from court deadlines and things like that. They're after every drop of sweat.

At the university the pay is incredibly low. They pay $11,000 for a job you'd get paid $16,000 for downtown, so of course the turnover is very high. Although my immediate bosses don't have a personal profit to make off me, they do have a stake in the department running smoothly and within budget, having the professors satisfied, getting papers published, and getting grants from well-done proposals. So there is pressure, and there are crises, but if you're lucky you're getting less of that at the university — with the trade-off being that the pay is a lot worse. I felt like I was getting an ulcer during my last year at the law firm; I didn't like feel like that at the university up until the workstudy cuts hit — the past month that feeling has been coming back.

Anyway, any boss can be a bastard, even if they're not convinced your pay comes out of their pocket. I know a lot of people in horrendous situations in other departments, especially in the bursar's, registrar's, and controller's offices — all of which have VDT pools — where the work is more "rationalized" and directly under the thumb of the central administration. The administration would love for all the other departments to be just as harsh as they are, and some departments are bad, but a lot of the department administrators don't see this as a profit-making institution — they only see the ivy camouflage and not the corporation behind it, so they don't push us so hard.

I've done "temping" at corporations and big law firms, where I saw the way big pools are set up. For example, they might have a big group of people that just does initial input, then another group that just proofreads all day, then a third group that just makes corrections and changes. That seems so horrible to me. It's like an assembly line. I think assembly line workers and VDT operators are supposed to be the job categories with the highest stress, so that situation — being an assembly line VDT operator — would just multiply it.

Ellen: That's the direction things are going all over; it's the extension of the pool situation I work in. There will be gigantic pools, where all the typing goes to word processing, and you never see the boss who generates it, and the work is incredibly subdivided. I saw a little of this at the bank, even though we only had one word-processing machine. I wasn't attached to a particular boss, like the other secretaries were, so I ended up doing most of the word processing. This left the others handling mostly things like arranging plane trips, placing long-distance calls, xeroxing, filing, and arranging luncheons in the executive dining room. Of course most of the time I was dying to get off the word processor, and they were dying to get away from the shrimp cocktail menu planning and onto the word processor. Doing any one thing all day is very boring, plus you lose any skills you have in other areas.

Sally: The jobs of people who don't go onto VDTs are really worse where I work, at least I would think so if I had them. Instead of everybody sharing the typing, now some people just stuff envelopes and do mailing, and others get stuck with all the typing on the word processors. Bosses get so they want everything to go on it, and it just takes over.

I believe those gigantic pools will happen, too. It has some good points, though, in that people in the same situation are thrown together, and can support each other, and talk about gripes — which is absolutely essential to your mental health, checking out that *you're* not crazy, the *job* is crazy. And I hope a lot of people will come out of that determined to unionize.

Ellen: But there's also the potential for further dividing people and turning them against each other. For instance, where I work now, all the major typing comes down to our word-processing center. The clerical workers who used to type things now just carry them down to us, and get sent down to bug us by their bosses. So they think, "Oh, those word processors, they never get anything done on time," and the word processors think, "Oh, those incompetents, why can't they get anything right the first time."

Sally: I'm active in a union organizing campaign where I work, with District 65/UAW, and I'm really committed to it. But it takes an effort to get up from the machine and spend my lunch hour going around talking to other people about the union, or going to meetings after work. I do it, but it's harder when I come out of work really wrung out.

And part of why I do it is because the only hope I see in the near future for making better conditions in my job is through a union and a written contract that we negotiate and can enforce. I've read contracts of unions at other universities where they've won provisions for things like a lot of prior notice to employees when machines are contemplated that will affect their jobs; the right to training, and to move to another job if yours is eliminated or you can't learn the machine; adequate break time; automatic grade and salary reviews; free regular eye exams; and regulations that cover things like detachable keyboards, flexible lighting, and other things to make it more comfortable. And just knowing that you have other people to back you up when you have a problem.

It's been unions that have led the way in pushing for investigation of possible physical hazards from the machines, and who've recommended guidelines for their physical set-up, and informing workers about them.

A union would guarantee we have a say in making decisions, which we don't have now. A union won't make it perfect, a boss is still going to be a boss trying to get the most out of you, but at least you can tell him your workload is physically impossible without feeling you're risking your job.

Ellen: The system is set up so that you really think of yourself as your job category, not as a worker in such and such a place. It really takes an effort to overcome that, to say "hey, why don't we all have more time to do our jobs and do them right; why are we under this kind of pressure?" and not take it out on each other.

Sally: This job and the last one I had both started without word processors, and then they brought them in. So in both cases, I could directly compare the level of stress and physical comfort and so on. I have this nightmare that my future will consist of chasing one step ahead of VDTs, because I really don't want to do them full time. They'll keep coming after me.

We've got to get a union contract, to help us make our bosses understand that there's a bottom line. That we are not a limitless source of production. We are human beings who can't just be plugged into an electrical outlet.

Notes

The following people read this paper and felt it reflected, at least in general terms, experiences they've had on their own jobs: Nelly Burlingham, Orly Fudell, Michelle Grossman, Meredith Hermann, Charles Hodge, Desma Holcomb, Ellen Houlihan, Felicity Howlett, Flaurie Imberman, Della Joseph, Brett Kingsley, Christina Larkin, Amy Manso, Julia Meyer-Orozco, Chris Pahigian, Maida Rosenstein, Harry Saint-Preux, David Sheldon, Barbara Solow, and Joan Ulrich.

For further information, see:

Cold Type Organizing Committee, *Don't Sit Too Close to the TV: VDTs/CRTs and Radiation* (Cold Type Organizing Committee, P.O. Box 40, Jerome Avenue Station, Bronx, NY 10468, $1).

New York Committee for Occupational Safety and Health, Inc. (NYCOSH), *Health Protection for Operators of VDTs/CRTs* (NYCOSH, Box 3285, Grand Central Station, New York, NY 10017, $3, $1 for individual VDT operators).

The Newspaper Guild, *VDT Health Collective Bargaining Kit* (The Newspaper Guild, 1125 15th Street NW, Washington, DC 20005).

Jeff Sorensen and Don Swan, "VDTs: The Overlooked Story Right in the Newsroom," *Columbia Journalism Review* (January/February, 1981).

U.S. Department of Health and Human Services, National Institute for Occupational Safety and Health (NIOSH), *Select Research on Health Issues in Video Display Terminal Operators* (Cincinnati, OH: April 1981); also published in *Human Factors Journal* (August 1981).

— , *Potential Health Hazards of Video Display Terminals* (Cincinnati, OH: NIOSH Publications Dissemination, June 1981).

Women's Occupational Health Resource Center, *Clerical Factpack* , (New York: Columbia University School of Public Health).

Working Women's Education Fund, *Warning: Health Hazards for Office Workers* (Cleveland, OH: Working Women's Education Fund, April 1981).

Chapter 18

Women's Work in

The Office of the Future

by Barbara A. Gutek

Computerization of the office could be the most influential change in the workplace in the 1980s and 1990s. The "office of the future" is a term used to describe this office environment, characterized by large increases in the use of computer-based technologies that will make office workers more productive and have the potential for increasing or decreasing the quality of working life for people in the office.

The office of the future represents the confluence of two developments. The first is a growing concern about lagging productivity in the United States, explained simplistically by the statements that U.S. workers today do not work as hard as U.S. workers in the past; or that the proliferation of government red tape and the workers required to process that information have diverted valuable resources from the production process into nonproductive information processing activities.

A second development is the coming availability of office technology. The proliferation of computer-based technology for filing, retrieving, storing, manipulating, sending, and receiving information provides a means for dramatically increasing the efficiency of secretaries, professionals, and managers in offices. In the past, there were separate tools for producing text, producing graphics, storing information, talking with people, sending information to people. Now all of these functions can be handled by the same system, one which will not only make these operations more efficient but will also integrate them. Most of these tasks will be done with the help of a computer terminal. According to one estimate, there was one terminal for every 48 U.S. workers in 1981; by 1986, there will be one for every 10 workers.

Justification for Office Automation

In order to define the office of the future, one must first be able to define "office." The word office can, of course, refer to a physical space, but as a more abstract concept, it refers to a work unit with some common information-handling activities; it generally encompasses at least two levels of hierarchy; that is, there is at least one level of supervision. An office may contain two workers or several hundred.

In the office of the future, many tasks will be automated. Information will be integrated and connected through a network: a professional will be able to compose a report at a terminal, draw data from databases in the same or some other computer, and send copies of various stages of the manuscript electronically to other terminals with personalized notes to the various receivers. ("Please check this price." "Know any more recent market share figures?")

Perhaps the most obvious visual difference in the office of the future will be the ubiquitous terminals at desks and work stations, although they will most likely come in a greater variety of forms than the ones people use today. There may be large, flat screens on walls or horizontal screens built into the surface of a desk or table.

A variety of configurations will co-exist in the office of the future. Some units will be stand-alone word processors; others will be connected through a network. Some will be personal computers; others will be dumb terminals connected to a mainframe or large central computer. Still others will be intelligent terminals. The much ballyhooed "paperless office" is not likely to emerge for a while, so manufacturers are also producing an impressive array of printers. In fact, the implementation of the office of the future is likely to be as varied as the offices that are being automated.[1]

All of this equipment is expensive, although the decrease in the cost of computing power is one of the factors that makes the office of the future feasible. Still, in 1982 personal computers cost several thousand dollars; small business computers cost about $5,000 to $10,000. Software packages, customized software, and repair and maintenance of equipment also add to the cost of systems.

At least five different factors can be cited as justification for implementing the office of the future. One is cost savings. Use of paper and other office supplies, telephone costs, photocopy equipment, typewriters, and the like may decrease enough to compensate for the cost of new equipment. Business travel may be partially replaced by video teleconferencing and companies may be able to build plants in less expensive locations and communicate with other plants electronically.

A second factor is labor savings, of which one of the most dramatic examples is word processing. "Saving labor" inevitably means either doing much more work with the same number of workers or using fewer workers to do the same amount of work. The development of a new technology in the workplace renews the debate about whether technology will eliminate more jobs than it creates. Paul Sniger, editor of **Digital Design**, wrote in an editorial in December 1980 that "computers kill jobs!"[2] Although most people are not as straightforward or outspoken as Sniger on this issue, it seems likely that the office of the future will probably contain fewer total workers than the office of the present. Furthermore, the mix of office jobs that exists today is likely to be different in the office of tomorrow; perhaps fewer clerical people will be needed relative to the number of professionals and managers. Perhaps top executives will no longer need as many middle managers.

A third justification for introducing automated office procedures is that better quality work will result. Electronic communication, for example, allows people to work on reports longer and transmit them right before a deadline or meeting. Of course, not all the capabilities of new technology will result in better quality work. People will probably compensate for the increased flexibility by starting later or allocating less time to some tasks. And such dependence on the computer results in total chaos when the system malfunctions.

A fourth justification for computerization in offices is that computers will provide more information for decision makers, thus aiding them in their work. The versatility of the computer is demonstrated in the ways that data and text can be arrayed and displayed, allowing managers, professionals, and administrators access to information they would not have been able to access before.

A fifth justification for the office of the future is that it will provide management with better feedback on the productivity of office workers. While office workers have been blamed recently for being less productive than other segments of the labor force, the fact is that office productivity is extremely difficult to measure, except in a few cases of straightforward tasks such as typing. Office computers can automatically provide management with logs of frequency and type of use (for example, number of key strokes or messages sent, orders filled, or pages of manuscript prepared). This can be done without the employee knowing if or when performance is being monitored. Furthermore, the ease of measuring "productivity" this way encourages employers to use such a method and reduces the complexity of many office jobs to measurable units. The extent to which these measures are a good assessment of productivity is debatable.

In sum, computerization of offices can be justified on the grounds that it will save money and labor, result in better quality work, aid executive decision making, supply information for other workers such as sales and public relations staff, and provide a way of assessing some types of productivity in the office.

Scenarios for Tomorrow's Office

The office of the future can be portrayed in glowing terms, by showing that computers can provide additional information to facilitate decision making, offer flexibility in physical location of work, eliminate many tedious tasks, give workers more control over their own tasks, and improve communications. On the other hand, the office of the future can be portrayed in depressing terms, by showing that computers can alienate and depersonalize workers by routinizing and fractionating jobs. Job fractionation occurs when one job involving many tasks — a secretary's, for example — is replaced by many jobs, each involving one task — typist, receptionist, file clerk. Thus, computers can decrease worker control and create tedious jobs. Mankin, Bikson, and Gutek have presented elaborate examples of each of these futures.[3] Similar examples designed to illustrate aspects of the office of the future follow.

Loren arrived at work at 11 p.m., ran down to the basement level of the office building and sat down at terminal 74. Loren logged in one minute late and saw displayed on the screen the month's listing of days tardy, time spent on breaks, number of key strokes made each day, and average number of key strokes per day, averaged over the month. Loren was depressed; pay was tied to the number of key strokes and Loren was below average. Once again, Loren's paycheck would be lower than anticipated, and not enough to pay all the bills. Loren began entering text. Loren did not know who left all that material, but it had to be entered before the managers and professionals arrived between 8 and 9 a.m.

Loren worked for 50 minutes each hour and had a 10-minute break; the computer "announced" breaktime. Several people were "swing" workers. They didn't have their own terminals but covered a terminal when someone else took a break. Breaks were staggered so that all terminals would be in use all the time. Loren wasn't sure when breaks would be scheduled for anyone, so it wasn't possible to plan to talk to anyone else who was a text entry operator (TEO). Loren didn't know very many of the other TEOs, in part because breaks were short and different people went on breaks at the same time, but also because turnover was high among the workers. When Loren took the first break, a new TEO was in the coffee room. The new TEO struck up a conversation. "Have any of the TEOs ever tried to sabotage the system?" the new worker asked. The way the new worker figured it, if management used the computer to keep track of the TEOs, then the TEOs had a "right" to try to outsmart the system.

Billie awoke in the beach house and decided it would be a nice day to work at home. Billie walked over to the terminal, logged on, and checked the calendar. No meetings were scheduled until 11 a.m. and that one was with Frank, so Billie sent him a message on the terminal: "I'm going to work at home. Will you check into my department to provide a little advice and moral support? Crack the whip, too, if you think that's appropriate. Let's hold our brainstorming session via terminal. If I feel like coming into the office before 11, I'll drop you a line." Billie started the coffee and went back to the terminal to scan the productivity sheets of the second shift text entry operators. Productivity was about the same and turnover was still too high. Billie decided to consult some of the psychological literature on productivity. Yesterday, Billie had perused the popular literature that provided advice to managers but was disappointed with the advice. Billie thought academicians might have more to offer.

Then Billie decided it would be nice to check the entertainment guide first. Billie and friend had planned dinner and entertainment for the evening and hoped there was a moderately-priced restaurant and jazz band somewhere between their two homes. Billie was happy that the company had provided the terminal and access to over 20 external data bases. They were helpful to Billie's job but they were also a nice fringe benefit. Billie found a restaurant and jazz band in the desired location but the band didn't begin to play until 10 p.m. Billie hesitated and then made a reservation. Billie was concerned about falling asleep before the band began. The previous three nights, Billie had worked on writing a report until 2 a.m. each night. Billie didn't really need to work that late but the terminal was there, all the information was available, the report was important, and Billie wasn't sleepy. Also, Billie knew that most other managers were working such long hours. It was hard to get away from work. Billie decided it was getting hard to tell home from work, and then called up **Psychological Abstracts** on the terminal to see what had been written on office productivity.

Neither of these examples is science fiction; the technology is currently available. The first example shows what computers can do *to* people. The office worker has become a machine operator, work is paced by the machine. Machine use is optimized at the expense of the operator's needs or wishes. The worker is completely alienated from the tasks and objectives of the company, as well as from other people in the company. Furthermore, there is no opportunity for these workers to advance, except perhaps from being a "swing" operator to having a terminal of one's own. The worker is not acquiring skills or knowledge that will make her or him more valuable to this organization or to some other organization. This "lower level" office job is probably more unpleasant for the worker in the office of the future than in the office of the present.

The second example shows what computers can do *for* people. They can provide the employee with more control over work, and provide information for doing one's job and making decisions. Furthermore, they can provide information about subordinates' productivity so that managers may not feel the need for direct interaction with subordinates or other employees. They can also be so "helpful" that it is hard to get away from work. When people have terminals at home, work comes home with them. When they have portable terminals, it even follows them on vacation. More important, the computer provides information and experiences that make this employee more valuable to the organization or to some other organization. The employee's use of the computer can increase her or his visibility and sphere of influence. Other things being

It is quite possible that Loren and Billie may be sitting in front of the same equipment. Thus, these examples should not be taken as instances of technological determinism, the belief that it is the technkky that makes people behave a certain way and that people have little leeway in responding to technology. An alternate explanation of the role of technology is that it provides for a range of responses or set of constraints on people's behavior. People make decisions about how equipment will be used; people in organizations create the settings in which Loren and Billie work. Someone or a group of people made a set of decisions that resulted in Loren's oppressive work environment and Billie's enriched one. How and why these dissimilar work settings develop should be of particular interest to women.

Potential Impact on Women

At least in the short run, more women workers than men are likely to be affected by the office of the future. First, the majority of women work in offices. A representative survey of working women in Los Angeles County in 1980 found that 46.7 percent of women are employed in the broad category of "clerical work" and the percentage of women in clerical work is increasing, not decreasing.

Furthermore, women tend to work in low-level office jobs. While almost half of all women work in clerical jobs, only 17 percent of men do so. Women are under-represented in managerial positions (16.5 percent of men versus 8 percent of women are in managerial jobs), and within that category, women are more likely than men to be in beginning and middle-management jobs.

Women who work in offices make less money than men in offices, are more likely than men to be supervised, and are less likely than men to supervise others. Thus, women are not likely to be in positions to decide how the office of the future is implemented. They may be in a position to select the particular equipment in a word-processing (WP) department, for example, but are unlikely to be in a position to decide that there *should be* a WP department. Thus, the work settings of Loren and Billie are likely to be developed by men, not women.

An equally important point is that Loren is quite likely to be a woman; Billie is quite likely to be a man! The work roles of men and women in offices are already polarized: men tend to be in high-paying, supervisory, or professional jobs, with opportunities for advancement; women tend to be in low-paying, subordinate, clerical positions, with little opportunity for advancement. In the office of the future, this polarization could increase, not because of any characteristic of the technology, but because of decisions made by upper level managers who are overwhelmingly male. These decisions are usually made without any intention of discriminating against women, but the results of decisions made so far have had the effect of creating an underclass of female office workers. There is no reason to think that the future will be any different unless there is a conscious effort to change.

Issues in the Office of the Future

A variety of issues determines whether a person's work will be enriched or impoverished as a result of using computers in the office.

The first issue has to do with the purpose of the terminal. Is the terminal there to facilitate the work of the employee or is the employee there to work on a terminal? Data entry operators (DEOs) are hired to work at terminals. So is a person who accepts telephone orders from customers and enters those requests into a computer. On the other hand, a professional writer uses a terminal to help her or him write. Likewise, a manager uses a terminal to access information and communicate with people throughout the organization. In general, clerical workers are more likely to be hired to work on a terminal than managers or professionals. Those workers are not likely to acquire skills in their work that will allow them to advance. In fact, becoming skilled in one's work is likely to make one *less* upwardly mobile, not more. An employer will want a fast, accurate data entry operator to stay in that job, and is not likely to advance such a person.

The second issue has to do with the kind of terminal the person uses and kind of tasks the person is doing. Some systems are very complex, can perform a great variety of tasks, and usually require extensive training periods. Other systems, dedicated to only a few simple tasks, require only a short training period. Clerical level office workers are more likely to use dedicated and/or simple systems. In fact, under computerization, several workers who had done a variety of noncomplex tasks may now each do one different, simple task, thereby reducing the amount of variety on the job. The tasks that such an employee performs are generally not transferable to other jobs because they may be specific to the requirements of the particular office. Likewise, the simple system does not provide the user with opportunities to learn more advanced skills.

The third issue is concerned with the "user friendliness" of the system. "User friendliness" is an overworked term that refers generally to the ease with which an untrained user can learn to interact with the system. User friendliness can encompass characteristics of the software (computer programs that are easy to use), or the hardware (a nonglare screen or well-designed keyboard). The person who is hired to work at a terminal may be less likely to have a friendly system than someone who has the freedom to choose whether or not to use a computer in the course of work. The person who has a choice may simply reject an "unfriendly" system in favor of tried-and-true methods that do not involve computers.

The fourth issue concerns control: does the terminal control the worker or does the worker control the terminal? A computer can keep track of the time a person is "logged on"; with a computer-aided telephone interviewing system (CATI), it can even automatically dial another telephone number when an interviewer finishes one telephone marketing survey.

On the other hand, the computer can access information sources that will help a newspaper reporter write a better, more accurate story and help managers forecast sales or profits. It can facilitate communication between people so that a person may be allowed to get more information from people as well as from databases. Some workers may be allowed to use computers provided by their companies to play games, keep personal records, write personal documents, and the like, while other workers may not have these privileges.

A fifth issue is whether or not the computer is used to monitor a worker's behavior. Behavior can be monitored for general patterns such as volume of sales per month and number of orders taken per month. Behavior can also be monitored in minute detail: number of keystrokes, number of errors on entry forms, total minutes "logged on."

On the other hand, a worker may be given a terminal to use or not, to take home or not. Under these conditions, the worker is still being evaluated, of course. But there is an assumption that the worker is motivated, committed, and reasonably efficient. The person is given more latitude in the kind of work he or she is doing and the methods of doing that work.

The sixth issue concerns the kind of training the employee receives. Not everyone who is trained to work with a computer is a computer scientist or programmer, although sometimes people assume that a job involved with a computer will provide them with valuable, new skills. Many of the jobs are tedious and involve little skill or knowledge. The training for these jobs is likely to be brief, and oriented toward the tasks to be done. Training may be done in classes if there are numerous people doing the same job. There is little opportunity to learn advanced skills and little opportunity to learn how the worker's tasks fit into the objectives or goals of the organization.

On the other hand, training may be personalized and offered at an individual's convenience. Or the person may be given a lot of leeway in learning on his or her own. Some computer companies encourage programmers to take terminals home on the grounds that the programmers may come up with something useful to the company while they are learning new skills or generally playing around.

These six issues form clusters that describe two groups of workers. One group of workers is hired to work on a terminal; they do a few selected tasks on a terminal that is not particularly "friendly" to the user. The computer both monitors their behavior and controls it to some extent. The worker receives little training and that training is very specific to the tasks to be done. This describes Loren's work environment.

A second group of workers uses terminals to facilitate their work. They have a complex workstation terminal which handles many different tasks. They exert a great deal of control over their "friendly" systems;

they have received personalized training and have the opportunity and time to learn more advanced techniques if they wish. This describes Billie's work environment.

The environment of Billie sounds attractive but Loren's sounds dreadful! Not everyone is likely to work in Billie's environment; there seem to be far more jobs for DEOs or TEOs. However, even the less skilled jobs need not be done in an environment as oppressive as Loren's. Yet it is possible that office work will be divided into these two classes, with men dominating the desirable, high-paying jobs with advancement opportunities and women dominating the undesirable, low-skill, dead-end jobs. Women need to be involved in designing jobs in the office of the future to avoid this distinction.

What Women Can Do

Since over 45 percent of working women are in clerical work, women are particularly vulnerable to changes in the office, just as a city like Detroit, whose economy rests on one industry, is vulnerable when that industry is doing poorly. Many women are in clerical work, not because they all choose clerical jobs, but because that is where they can find work; women with college degrees and even advanced degrees in traditional fields such as humanities and social sciences are in clerical or administrative jobs. If many of these jobs are eliminated, where will those women find employment? Opposing the new technology is likely to be a futile and misplaced effort. Other jobs must be made available to women.

Second, within companies women can take a strong position about instituting the office of the future in a sensible manner that not only takes into account the efficient flow of work, but also provides career opportunities for all employees in the organization. Providing opportunities for employees is one way that employers can foster commitment, loyalty, and effort in employees and thus is sound management policy. It is in women's best interest to point out to managers that management has much to gain by providing career opportunities for all workers.

Since automated office technology provides considerable leeway in the design of jobs, it is up to workers to see that the technology is implemented in that manner.[4] One way for women to try to ensure equitable treatment for women office workers is to organize within a union (see Chapter 29).[5] Women may also be able to organize within a given company. At the very least, women workers need to know what legal rights they have as workers.

The bottom line is the need for women workers to support each other. Over 50 percent of women are now working outside of the home, while the percentage of men in the labor force is declining. Women are a large enough sector of the labor force to ensure a humane office of the future with opportunities for everyone, if they are aware of the issues and willing to take a stand.

Notes

1. T. K. Bikson, B. A. Gutek and D. Mankin, *Implementation of Information Technology in Office Settings: Review of Relevant Literature* (Santa Monica, CA: The Rand corporation, 1981), p. 6697.
2. P. Sniger, "Computers Kill Jobs!" *Digital Design* (December 1980): 14.
3. D. Mankin, T. K. Bikson, B. A. Gutek, "The Office of the Future: Alternatives and Choices," *The Futurist* (June 1982): 33-37.
4. Jan Zimmerman "How to Control the New Technology Before It Controls You," *Ms.* 9 (January 1981): 81-83.
5. R. L. Hanauer, "The Terminal Secretary," *Science for the People* (November/December 1981): 19-24.

See also:

L. Branscomb, "Computer Communications in the Eighties — Time To Put It All Together," *Computer Networks* 5 (1981): 3-8.

B. A. Gutek, *Sexuality at Work: An Empirical Analysis*, book in preparation.

R. R. Panko, "Office Automation Needs," *Telecommunications Policy* (December 1981).

P. Strassman, "The Office of the Future: Information Management for the New Age," *Technology Review* 82 (December 1979/January 1980): 54-65.

D. Whieldon, "How to Pick 'Friendly,'" *Computer Decisions* (September 1980): 42-44, 48, 56, 60-63.

Chapter 19

Cold Solder on a Hot Stove

by Rebecca Morales

Perhaps the public's easy acceptance of emerging high technology employment is in part due to its association with "progress." The term "high technology" encompasses industries producing computers, communication equipment, test instruments, aerospace equipment, and electronic components. Microelectronics, the building block which supports the growth of these industries, imparts the characteristic of being technologically advanced. Microelectronics is so important that it is changing the production process in a variety of other industries, ranging from fast foods to education, automobiles, and medicine. Work that previously depended on human labor now can be done by computers or robots guided by tiny electronic devices. In fact, in the past two decades, microelectronics has transformed aspects of production to the extent that some claim we are on the threshold of a second industrial revolution.

The popularity of microelectronics has accompanied the growing importance of computers and information systems in industry. Development of semiconductor material improved the ability of transistors to amplify, modify, and retain massive amounts of electronic information or "bits," without generating heat. One type of semiconductor, known as the "silicon integrated circuit," is composed of numerous interconnected transistors and other components. Through constant innovation, the number of transistors stored on a tiny "chip" of silicon (less than one-quarter square inch in size) grew from 10 in 1960 to 100,000 by 1980, and may reach 1 million by 1985. Microtechnology quickly surpassed human capacity for exchanging information, at a fraction of the time and cost of conventional vacuum-tube technology.

Yet for all the promises of increased productivity in the coming era, emerging employment patterns suggest that the historical patterns of job differentiation between the sexes will be preserved. The "high tech" employment that consists of challenging, sophisticated research is typically dominated by male employees. On the other hand, most of the high tech labor force confined to dangerous and unrewarding assembly line work is female and minority. In response to intense competitive pressures, part of this production process is being transferred to low-cost female labor overseas. Ironically, many of the jobs that remain in the United States are being organized into a method of production once thought to exist only among older industries — homework, or the practice of taking assembly work home.

Furthermore, it is predicted that, over time, the penetration of microelectronics into different sectors of the economy will ultimately displace more workers than it will employ. Microelectronics has advanced at a lightning pace in the last two decades, but this has been at the expense of low-wage female workers in the United States and abroad. As microelectronic technology transforms other industries, it is expected to create serious limitations on employment opportunities for these workers in the future.

This suggests that the transformation of our economy will not be smooth, or simple, or uniformly beneficial. Rather than advancing all segments of society equally, the effects will be felt selectively. As a few men enter favored, technologically-based employment, the gap will widen between skilled and unskilled labor, further distinguished by differences in sex and race. Women who thought high tech would lead to good jobs may find themselves in competition with low-wage workers overseas, with sweatshop labor or homeworkers based in the United States, or even with robots. In light of such potentially bleak prospects, this paper will explore the evolving relationship between the growth of high tech microelectronics and the utilization of female labor, with a special look at why homework has become integral to the production process.

The Microelectronic Revolution in Reality

California's Santa Clara County, near San Francisco Bay, earned the name "Silicon Valley" because of its prominent role in electronic component production. The electronics industry originally grew in Silicon Valley in the 1950s to take advantage of Stanford University's engineering department, and to escape the high-wage New England labor that predominated near Massachusetts Institute of Technology. With more than 120 companies producing microelectronic circuits, each employing over 250 workers, plus a number of supplier firms, this area exceeds any other in the world in the manufacture of silicon chips. Approximately 200,000 people are directly or indirectly employed in electronics. Consequently, a careful look at the area provides an accurate picture of what expanded microelectronic growth might mean for women workers.

To understand and appreciate the almost sudden appearance of high technology industries in the Silicon Valley, it is essential to examine the industries' movement within a broad context internationally and within the United States. High technology industries are relatively free to choose their location because they are not tied to a natural resource base or energy supplies. The products they make are light in weight (have a high value-to-weight ratio), so the cost of transport to markets, wherever they are located, is relatively low. However, it is important for these employers to be located near labor, both highly-skilled, scientifically-trained workers, and low-wage assembly line workers. During its early stages, a product goes through continuous innovation and constant changes in design. As a result, research and production work need to be located near each other. But as demand for a product stabilizes, mass production can shift to areas where labor is inexpensive, while small, special order production is kept near home research facilities.

Any change that occurs in one product area — hardware (chips, computers), software (computer languages), or peripherals (terminals, printers) — stimulates development among the others. In this respect, the industry is highly integrated. With a potential for fast profits, and relative ease of entry into the production phase by new firms, there is a lot of competition. This has led to a continual search for reduced manufacturing costs, particularly among the producers of semiconductor components. Since component production requires an intensive use of low-skilled labor, employers will often cut costs by moving to low-wage areas of the United States and to other countries.

The actual chip manufacture is first done in the United States, then exported for testing and assembly, and later re-imported for incorporation into other products. Because these imports are "intermediate goods" that go toward the making of a final product, the companies can take advantage of U.S. tariff codes that tax only the value added abroad, chiefly the value created by very low-cost overseas labor. (In 1980 wages in Hong Kong plants were about $5 per day, which was high compared to Indonesia at $.80 and the Philippines at $.86 per day. In contrast U.S. Assemblers averaged over $4.50 per *hour* .)[1] The incentive to go abroad is further enhanced by low shipment costs. The result has been the industry's dramatic penetration into international labor markets since the early 1960s.

In addition to a clearly demarcated international division of labor, the industry is characterized by a sexual division of labor. Women work in production, while men are responsible for research and management. In one study of five Silicon Valley semiconductor plants, nearly half of the workers were low-skill assemblers. Women constituted 85 percent of the assemblers, and more than half of these assemblers were minority women, primarily Latinas and Asians. While women in general were concentrated in the clerical and assembler categories, minority women registered extreme isolation at the occupational bottom. In contrast, 87 percent of the professional and managerial staff were white males. Table 19.1 summarizes the results of this study.

The pay received by these workers shows significant disparities. For assemblers, wages began at the legal minimum, which in 1977 was $2.50 per hour (or $5,200 per year), while professionals earned $12,000 to $35,000 per year. Since 1977 the differential has actually grown wider. By 1979 assemblers earned an average wage of $4.52 per hour (or $9,402 per year for a 40-hour week), while engineers were drawing from $20,000 to $40,000 per year, or more. From the employer's point of view, the reason for such extremes in pay has a certain logic, albeit a socially perverse one when implemented. They argue that since the key to prosperity in this industry rests on innovation, good researchers are worth a premium; a high wage is necessary to retain skilled personnel. On the other hand, assemblers' tasks have become so fragmented, reduced to such simple steps, that very little skill is needed to complete the work.

Table 19.1
A Survey of Five Semiconductor Plants

	Total	Professional and Managerial	Technical and Craftspersons	Clerical	Assemblers
Total	2837	811	434	389	1106
Male	1282	786	327	67	52
Female	1555	25	107	322	1054
Minority	796	91	83	51	571
Male	168	82	58	12	16
Female	628	9	25	39	555

Source : Alan Bernstein, et. al., "Silicon Valley: Paradise or Paradox" in *Mexican Women in the United States* . eds. M. Mora and A. del Castillo (Los Angeles: UCLA, 1980), p. 108.

While stability, or lack of turnover, in the professional labor force is highly valued by employers to ensure continuous and consistent research, just the opposite is true for assemblers. It is important for an employer to be able to release assemblers easily during downturns in the market, or during periods of retooling due to product changes. The way in which an employer can have access to both a flexible and low-cost labor force is through a ready supply of labor; women, especially minority women, provide that supply.

The overseas movement of intermediate assembly was, in part, a response to pressures in the Valley that constrained the labor supply and threatened to drive up wages. As Silicon Valley experienced rapid growth, people moved into the area at a phenomenal rate. Employment mushroomed particularly during the 1960s and 1970s: from 1960 to 1975 "the county's employment grew 156 percent, three times the national rate of 46 percent and more than double California's 65 percent increase."[2] Displaying a classic "boomtown" phenomenon, housing and local infrastructure were barely able to keep up with demand. Chronic housing shortages drove up costs to inflated levels that exceeded the reach of low-income persons. As noted in one report, "by 1980 there were over 670,000 jobs, but only 480,000 housing units, and the *average* home price was well over $100,000." Low-wage, low-income workers were forced to locate further and further from their jobs. Even some professional workers found housing priced beyond their means, and employers began to offer such incentives as housing assistance and lucrative benefit packages to bring people into the area. But no one subsidized the cost of housing and long commutes for production workers, so as these costs rose, the pool of available workers decreased, thereby inhibiting further industrial expansion.

Local "no growth" policies that began in the 1970s added another constraint on industrial development in the Valley. Following a moratorium on industrial growth, some communities started to require fees from new industrial developments for application towards the building of housing, while others used this revenue for upgrading streets. The labor shortages and high cost of development forced the industry to restructure its production in ways that would minimize costs and also ease growth pains in the Valley. Since companies clearly did not want to decentralize research facilities, production became the choice for relocation. Intermediate assembly had already begun moving overseas, but now other aspects of production began to be transferred to Idaho, Arizona, and other right-to-work states with anti-union laws. As an alternative to exporting production, some employers turned to what abstractly can be thought of as importing labor, or the employment of Third World women within the United States, to do work in their homes as a means of lowering labor costs during the final stage of assembly.

There are actually several ways production costs can be cut, some of which have already been mentioned: through the employment of women and minorities; by minimum health protection at the workplace; by internationalizing part of the assembly; and by subcontracting part of the work to home manufacture. These tactics become important during different phases of production. A breakdown of the basic stages of chip manufacture clarifies why this is so.

In the initial stage, silicon wafers are prepared as integrated electronic circuits through a complex process of crystallization, gas diffusion, electroplating, and acid washing. During this process workers are subjected to cleaning ovens and numerous corrosive materials. The work is notoriously hazardous, but workers are not provided with much protection, which employers allege can be quite expensive.

In the second stage, the wafers (now integrated circuits) are cut into microscopic chips and "bonded" to lead frames by gold wires, to permit them to be soldered to other electronic parts, and covered by a protective material. The attachment of fine, gold wires under high-powered microscopes is generally done by overseas labor.

To complete the process, the various integrated circuits are assembled, or "stuffed," onto printed circuit boards for eventual placement into computer systems. Much of this final assembly is labor intensive and time consuming, unless very expensive automated equipment is used. Each board has a different pattern, and the circuits must be placed in the boards one at a time. Contractors have learned it is more cost effective on small production runs to relegate stuffing to homework.

In each stage corners are cut to lower production costs, and it is usually the female labor force that feels the consequences. Although the organization of work in the internationalized intermediate phase will reflect very different labor relations and conditions than apply in the

United States, analysis of each production phase shows how women workers are *crucial* to the economic structure of the industry. For comparative purposes, foreign and U.S. female workers will be discussed separately.

International Labor

In the global arena, most microelectronic production is concentrated in industrial areas, called Export Processing Zones (EPZs), usually located within Southeast Asian countries or Mexico (See Chapter 3). With the same multinational companies scattered throughout various countries, nearly identical employment patterns have appeared among plants around the world. Drawn from one of the least expensive pools of labor, the production workers are almost exclusively young women between the ages of 16 and 25, who are expected to conform to traditional roles defined by their families. Workers identify with their plants, making it difficult for them to rebel against an employer with whom they have inadvertently established a submissive relationship. Employers exploit women further by establishing strict daily and monthly quotas on their output, and by providing only the minimum of relief, such as giving them only one 45-minute rest period during a straight eight-hour shift.

A combination of sexual exploitation with repressive disciplinary measures has resulted in an alienated labor force, disassociated from cultural ties, yet constrained by employers who virtually dictate the pace of their lives. Nevertheless, even these workers have begun to initiate claims against their employers through strikes and demonstrations.[3]

With agencies like the Organization for Economic Cooperation and Development calling for restraints on multinational corporations, and in anticipation of growing militancy among workers in their various plant sites, electronics companies have begun to further automate and consolidate their production. Jobs that were once labor-intensive are now slotted for mechanization, with the intent of making the most modernized U.S. plants competitive even with those plants using low-cost overseas labor. As one International Labor Organization report noted, the advantages to producing abroad are being eroded.[4] The introduction of automation and robotization will also displace workers in the United States who perform dangerous or tedious jobs. But for now, semiconductor production workers remain among the lowest paid of industrial workers in the United States, with some of the highest exposure to occupational hazards. They are linked with the international women's labor force by a continuous process of production.

A Profile of U.S. Production Workers

Production workers in the United States may be materially better off than their overseas counterparts, but domestic and foreign assembly workers are equally powerless in the organization of their work. Because they are *female* assembly workers, the objective conditions that define their work environment are fragmentation and a sexual and racial division of labor. When work is divided into simple, repetitious steps, it results in deskilled workers who are easily substitutable and who lack control over the design of the product or the production process. This function is retained by male research and management staff; the most unstable, least remunerative production work is "feminized."

These are generally Third World women who have not been the concern of mainstream North American society. One indicator of their alienation is the lack of unionization in the Valley. Union officials who say the Valley is unorganizable will sometimes allude to the fact that the female labor force is tied to traditional social models that prevent them from challenging male authority figures. These women, they complain, are hungry enough to break strikes, regardless of long-run effects. However, this is simply another instance of blaming the victim. The problem is based on the structure of the industry, which needs to constantly release and rehire production workers to stay competitive. To insure that workers do not organize, the American Electronics Association, which looks after the interests of these firms, has been sponsoring notorious seminars on union busting and monitoring union activity in plants. In this hostile climate, women workers have found constant job mobility and homework to be a different means for achieving a balance between earning an income and retaining dignity through work.

As previously noted, many U.S. electronics assemblers are minority females. The ethnic groups that contribute to this labor force include Koreans, Filipinos, Vietnamese, and Mexicans. A significant number of these workers are recent immigrants or refugees for whom electronics assembly represents their first U.S. job. Sometimes one ethnic group will predominate. For example, at Advanced Micro Devices, Filipinos reportedly constitute the majority of the assemblers, while at Hewlett-Packard, it is Vietnamese. The subtle message conveyed to workers is that they should be grateful the employer prefers their ethnic group, an appreciation best returned if employees do not make demands. An alternative strategy is followed by the Rolm Corporation, where Latinos, Filipinos, and Vietnamese are concentrated in separate departments, making it possible to prevent worker unity and to aggressively create competition among the workers.[5]

Because they are denied the power associated with collective action, these workers find that their only recourse in the face of endemic job loss is to move, rather than extract compensation or force a restructuring of employment patterns. Given this and the fact that there is very little opportunity for advancement into better-paying occupations, it is understandable that an increase of five cents per hour will be enough incentive for a worker to change jobs.

Chronic job mobility is also a response to workplace conditions. Electronics is noted for creating complicated health hazards for workers, due to constant exposure to toxic chemicals. Acid burns, headaches, and nausea as a result of chemical fumes and vapors are frequent complaints, and there are many long-term effects that have yet to be acknowledged. Illness rates are four times the average for manufacturing. Some ailments are so new that occupational health experts have been unable to keep up with the problems, much less anticipate potential bodily threats. Workers complain that protective legislation is not enforced and that when they try to force workplace improvements, they are fired. Therefore, job mobility is sometimes simply a reflection of a worker's search for a more healthy environment.

There are several other sides to women workers' lives that affect job location decisions. A working mother has to think about the cost of childcare, which can take a sizeable chunk out of a minimum wage paycheck. Since the commute for many is very long and public transit is often not available, transportation takes away time and money that could be used for household purposes. A working mother also usually performs double-duty — she comes home tired and still has to care for her family. These women are willing to make the trade-offs required to engage in work at home.

For a significant number of women, homework also makes it possible to earn an income without having to submit to the gender stereotyping prevalent at the factory. White men gain satisfaction through promotions and job stability; minority women gain that satisfaction by acting as entrepreneurs outside of the plant.[6] Status devaluation is less apparent if a woman doesn't have to consciously acknowledge gender and race stratification on the job. Thus homework flourishes because of the competitive structure of the industry, discriminatory behavior in the workplace, and the double burden on women workers to both earn an income and raise a family.

For the average person, the idea that homework exists in such an advanced field is incomprehensible. Yet in many ways, the electronics industry has come to resemble the garment industry, in which it is common to find firms resorting to work done at home. These industries share highly competitive market structures and a routinized assembly process that relies on female labor. As a shelter against the costs of releasing and rehiring workers or carrying inventory during market fluctuations, manufacturers contract out circuit board assembly work to low-overhead firms.

Homework can be initiated in a number of ways. Sometimes a company will given "cash bonuses" to employees who hire home workers at low cost. Sometimes an employer will pay its part-time workers cash for work they do at home, an attractive offer to workers who don't want to report their full income. Or perhaps a broker will approach an employer with an offer to assume the "stuffing" for a low rate; the broker, in turn, will charge workers an initial sum of $150 to $250 for jobs that will be done in the workers' homes.

The black market for homework survives on housewives, refugees, undocumented workers, and limited-income persons who find that in a cash economy, not paying Social Security or Workers' Compensation leaves them slightly more income than a minimum wage paycheck after taxes. They are usually paid at a piece rate, which during 1980 was reportedly 50 cents each for assembling 300 printed circuit boards.[7] For the employer, work that might cost $9 per hour plus benefits in the factory may total only $6 per hour with no benefits if done at home. But someone has to pay for the costs of unexpected injuries, unemployment, and exploitation: that someone is usually the woman worker.

Although some homeworkers will earn as much as $5 or $6 per hour, the majority end up earning less than the minimum wage. Subtracting an initial entry fee of $250 for "basic materials," (another name for a kickback), workers' incomes drop even more. To bring their income up to subsistence levels, some will draw unemployment insurance or work part-time, while working at home on the side. But if they work days, nights, and weekends, and require their children, in-laws, and other members of the household to participate in the labor, the unrecorded income can reach as much as $3,500 in one month. The incentive to earn as much as possible means that any leisure time, whether a rest break or a vacation, is lost income. At that pace, burn-out is an occupational hazard.

Others are less concerned with making as much money as possible than with earning enough to make ends meet. But they forget they are absorbing the cost of electricity, rent, and heat. If they are using dangerous chemicals at home, the entire family, particularly young children, is at risk. From the workers' point of view, homework is satisfactory because it allows them independence in setting their schedules, the opportunity to oversee their children, freedom from transportation problems, and flexibility in deciding their own work goals. In this respect, the worker becomes her own supervisor, free from the petty hierarchical controls of the workplace. Futurist Alvin Toffler and economist E. F. Schumacher warn that cottage industries will become more significant in the future, and some political conservatives see this as an expression of individual choice. But freedom to determine the pace of one's own work comes at a high price.

Once people agree to work without provisions for childcare, safety protection, and economic security for when they are old or disabled, they agree to work under conditions that approximate economic slavery. Moreover, homework opens the door for further erosion of the standards governing working conditions. If poorer working conditions become acceptable to the public, what is to stop passage of legislation that will institutionalize these arrangements? Without the potential for collective action, attempts to unionize are impossible.

Currently, women are seen as undermining strikes and union demands by working at home. But perhaps a different kind of union is needed. Recently, the United Domestic Workers of San Diego proved that even hard to organize service workers can form a union. A union can act like a hiring hall, dispensing with organizing at the workplace. Homeworkers present a creative challenge that will force unions to define new structures and to incorporate childcare as integral to workers' needs.

Not all homework is illegal — a section of the California Labor Code assures industrial homeworkers coverage under labor standards legislation. But as of July 1981, only seven electronics firms in California had valid homework licenses. The remainder of the firms skipped the $100 licensing fee and operated illegally. Although underground employment is pervasive, not all companies engage openly in either legal or illegal homework. Larger companies, in fact, rarely enter into homework directly. Instead, they subcontract with brokers who initiate homework, or who contract it out again. According to Pete Carey and Michael Malone, although an estimated ". . .thousands of people and millions of dollars are involved, there are no large factories involved in this underground, nor do the names of many of these firms appear on state or federal records."[8] Those companies that do not compete through homeworking do so in other ways, such as moving to low-wage places, or finding ways to automate more of the production process.

Prospects for the Future

The contemporary debate over whether homework legislation should be relaxed to allow more women to work has no easy resolution. From the union perspective, the problem appears to be one of trying to prevent the further degradation of working conditions. Less apparent, but integral to this issue, are the problems of women who work out of financial necessity while caring for their families, and of employment for minorities who are crowded into the lowest level jobs. Since women of color do not generally enter into clerical positions in the microelectronics industry, homework is one of the few alternatives open to them beyond the assembly line. So while the exploitation of *female* labor in their homes is one facet to consider, another is the exploitation of *minority* women or new immigrants who are culturally different or seen as of an inferior social status. Society has related these women to the worst jobs in the factories, so their employment at home is justified by suggesting that these women can't do any better, or that they work in conditions they deserve. Eliminating homework in an effort to stem the erosion of employment conditions in general means destroying jobs available to people with limited options, for whom automation will squeeze options even further.

The role of cheap female labor in high technology must also be understood as part of the worldwide trend toward automation. Although minority females already constitute the least expensive labor force, firms, in the quest to cut costs even more, continue to automate or find other ways for their workers to cost even less. Automation is ultimately cheaper than even this labor, but as yet cannot be applied to the detailed manual work that "stuffing" involves. So for the moment, semiconductor manufacture will continue to depend on low-wage, female labor, while plans for automation are on the drawing board.

Developments in microelectronics are the leading edge of technological advancement in other fields. Consequently, women who work in microelectronics are caught in a cog of the wheel that is turning to displace other female workers, such as office workers (see Chapters 18 and 29), even as they work to replace themselves. The social and economic imbalances that may result in the long run are serious. And so are the solutions. These are by no means clear, but as one International Labor Organization report suggests, new social and political systems are one potential scenario that may arise out of these revolutionary trends in the economy, as the issue of employment becomes increasingly prominent. This issue is especially imperative for women as the lower and unstable occupations of high technology industries are increasingly defined as women's work, and even more specifically, as minority and immigrant women's work.

Notes

1. CSE Microelectronics Group, *Microelectronics: Capitalist Technology and the Working Class* (London, CSE Books, 1980), pp. 12, 19.
2. Anna Lee Saxenian, "Silicon Chips and Spatial Structure: The Industrial Basis of Urbanization in Santa Clara County, California," Working paper no. 345 (Berkeley, CA: Institute of Urban Regional Policy, University of California, March, 1981), pp. 63-64.
3. Alan Bernstein, Bob DeGrasse, Rachel Grossman, Chris Paine, and Lenny Siegel, "Silicon Valley: Paradise or Paradox" in *Mexican Women in the United States: Struggles Past and Present*, eds. Magdelena Mora and Adelaida R. del Castillo, (Los Angeles: Chicano Studies Research Center Publications, University of California, 1980), p. 111.
4. J. Rada, *The Impact of Microelectronics: A Tentative Appraisal of Information Technology* (Geneva: International Labor Organization, 1980), p. 23.
5. Robert Howard, "Second Class in Silicon Valley," *Working Papers* (September/October 1981).
6. Naomi Katz, "Join the Future Now: Women and Work in the Electronics Industry," working paper (San Francisco: San Francisco State University, 1981).
7. Pete Carey and Michael Malone, "Black Market in Silicon Valley," San Jose *Sunday Mercury News*, (August 31, 1980).
8. *Ibid.* .

See also:
   Peter Baird and Ed McCaughan, *Beyond the Border: Mexico and the U.S. Today* (New York: NACLA, 1979).
   Jeremy Brecher, "Roots of Power: Employers and Workers in the Electrical Products Industry" in *Case Studies on the Labor Process*, ed. Andrew Zimbalist (New York: Monthly Review Press, 1979).
   Barbara Ehrenreich, Robert Appleyard, A. Siranandan, and David Snider, "Capital and Labor in Silicon Valley," *The Witness* 64 (November 1981).

Hardy Green and Elizabeth Weiner, "Bringing It All Back Home," *In These Times*, March 11-17, 1981.

Judith Green, Ursula Murray, and Bob Davis, "The New Sweatshops," in *The State and the Local Economy* (London: Community Development Project Political Economy Collective, 1979).

John S. Hekman, "The Future of High Technology Industry in New England: A Case Study of Computers," *New England Economic Review* (January/February 1980).

Emma Rothschild, "Reagan and the Real America," *The New York Review*, February 5, 1981.

Saskia Sassen-Koob, "Exporting Capital and Importing Labor," New York Research Program in Inter-American Affairs, New York University, Center for Latin American and Caribbean Studies, September 1981.

SRI International, "High Technology and the California Work Force in the 1980's," prepared for the California Department of Economic and Business Development, March 1982.

Chapter 20

Blue Collar Women

by Mary Lindenstein Walshok

There are three issues I would like to address. The first concerns the ways automation has affected women's labor force participation. By looking at areas of increased participation of women workers and at discussions about the impact of technology on domestic roles, we can get some insight into the question of labor force participation.

The second issue relates to the question of what, if any, expanding opportunities there are for women in light of technological developments. I would like to point out the new functions and activities that appear to be evolving from technological developments and the ways many traditional jobs are being transformed by technology. These developments represent potential new pockets of opportunity for women if, and I underline *if*, women are assured knowledge of and access to positions. I would like to examine the qualities women seek in their employment. When we evaluate the qualitative impact of technology on women's work, it is terribly important to have a clear understanding of what women seek from their work; I am not sure we have that understanding.

The final issue is the question of how we as educators, employers, and generally concerned women can ensure women knowledge of, access to, and adequate training for emerging and changing jobs. Technological advances mean nothing if they simply end up displacing women from their traditional jobs, while new and transformed work remains closed to them. A strong social consciousness and an aggressive social policy can ensure that technology will mean increased opportunity for women rather than more limited employment options.

The Impact of Automation

A number of important studies touch, directly or indirectly, on the impact of automation on women's lives. Let us look at housework. People assume that the automation of domestic duties — cleaning, food preparation, laundering — has been one of the factors propelling women into the paid work force. However, in an article in **Scientific American**, Joann Vanek argued that despite the proliferation of labor-saving devices, women spend as much time today in domestic work as they did 50 years ago.[1]

Technology has also affected work force participation on the job in ways that contradict common sense. Valerie Oppenheimer was the first to demonstrate that the increased participation of women in the labor force is as much a result of demand for workers as it is of a supply of idle housewives.[2] Even if every able-bodied man in the United States were employed, still only about 70 percent of the available paid jobs would be filled, because there has been such an enormous expansion in fields such as banking, clerical services, and in new technology areas such as computers, medicine, and health sciences.

It is important to understand the points made by both Vanek and Oppenheimer because these facts suggest an important indirect relationship between automation and technological innovation, and women's work. The technological innovations of the middle and latter part of the twentieth century have not only freed women to pursue paid employment, they have also created jobs and transformed and expanded job sectors so that the economy actually needs women in paid employment. The quality of work currently being opened to women is another important question. But the increased productivity coming from automation has transformed the economy so there are many more service-oriented occupations and expanding opportunities for all persons, especially women.

The innovations in industry and office procedures have also expanded in the overall economy; jobs are expanding rather than contracting. What we also need to be willing to acknowledge about technology is that even though some areas of employment have been dramatically deskilled, others have been transformed into more complicated and interesting options. An example is the work done by skilled blue collar workers at the General Motors Corporation. Even though computers are now running certain aspects of the assembly line, many of the former assembly line workers have moved up into jobs which involve maintaining and repairing those computers. These new jobs are qualitatively different from working right on the assembly line.

The ripple effect of technology has been far-reaching. Jobs have been created in a variety of sectors. The creation of jobs is a very important question, particularly in the context of future technology and women. When we begin to look at the differences in social class and at the limited opportunities minority group members face, it appears in absolute terms that the employment position and the earning of women have improved as a result of technology. But relative to men, working women are still in as bad a position. Despite this, the attitude of working class women is that technology has improved their circumstances.

New Jobs, New Challenges

Let us look at the expansion and transformation of women's employment opportunities due to technology. The significance of automation and technological innovation is that they could potentially transform the nature of the opportunities open to women and equalize access to varied jobs. Figures from the Department of Labor suggest a number of exciting, positive opportunities for women, at least in the short run. The first is that there will be sufficient jobs in the economy to employ better than 90 percent of eligible males and close to 50 percent of eligible females. This was, of course, prior to the change to the Reagan Administration. I don't know if we can continue to believe this.

Holding aside for a moment the persistent problem of youth and minority unemployment, jobs appear to exist and to be expanding. The problem is that while automobile assembly line workers are unemployed in Michigan, companies in Orange County, California, can't hire enough electronics assemblers, technicians, and supervisors in the electronics industry. These are very real problems, but if we look at the overall picture, the electronics field is expanding more rapidly than the automobile industry is declining. On a society-wide level, jobs seem to be expanding, and the Department of Labor points to these rapidly growing fields: computer programming, sales, maintenance, and repair. Most of us don't notice all of the office machine and computer repair people who wander around the offices and buildings in which we work, but they are the new skilled blue collar workers of the 1980s and 1990s, and jobs are rapidly expanding in those fields.

There are also many jobs expanding in the health area, particularly among technicians and laboratory workers. A proliferation of all kinds of medical equipment and machines, which need to be used, maintained, and replaced, creates new jobs. In dentistry, architecture, science, and engineering there is vast and very promising growth.

It is quite interesting that over 20 years ago a sociologist at Berkeley criticized most of the research on work because it had a narrow image of who the blue collar worker was. We think of automobile and steel workers as prototypical blue collar workers; sometimes we include carpenters and plumbers. But it is important to acknowledge that in addition to these kinds of jobs, which actually are on the decline, there are many expanding jobs in repair and maintenance. This includes mechanics working on the Bay Area Rapid Transit System, who are responsible for monitoring and repairing the electronic equipment which runs that system, as well as airplane mechanics, telecommunications operators and repairers, and office machine repair people. Thus, automation may be deskilling some areas by replacing assembly-line workers with machines, but the machines still need to be operated and maintained.

Women are interested in these technical jobs now more than ever, particularly when they are presented with the opportunity to pursue them. There are a lot of emerging studies which bear this out, including research done by Sylvia Navari at Sacramento State,[3] Bridgit O'Farrell at Wellesley,[4] Myra Max Ferree at the University of Connecticut, and myself.[5] We have been watching women as they move into skilled blue collar jobs. All four of us, working in different parts of the country with different populations, are coming up with similar findings.

First of all, the increased participation of women in these jobs is three and four times greater than the increase in participation of women in law or medicine. There has been an enormous increase in women moving into skilled blue collar and technical jobs. They began with such a small number that the absolute number is still small, but they are increasing at enormous rates all over the country. The reason they are increasing is not because there are thousands of women dying to be skilled blue collar workers, but because opportunities are opening up for jobs that pay very well and offer women a lot more autonomy, independence, and challenge than traditional work.

Women who go into these nontraditional jobs have a strong personal identification as working persons — they see themselves as lifelong workers. They are money-oriented because they have three or four children, because they are divorced, or because they are supporting sick mothers. Conforming to the typical stereotype of unskilled female workers, they have not held jobs for more than nine or ten months at a time, even though they have been working all their lives. They might have clerked in a drug store, cleaned motel rooms, or worked at a fast food service operation. Maybe they were secretaries in an office, but few of them had stable employment.

The group I followed over a four-year period ended up having very stable employment because at last they were in jobs that paid them well, challenged them, and gave them some security. This is what people are discovering about the satisfaction and stability of employment in jobs that provide meaningful work. Meaningful, nontraditional, blue collar work for women covers everything from auto mechanics to office machinery repair, telephone installation to engineering, drafting to airplane instrument repair.

Automation in the office context is another impact of technology. It is an area that is greatly debated, but I would like to refer to the results of some research done by two women at Boston University, Evelyn Glenn and Roslyn Feldberg. Both of these women are radical feminists. Both of them went into major Boston insurance companies convinced that they were going to find that secretarial and clerical workers felt increasingly alienated by the introduction of word-processing machines. They found just the opposite.[6]

They found that word-processing machines, rather than alienating or routinizing the work, freed the women in those insurance companies, giving them much more discretion over the pacing of their work. Because this work involved learning a certain minimal amount of programming language and some new skills, the women got the impression they were moving out of the secretarial sphere into technical jobs. The women no longer defined themselves as secretaries, but as technicians. And because not all of the office had as yet been automated, the women who worked the machines saw themselves as differentiated from and better than the other office workers. This gave them some sense of satisfaction. Secretaries said they felt they had more control over their time. They were able to pace their work much better, and there was not a supervisor looking over their shoulders the way there had been when they worked in the typing pool. They took coffee breaks when they wanted; there was more freedom.

We still have to wait to judge the impact, qualitatively, of automation on women's work experience. Some of the early research suggests that qualitatively women see their jobs as improved when they move into more technical spheres. That may be because women have had such lousy jobs prior to having these technical jobs. One woman I interviewed said, "The job I have now requires me to do eight different things, and the job I had before required me to do three different things." She reasoned her new job was more than twice as challenging and twice as satisfying.

All this is a sad commentary on the history and status of women in the world of work. But we are learning that automation is not considered as negative as many of us originally believed it would be. Even though automation is giving rise to high growth areas and high growth industries, we need to be cautious about what level of participation women are going to have in these high growth areas. Francine Blau points out that in the Boston electronics industry, hundreds of new jobs are being created in what previously was a declining industrial economy. The problem is that 70 percent of the operatives jobs, the least skilled and the most routine, are held by women, while women hold less than 10 percent of the skilled crafts jobs.[7] So even though technology may be creating jobs, even challenging and interesting jobs, women are still disproportionately channeled into the most routine and lowest-paying ones. Blau argues that to overcome this inequality in access, more attention should be placed on new jobs created by the growth of the economy. If we allocate job openings on the basis of sex distribution in the labor force, 40 percent of the jobs would go to women, and 60 percent to men. The operatives jobs should be distributed 40/60 percent by sex, as well as the crafts jobs. They are not and they should be.

Satisfaction on the Job

The qualities of work valued by women underscore why some of these new technical jobs can be very satisfying. There are basically four qualities of work valued by women that I've identified in my research, and they are not typical qualities identified with women. In past research on what women want from their work, priorities were convenient hours, proximity to home, few demands, reasonable pay, and a sociable work environment. But there is emerging research that provides a much more honest and complicated picture of what women are looking for and why many of these technical jobs, at least in the short run, are very promising and exciting.

Over 100 women continuously identified four criteria for their work. First, a sense of productivity, defined in terms of sensing some kind of accomplishment, producing something at the end of the day. A plumber who had previously worked as an electronics assembler said, "You know, I go into the house, I pull the toilet out, I change the pipes, I put the toilet back, and leave. I've accomplished something, and that matters a great deal.''

Challenge was the second important quality the women identified. Challenge was defined in terms of newness, variety, and problem solving. One of the positive attributes of many of these automated or more technologically sophisticated jobs is that they do change, allowing the worker to become a problem solver. When people have to repair the instrumentation in an airplane panel, they must sit down and figure out what the problem is, maybe do a little testing, put different wires together, find the right solution, and repair it. This sense of challenge is satisfying.

A third factor is relatedness, making women feel they are in the mainstream, rather than backstage. It also has to do with women getting feedback and recognition for what they do. In many of the technical jobs, women said they had this feeling of significance.

A fourth characteristic, perhaps most important, is autonomy, described by the women in terms of control over the pacing of their work, discretion as to the sequencing and frequency of tasks, and feeling they define what is going to happen in their own day. The vast majority of working women are caught in other people's timetables and priorities. The plumber who can take a two-hour lunch, or the appliance repair person who can stop at McDonald's and get a hamburger and a coke, or go to the children's clothing store and pick up a pair of pants for her boy on her way to repair someone's washing machine, has a lot more discretion than the woman in the typing pool who clocks in at 8:00 and clocks out at 5:00, gets two 15-minute breaks and a half hour for lunch. Women combining paid employment with their family lives, childrearing, and some sense of personal space can find an awful lot of jobs that give them the discretion to do this. These jobs are a promising avenue for the new woman who is trying to do it all.

Guaranteeing Access for Women

I have suggested some of the potentially positive sides of technology for women's work, summarized some of the employment spheres where jobs are expanding, emphasized the qualities women seek in their work. Now, what can be done to assure women information about and access to opportunities and success in jobs? I think the following represent some minimum steps we can take:

- broaden the general and female public's knowledge of technology and its consequences for employment options;
- support early basic skills development essential to preparation for a technical future;
- help women plan for the future in light of technology;

- help organizations plan for the future by training men and women employees equally and placing women employees in new positions;
- keep the pressure on for equal employment opportunities at all levels, in all categories of jobs;
- assure proper recruitment, orientation, competency-based classroom and on-the-job training for women in skilled and technical jobs.

I am not suggesting that the future is bright — only that the future for women can be brighter than it is today if we have a fuller understanding of the range of choices, the costs and benefits of these choices, and what must be done to realize our choices in a postindustrial, technological future.

Notes

1. Joann Vanek, "Time Spent in Housework," *Scientific American* 231 (November 1974): 116-20.
2. Valerie Oppenheimer, *Female Labor Free in the U.S.: Demographic and Economic Factors* (Berkeley: University of California Press, 1970).
3. Sylvia Navari, "Women in Skilled Labor," Institute for Human Service Management Monographs (Sacramento, CA: Sacramento State University, 1967).
4. Bridgit O'Farrell, "Unions and Women's Mobility in Blue-Collar Jobs," paper read at the Society for the Study of Social Problems, annual meeting, 1979, Boston.
5. Mary Walshok, *Blue Collar Women: Pioneers on the Male Frontier* (Garden City, NY: Anchor Books, 1981).
6. Evelyn Glenn, and Roslyn Feldberg, "Orientations to Work: Rationalization, Technology, and Women Clerical Workers," paper read at the Society for the Study of Social Problems, annual meeting, 1979, Boston.
7. Francine Blau, "The Data on Women Workers, Past, Present and Future," in *Women Working*, eds. Ann Stromberg and Shirley Harkess, (Palo Alto CA: Mayfield Press, 1978), pp. 29-62.

Chapter 21

New Jobs in New Technologies:

Experienced Only Need Apply

by Diane Reynolds

There is a cigarette ad that claims "you've come a long way, baby." We all know we have not come nearly far enough, particularly on the economic front. Figures show women earn $.59 for every $1.00 a man makes. Moreover, half of all working women hold jobs in occupations that are at least 70 percent female. Emerging technologies can either raise women out of these pink-collar ghettos, or can create new ones.

Let us look at some early technologies. The telephone and the typewriter, marvelous new inventions in their time, were originally operated by men. The technical nature of these inventions appeared to be just too much for the delicacy and simplicity of the female mind. But this philosophy changed; women moved into these occupations of telephone operator and typist and their wages stagnated. To say that this stagnation occurred, however, merely because these occupations are predominantly female is far too simplistic.

Two critical items must be present, available, and operating for women to make today's new technologies positive rather than negative forces. The first is recognition of the importance of the trade union movement and of the benefits of collective bargaining in achieving full value for labor. The second item is skill training as opposed to formal education.

These two factors explain why two women with the same basic ability, intelligence, and formal education can make very disparate wages. One may earn $4 an hour as a clerk or an electronics assembler while the other may earn over $20 an hour as an operating engineer. What does the operating engineer have going for her that the clerk or electronics assembler does not? A strong tradition of unionization is one major difference. Although the occupation of operating engineer has been predominately male, that issue, I would suggest, has possibly less significance than its long history of collective bargaining and negotiation for improvements in wages and benefits, culminating in the threat of strike. Thus, wages for operating engineers have risen at a rate that compares favorably with many so-called "professional careers."

The other important determinant is skill training, more particularly, on-the-job training. Let us use the example again of two women who have the same basic abilities and intelligence. Let us say both of them enter the labor force at the same time. One enters a job situation with a complete formal education, but without any opportunity to upgrade her skills or wages; the other begins a skill progression that will lead to economic rewards rivaling the salary of any professional woman — often in much shorter time, considering that the professional woman pays for her own four-year college education. The skilled tradeswoman earns a wage from her first day on the job and receives regular periodic increases through the course of her four-year apprenticeship. This comparison is not meant to suggest that everyone scrap the four-year college degree, but clearly the college degree is not the only avenue of entry into highly technical occupations.

I do want to suggest, however, the very tremendous significance of what California's Governor Jerry Brown called "employment-based training." This kind of training, whether it is entry level or upgrade, is the only mechanism available to the vast majority of women for moving out of a clerical, white- or pink-collar ghetto. The governor's concept of employment-based training was embodied in his administration-sponsored piece of legislation passed in California in 1979, entitled "The California Worksite Education and Training Act," or CWETA. In California this program operates out of a $25 million state fund.

The legislation is based on the apprenticeship concept. It has increased employment-based training, providing a mechanism for moving up and out of low-skilled, low-paying, dead-end jobs by utilizing internal advancement opportunities within most large industries, particularly high technology industries. In the electronics field, for example, the most prevalent and lowest paying occupation is electronics assembler, an occupation dominated by women.

Fewer and fewer women are found up the occupational ladder. The problem is that the rungs of this ladder are shaky at best and, in most cases, totally nonexistent for either women or men. I remember one woman who told me she was looking forward to a seminar offered by her employer which would outline promotional and upward mobility opportunities within her company. She went and found, to her great dismay, that the entire seminar consisted of an explanation on how to progress from junior clerk typist to senior clerk typist. This is indicative of the real problem.

Women and other workers need a mechanism to make that critical quantum leap in the employment market, be it from clerk to professional, from semiskilled to highly skilled worker, or from electronics assembler to electronics technician. And this need not be exclusively through a formal academic program.

Internal labor markets exist in most of the new technological industries: electronics, data processing, computer occupations, telecommunications, and aerospace. But women are clumped at the entry-level, bottom rung in these industries, and will stay there unless internal upward mobility ladders are established. This is what the CWETA legislation endeavors to do by establishing financial incentives to employers who provide in-house, employment-based, formal, on-the-job training, supplemented at community colleges by related classroom instruction taken by the individual employee after working hours. For the employee, this legislation comprises a total program of skill progression and salary advancement. For the employer, it provides the skilled work force so desperately needed to keep up with accelerating demands.

It is interesting to note that after its first year and a half of operation, and without being specifically targeted to women, 60 percent of the participants in the program turned out to be female. That is because the legislation is targeted to upgrade skills in the labor market, and as we all know, women are down at the bottom.

Although the governor's initiative was aimed at providing a generic apprenticeship approach to new and emerging high technology industries through CWETA, we must not overlook the impact of new technologies on many traditional apprenticeship programs, and the desire of many women to enter nontraditional female occupations: plumber, carpenter, electrician, tool and die maker, operating engineer. These are high-skilled, high-paying jobs that women are finally getting a crack at. In 1976 California became the first state in the nation to have goals and timetables for the participation of women in apprenticeship programs. In 1978 the federal government passed even more stringent goals and timetables; the formula is complex, but basically, the guidelines require that approximately 20 percent of every trade's entering apprenticeship class be female. In 1975, before either the state or the federal legislation, there were almost 300 different kinds of apprenticeship programs and there were only 300 women involved. By 1980 we had a gain of 350 percent, though the actual number of women is still relatively small. There are about 45,000 apprentices statewide; just a little over 2,000 are women. We have made a beginning and we are moving along, but there is still a great deal more to be done.

Even the traditional building trades and machining occupations are affected by the new technologies. We now find plumbers and sheet metal workers who are installing solar systems. Machinists are learning to operate advanced numerical control equipment. And as technologies continue to change more and more rapidly, training and retraining for jobs that did not exist 20 years ago will assume greater importance. For the women who can avail themselves of these opportunities, training means a bright economic future.

Notes

For more information contact: Division of Apprenticeship Standards, Department of Industrial Relations, State of California, 525 Golden Gate Avenue, San Francisco, CA 94102, (415) 557-2950.

Chapter 22

Paths to Power

In High Technology Organizations

by Natasha Josefowitz

There is no doubt that prejudice still exists against women who choose to work in technological fields. Like all working women, they confront two types of barriers: dysfunctional socialization or internal barriers, which require awareness to diminish them, and external barriers of discrimination and prejudice. But for women in high technology organizations, there are still other dimensions they need to deal with specifically as women scientists or engineers. Before I turn to those, let me first review briefly the barriers to power due to women's socialization — the internal barriers. I call them the "Seven As."[1]

Internal Barriers

The first "A" deals with the issue of *authority*. Because women have always seen authority in the hands of men, there is no role model for what authority may look like in the hands of women. Therefore, they must invent it. Anything that must be done for the first time is a much higher risk than modeling behavior on others' tried and true way of doing things. Women who feel powerless must overcome the issue of the legitimacy of their authority.

The next "A" deals with *assertion*. Assertiveness is an issue which arises from role expectations. Women are in a double bind. If they act as assertively as men do, they may be seen as aggressive by many men and by some women who are not accustomed to seeing women assert themselves. However, if a woman is not assertive, then others assume she has no leadership qualities. No matter which way women go, they encounter either anger or resistance, discounting behavior or indifference, so they might as well please themselves.

The third "A" I call *accountability*. This deals with the fact that women are carrying more emotional responsibility than many men. Women are expected to be harmonizers, mediators, the ones who understand. If there is a conflict, women are expected to smooth it over. As a result, women managers may have trouble delegating responsibility, and instead feel they ought to "do it all" themselves. If they do delegate, they may feel guilty or worry about whether the work is being done properly, and thus supervise too closely. Women need to learn to unburden themselves and to trust others more.

The next "A" is *accessibility* . The issue here is the difficulty that many women have in setting boundaries. Women are used to meeting the needs of other people, be they husbands or children, family, or friends. But what about women's own needs? Are they fulfilled by meeting everyone else's? Or do women, in fact, neglect themselves by doing so?

In interviews with 102 female and 68 male managers, I found women were twice as accessible to their peers, subordinates, clients, and suppliers as their male counterparts. What did I measure? Open versus closed doors. Women keep their doors open more often than men do.

Women have a harder time having their phone calls and visits screened by a secretary; they allow more interruptions and the interruptions last longer. They have a harder time cutting off conversations when the topic is finished. They give their home phone numbers to their staff, saying they can be reached at home evenings and weekends if necessary, while no male manager ever does that. When women are accessible *consciously* , their accessibility is functional, but when women are controlled by their unconscious, they are not in charge of their decisions and behavior.

Another "A" deals with *affiliation* . Here the problem lies in the feelings of dependence many women have on existing friendships. Friendships are important for women who early in life develop the prerequisite of liking other children in order to play with them. Not so for boys. Boys tend to play for the pleasure of the sport, girls for the pleasure of being with each other. If we translate this on a managerial level, women feel loyalty to their colleagues and peers, and therefore find it more difficult to change from one department to another, to move on, to move out and leave their colleagues behind. Of course, upward mobility is not the only way to go. Some prefer horizontal enrichment or prefer not to add responsibilities, even if it would mean higher pay or a better position. This is a decision only the individual can make.

The sixth "A" is *approval* . If women do not think of their jobs as part of a career path, then the rewards for work well done need to come from someone else's recognition of that fact. Therefore many women tend to seek approval rather than constructive criticism. Any disapproval is considered to be directed at the total person, rather than at a single action. In other words, women tend to personalize criticism. In order to know how they are doing and how they are perceived, women *should* seek feedback from their superiors.

The last "A" is, in fact, three, but they all deal with the same issue: affability, apology, and anger. *Affability* is the way women have been socialized to smile. Women are not supposed to muddy the waters, stir up conflict. Instead they are supposed to be nice, polite, gentle, calm, mild, helpful. In fact, women often smile even when they are angry.

Apology deals with the fact that women very often discount their own actions. For instance, they use disqualifying statements before questions, such as, "I may be wrong but. . ." "This may have been said before but..," "I'm not sure of this but. . ." Ending statements with question marks, such as "right?", "yes?", or "okay?" is, of course, a safer thing to do.

If there is only one woman in the audience or in the lab or at a meeting, she speaks for all women. She represents the woman's point of view. No man has that burden. In fact, if a woman does poorly, one will often hear "we should not have hired a woman." Ten men can do poorly and no one will say "we should not have hired a man."

If *anger* is not ladylike, but is an acceptable expression for men, and tears are fine for women, but an expression of weakness for men, how are the sexes to learn to broaden their range to both cry and be angry when appropriate? If a man is angry, he is strong, forceful, and respected. If a woman is angry, it is "that time of the month," she's being overemotional, making mountains out of molehills, unreliable. On the other hand, men have lost elections because they have shown tears in public.

The paths to power, self-confidence, and self-realization are many, but they all have one starting point: awareness. We need awareness of ourselves, our needs, our rights, and our aspirations. This awareness does not come full blown into our consciousness, but develops slowly, one step at a time. And even though there is not much women can do about the way they were brought up, women may choose not to repeat dysfunctional patterns as they become conscious of them. What helps is to talk with a trusted friend about some of the "Seven As"; it is very hard to go it alone.

External Barriers

Besides the internal barriers of socialization which burden women in high technology organizations, there are strategies for conquering external barriers that need to be known by women in all types of work and in all kinds of organizations.

The major stumbling block is what I call the clonal effect in organizations.[2] If I ask you, "Who would you hire? Who would you promote?", the most likely answer would be "someone whose behavior is predictable, someone whom I trust, possibly someone whose values or interests I share." Well, who is that person? Probably someone who is most like you, because that is where the comfort level exists. Most organizations tend to replicate themselves. If the power base is in the hands of white males, they will tend to hire other white males who are similar to themselves. This creates barriers for anyone who is different; women, Blacks, minorities, or even other white males who somehow do not fit the image of the organization. A much older or a much younger man, or an obese one, or one with an accent or a handicap may have a much harder time being accepted. The clonal effect is unconscious, by definition. Therefore it works against the person who is different unless that person decides to bring up the difference in the open and talk about it. Blacks are not going to look white, people are not going to lose their accent, and no matter how many three-piece suits women wear, they will not pass as men.

One of the things we know about organizations is that heterogeneity promotes creativity. And nowhere more than in scientific organizations is there a need for heterogeneity, as opposed to homogeneity. The different person, the woman, needs to celebrate her difference and say what it is she is bringing to the organization that is different, that is not there yet. There is an oft-quoted myth that because little boys had opportunities to play ball and little girls did not, little boys grow up to be marvelous team players and poor little girls don't know about that. However, no one asks what little girls were doing while all those little boys were playing ball. The little girls were talking to one another. They were perfecting their verbal and interpersonal skills, exactly what is most needed in scientific organizations. It is in their ability to share data, communicate, help others, talk about their findings, encourage disclosure, and elicit feelings that women can make an extraordinary difference in the scientific community.

I believe that familiarity brings promotion. If the tendency is to trust most those who are most predictable and those whom we know best, then it is evident that being known by the person who makes decisions about promotions or budgets is an important strategy. Knowing this, a woman needs to become as familiar as possible with the people who have power and influence in her organization. Choose a small office next to the person in charge rather than the lovely one two floors away. Seek occasions to be known by your bosses by interacting informally with them as frequently as possible and by asking to work on projects with them.

In other words, it is not only the type of project which is important, but also who is going to be on the team. As a woman becomes better known, she becomes more trusted, and therefore is eventually given responsibilities, money, and position.

Because most men have been socialized to see women in dependent, helpless roles or solely as nurturers, mothers, daughters, servants, or sex objects, women as equal colleagues violate their expectations. Whenever expectations are violated, people get upset and angry. And the tendency is to not hear, not see, not experience the behavior which is obviously there. For instance, a woman's contribution at a meeting is often later attributed to a man, or what she says is not heard at all. But if a man later says a similar thing, it is picked up and discussed. This is due to the fact that a woman saying anything worthwhile is so against learned expectations that when she does, it is seen as not possible and therefore discounted. Thus women need strategies to keep reinforcing their visibility.

For instance, if I have said something interesting at a meeting that I am afraid others might not remember originated with me, I will write a memo to all concerned that reads, "As I said at our last meeting, I would like to reinforce the point," or "I would like to add to it or I'd like to suggest." Visibility also includes visiting your colleagues in their offices, sitting down and chatting with them, and just generally being around.

Another important strategy is to know the difference between real and attributed power. People with the highest title or the largest office have obvious, legitimate power. However, power is also in the hands of people who do not seem to have any specific status or recognition. One can observe these attributes by the following clues: Who calls the meetings? On whose territory? Who sets the agenda? Whose agenda gets implemented? Whose topics are picked up and followed through? Who interrupts whom? Whose suggestions are heeded? Who has eye contact with whom? Whose work gets done first by the clerical staff? Who is most often with the people with the highest power positions? After a while, it is possible to become very good at noting the subtle cues which tell you who in fact already has informal power and who is on their way to getting it.

Another strategy is to be an expert in a very narrow field, to be the only one who knows how something is done, or how to retrieve a certain piece of information, so that people need to come to you if they want it. Whatever it is that you produce, be sure to put your name to it. If you congratulate a colleague about a piece of work, write a memo to that colleague's boss and send a copy to your colleague.

It is important to know the difference between mentors and sponsors as a specific strategy. Mentors can be your peers or your immediate superior. A mentor is a person who teaches you what you need to know and has a specific skill or knowledge. A mentor is present-oriented and talks to you. A sponsor, on the other hand, needs to have clout in the organization and be several rungs above you; she or he will speak about you to others and is future-oriented. If you need to represent your company, for instance, at a regional meeting, your mentor will tell you what to say. Your sponsor will introduce you to the regional vice-president. Everyone needs to have both functions filled: a mentor to show you the ropes every time a new project or step up in the hierarchy is undertaken, and a sponsor to represent you, to talk about you, and to see that your work gets recognition.

The last strategy deals with support. Again, everyone needs a brain to pick, a shoulder to cry on, and a kick in the pants. Because women in the fields of high technology are often tokens or the first to enter their field, there are few female mentors and sponsors and few, if any, female models or colleagues. I urge women in these situations either to form support groups outside of their organization or to join existing groups, preferably those dealing with their specific professions, such as the Society of Women Engineers, just so they can hear they are not the only ones who get bypassed, overlooked, not heard, misinterpreted, joked about, or whatever the particular discriminating factors are in each situation. It is critical for women not to feel that they are alone, getting the brunt of the stereotyping.

Special Strategies In Technical Settings

Finally, let us look at some strategies specifically useful to female scientists and engineers in organizations.[3]

Need for security . Security is stability and continuity, while challenge disrupts established patterns, resulting in creative tension or creative contradiction. The external source of security is acknowledgment from others; the internal source of security is self-confidence. This often is counterbalanced by fears that you do not know, or that you know less than others and may be found out. Women need to learn the difference between knowing and knowledge, in order to attain self-confidence.

Knowledge is content-oriented. To have specific knowledge is to have expertise in some area; this can be learned. Knowing, however, is process-oriented. Whereas content refers to what is being said, process refers to how it is said. To hear the content, you listen to the actual message. To understand the process, you listen to the tone of voice, the nonverbal cues, the reactions of others. Although knowing is a skill that can be sharpened, most women already possess it and use it unconsciously. To use it more effectively, women must acknowledge its force and use it consciously. When intuition speaks, we are conscious of knowing. I call it "gut is data." And "gut" is good data to pay attention to.

To gain external sources of security, women need to toot their own horns. No one else will do it for them. External sources of security provide recognition and prestige, which enhance self-confidence. There is a high risk for women who are breaking ground in new fields. This risk is so tremendous that it is an achievement in itself, but men do not recognize it and do not know how to reward it. To be willing to be in such a situation already says a lot about the woman who is there. Therefore women need to join professional groups or talk to friends and female colleagues to receive validation for what they are doing. Of course, the best external sources of security are prestige and recognition through promotions, pay raises, awards, publications, speeches, and applause.

Challenge . The internal sources of challenge are competence and natural curiosity, and the willingness to pursue this curiosity. It also comes from identifying the "Seven As" and dealing with them effectively.

The external source of challenge has to do with the opportunity to be exposed to new and/or unsolved problems, to be given resources. If a woman sees that she is excluded from the opportunity to solve problems, then she will have no way to prove herself and to prove that she in fact can do it; besides she will lose her motivation to perform. A woman needs to ask, demand, insist on being given the opportunity to deal with problems. Again, of course, she is at higher risk than a man would be. If she is not able to resolve a task she has requested, she may feel twice as bad as any man who had been given these opportunities. Technical performance is the result of two things: individual resourcefulness and environmental facilitation, each repeatedly reinforcing the other. Both are required to use challenge creatively.

Pure science versus application . It is important to maintain interests in both these worlds — pure science allowing deep exploration, and application allowing broader knowledge. It is even important to have some exposure to administrative tasks because having administrative skills helps you understand how your organization runs, gives you some decision-making powers, and recognizes you as part of an ongoing administration. It gives you visibility and influence. It also may be a way of gaining membership, of earning one's stripes, of becoming one of the gang, of getting into the inner circle — into the informal network.

Compatibility versus competitiveness . Like men, women need colleagues who are personally compatible, yet intellectually competitive. How to know when this is what is occurring? One clue is that arguments about ideas are good intellectual competition, but arguments about personalities may be a sign of incompatibility. Conflict around ideas is healthy; it is best done in a climate of mutual trust, when differences of opinion are not seen as discord or conflict, but as building on each other's ideas, as more resources providing better solutions.

Self-direction versus other-direction . Effective scientists, who are self-directed and value freedom, still need interactions with colleagues to test ideas. Contact with superiors and peers helps determine which direction to take, although relying extensively on supervisors for stimulation can result in below-par performance. For the best motivation, a balance is needed.

A positive correlation has been found between high performance and interaction with colleagues. In other words, the more opportunities a person has to communicate with colleagues, the better her performance. In my work in high technology organizations, I have frequently encountered the lone scientist who likes to sit in her or his cubicle and work in isolation, preferring not to be disturbed. A good manager should be aware that people working in related areas need to be knowledgeable about each other's activities, interests, and problems, and should structure opportunities for interchange. Short, frequent contacts with many are better than longer contacts with only a few. The autonomous, isolated individual who lacks stimulation just does not do as well as the person who has contact with peers and superiors.

Groups . The research done on groups in scientific organizations shows that after four or five years, groups seem to decline in usefulness. If the membership remains the same, the group becomes static. A good group is one which can maintain interaction and competition in an atmosphere of both friendly warmth and intellectual rivalry. How is that achieved?

Let us look at the behavior of men and women in groups. The same men tend to be active participants for the life of the group, while men who are low participants often miss meetings or drop out. Women, however, have a different pattern of activity and dominance. They change from meeting to meeting. Women who were dominant and active in one meeting tend to draw out other women and men at subsequent meetings, saying "it is your turn this time." Men tend to make remarks to the group as a whole, not to individuals. Their remarks are impersonal and indirect. Women address remarks to individuals 90 percent of the time; these remarks are personal and direct. Men generalize and speak for others. Women personalize and speak for themselves. Men's topics deal frequently with competition, aggression, superiority, and are task-related. Women's topics deal with self-revelation, expressions of feelings, and are process-related. Men achieve camaraderie through the discussion of events and through joking. Women achieve closeness through discussion of self and family.

Male identity is based on status and achievement. Female identity is based on relationships and how the women perceive each other. Men jump from one topic to another. Women discuss the same topic for half an hour or more. Men exhibit competition and attempt to win in a power-orientation. Women exhibit cooperation and attempt to please other group members in a support-orientation. Men show strength and hide weaknesses. Women exhibit weaknesses and show vulnerabilities; they hide or repress strengths. Men express anger with ease, women with difficulty. Men are out of touch with their own feelings, which are either repressed or denied. Women are in touch with their own feelings. Men verbalize feelings with difficulty, women with ease. And men exteriorize blame by saying "it's your fault" or "it's their fault," while women internalize by saying "it's my fault." Contrary to stereotypes, research has shown that topics initiated by men get more air time and that men interrupt women much more frequently than the other way around.

As we look at typical behaviors in groups, we see that a group made of all men, as well as a group made of all women, misses out on a lot of contributions the opposite sex brings in. In the particular case of a few women in a large group of men, these behavior patterns tend to discount women's contributions to a discussion. In a scientific or technical setting, where contributions to content are essential and explicit, it is particularly critical for women to receive credit for their ideas and become highly visible to their colleagues through the strategies described above.

Satisfaction is related to intrinsic and extrinsic rewards . The intrinsic rewards in a high technology organization include the opportunity to use one's skills, to gain new knowledge, to deal with challenging problems, to be able to follow one's own ideas — in other words, to self-actualize. The extrinsic rewards include a good salary, higher administrative position, association with top executives, and recognition from peers and superiors. Both intrinsic and extrinsic rewards are needed. Just as success breeds success, achievement stimulates further achievement. Some labs reward creativity. Other labs reward productivity. If only productivity is rewarded, scientists may have to take well-established paths and not risk making errors.

It is well to note that creative potential peaks in the late 30s to early 40s for abstract, research disciplines, such as mathematics and theoretical physics. In the applied sciences, such as geology and biology, creative potential peaks later. However, it is possible to maintain peak performance by introducing new possibilities for learning through transfers, opportunities to meet and work with new colleagues, new projects, or new responsibilities. Some women may have a tendency to wish not to move on, having found security where they are. After a long struggle to obtain membership and recognition, they may be weary of taking on new and higher risks. But if upward mobility or further scientific achievement is the goal, then women must keep their creativity level at a peak.

Hazing. Hazing is a common experience for males, but an uncommon one for females. This can take very subtle forms, from being given all the menial tasks, to more stressful kinds of hazing which occur in organizations where team spirit is important. For example, in one company new engineers were given the most boring tasks to do and were not allowed to handle anything important for a year. It often takes many months of feeling overqualified, doing routine work, before a new technical employee, male or female, is trusted to handle major projects and is considered a member of the team. Women who are not expecting this kind of treatment believe it is discrimination due to their gender or even sexual harassment.

It is important for women in these situations to find out if men who are new to the organization undergo similar treatment. If so, they are being subjected to hazing and must respond in one of two ways — either laugh about it good-naturedly or display indifference, as if they are not touched by it. Anyone who reacts by being upset or angry is seen as not belonging. Hazing is a rite of passage, which helps a person become a member of the organization; it is an initiation rite. If you pass it, then you are part of the team who will haze other newcomers as they arrive. It is possible for women to mitigate the severity of the hazing when other women come in, or at least to inform them that it is a usual company practice and that they should not take it personally.

When we talk about hazing, what we are dealing with are the norms of an organization. Norms are important for women to know because they are the unwritten rules stating what people should and should not do. Norms exist everywhere; although they are not posted or talked about, they are nonetheless pervasive. Norms lend stability and predictability to organizational life. Although they are neither good nor bad in themselves, they may be functional or dysfunctional for a particular purpose.

The only people who can break norms with impunity are leaders or people who have a great deal of seniority. A new person is sanctioned for breaking norms, so it is important for a new woman coming into an organization to "psych out" what the ongoing norms are and follow them until she has earned enough trust and credibility that she can deviate from the norms and set some new ones herself.

Women are entering high technology organizations in greater and greater numbers. They and the ones who are already there are creating precedents for those who follow. They are the groundbreakers without role models; they are the risk takers without support. These women have the added burden of sponsoring large numbers of women coming in who will make demands on them. They will have to balance their time between pursuing their own work and helping younger women learn the ropes and get established. Let us remember that everyone of us who looks good makes the others look better. My verse "Leadership" expresses this best.[4]

> If the best of me
> Can make more of you,
> Then the best of you
> Will reflect on me.

This is a time of challenge and excitement; as always in periods of transition, it is also a time of pain and confusion. The women who are the first to enter technical fields will experience both the difficulties and the rewards.

Notes

1. Adapted from Natasha Josefowitz, *Paths to Power: A Woman's Guide from First Job to Top Executive* (Reading, MA: Addison Wesley, 1980).
2. Natasha Josefowitz, "The Clonal Effect in Organizations," *Management Review* (September 1979).
3. Categories adapted from Donald C. Pelz and Frank M. Richards, *Scientists in Organizations: Productive Climates for Research and Development*, revised edition (Ann Arbor, MI: Institute for Social Research, University of Michigan, 1976).
4. From Natasha Josefowitz, *Is This Where I Was Going?* (New York: Warner Books, forthcoming).

Chapter 23

Bambi Meets Godzilla:

Life in the Corporate Jungle

by Sandra Emerson

The technologies that dominate our daily lives and international politics are the products of corporate America. Everything from tampons to television, from rifles to neutron bombs is proposed, lobbied for, and produced by the major corporations of North America. One key to women exerting control over technology is gaining corporate power. This is doubly difficult in the high technology corporations shaping our future because the career path to the top in such companies involves both managerial and technical expertise — areas in which women traditionally have been outcasts at best.

Unfortunately, simply choosing and training for a career in science or engineering is not enough to put a woman on the path to technological upper management, although such a choice may well suffice for a man. At some point the technological woman must come to grips with managerial science and more importantly with corporate politics. It is particularly in the arena of corporate politics that the technological woman is most apt, as Fisk and Barron say, to "re-create Bambi meets Godzilla."[1]

Given the functioning of the North American marketplace it is not surprising that there is an increasing number of management courses aimed at women (a veritable market of Bambis). Although some of what these courses offer is beneficial, they often fail to deal with the realities of corporate politics and more specifically, they fail to acknowledge the unique difficulties confronting women in technological settings.

In fact, most management training programs for women actually provide a disservice by pitching "survival" techniques, such as assertiveness training, as success techniques. As an example, most CEOs (chief executive officers) *are* aggressive to the point of being offensive — they are obsessed with notions of power and success; they are not even perceived as "nice" people by their subordinates. They would fail miserably on a test of the material that women so willing assimilate in the belief that it will take them to the top. Often these courses are offered by women from fields that are perceived by technologists as "non-threatening," such as personnel or training. Thus the experience these instructors bring to the classroom is only partially relevant and sometimes misleading for women aspiring to technological management. That many of these courses are sponsored by large corporations is not surprising. It is in the best interest of the existing corporate power structure to offer management training for women and minorities to teach them "their place."

In view of the lack of information on women, technology, and management, I offer this brief guide to things as they are in high technology upper management. This is not intended to be a manual on style or managerial technique, since most courses cover those topics *ad nauseum* . It is intended to be the link that's missing from most such courses: a description of the real world.

The Scene

The world of technological management is a grim and sterile one. The successful technologist is most often a person who prefers dealing with things to dealing with people. Things, after all, are predictable; volumes have been written classifying, graphing, and explaining physical phenomena with remarkably little debate about the conclusions. The world of things provides absolute answers to seemingly complex questions. Intuition is denied (although it is often used). *Analysis* and *synthesis* are the macho tools of the trade. Sally Hacker has shown that many men who self-select for technical careers are emotionally-stunted whiz kids incapable of coping with normal human relationships.[2] Technology, and by extension the technological workplace, have become vehicles of escape from reality in general and frequently from women in particular. Small wonder that women find themselves unwelcome in the technical environment.

From this body of emotional cripples a few rise to the ranks of management. That they possess few of the "people skills" normally seen in managers is acceptable in the technological environment. After all their colleagues and subordinates are all in the same boat. Even the most rudimentary techniques of manipulation are sufficient, if masked with a little managerial jargon. In fact, second only to "bussing posteriors" (in the jargon: kissing ass), it is the ability to deliver managerial buzz words with a macho stance that counts. This might seem a simple talent to master, but most technologists are amazingly inept at language skills. Needless to say, most women, although they have far greater verbal skills, have trouble with posterior bussing and the macho stance. A prime example of the macho stance is portrayed by one manager I know who attains a noticeable erection every time he gives a presentation to upper management. His condition is accentuated if anyone questions his material: a hard (forgive the pun) act for a woman to follow.

The linguistics of management deserve a brief digression. The following phrases are common: "got him by the short hairs," "got him coming and going (or front and rear)," "he got his whizzer caught in the wringer," or the most popular summary of corporate strategy: "when you have them by the balls, their hearts and minds will follow." It's no surprise that women have difficulty conquering this vocabulary or are viewed with suspicion if they do.

The distinction between technologists as workers and technologists as managers is an important one.[3] Unlike other fields of endeavor, technology offers no entry-level managerial positions which lead to the top. The managerial positions on the path to the president's office can only be entered by "crossing over" from advanced technical positions. True, areas such as personnel or contracts administration offer entry-level management positions, but these career paths "top out" far from the president's office in technical companies. Generally, once technologists reach the higher rungs of the technical career ladder, they are confronted with the need to "enter management," because pay and "perks" (perquisites) for technical positions are limited.

Strange as it may seem, in the high tech world the rewards for outstanding technical expertise are far lower than the rewards for mediocre management. Thus, many technologists who reach this point make the obvious choice and become managers — a career path for which they are uniquely unsuited. Some corporations claim to offer dual career paths, technical and managerial, but the interval over which a real dual option exists normally stretches across only a few pay grades. Beyond that range the few remaining technical positions are in fact managerial, at least in their requirements for political skill and their emphasis on other nontechnical issues such as marketing and budgeting.

For technologists as *workers* , performance and technical skills are important. Many corporations make a pseudoscience of measuring the performance and skills of their "worker bees." Astute workers, including most women in technology, quickly learn these formulas for measuring performance. Internalizing these formulas may suffice to bring some women part way up the corporate ladder, but as they approach the top of the technical ranks women frequently are confused by a subtle shift in the rules. The technical competence that is praised in a "worker bee" counts for little in the managerial ranks. There is more at work than the shift from dealing with things to dealing with people. All logic seems to be gone. The woman has now met corporate politics and without a long history of men's room conversations, she is most likely unprepared. The greater the technical skills that brought her this far, the greater the likelihood that she has been excluded along the way from the rudiments of the political process. She has arrived by brute force excellence into a world where excellence carries little weight. It is likely that her very technical excellence has frightened those with less technical and more political savvy.

The King's Court

Outside of Japan, most contemporary corporate structures are drawn
from feudal models. The chief executive officer (CEO) is the king. His
wife is the queen. The chosen few who immediately surround the CEO
(his feudal lords) pay tribute, bow and scrape, and perform other similar
duties appropriate for "upper management" or "senior executives." In
large multinational corporations this structure is re-created in divisions
or operating groups, in which case the CEO is replaced locally by a
general manager or president, who extracts tribute locally, but himself
bows and scrapes in the presence of the CEO at headquarters. Headquarters in any organization is the center of the corporate universe; divisions and subsidiaries are the provinces.

The resident king draws about him a court consisting of the heir(s) apparent, a court jester, a lackey, and a tax collector. For those not familiar
with the workings of such an inner circle it is easy to confuse the roles
(especially since the players invariably all dress alike). The heir(s) apparent in a technological corporation all have technical backgrounds and
may carry titles such as vice-president of marketing, programs, or
engineering. The vice-president of research is rarely an heir apparent as
a result of his (rarely her) emphasis on technology rather than business.
The titles in this category are varied, the trickiest being special assistant
to the president, a position that is a dead end if it's permanent, but an indication of someone moving either up or out otherwise. (Permanent in
this context is anything over three years).

The positions of lackey and jester are filled by those with nontechnical
backgrounds in personnel, law, or public relations. The tax collector,
often called the head "bean counter" is the comptroller or senior-most
accountant. Men in these latter categories may serve as good sources of
information, and because of their presence in the inner circle should be
paid the appropriate tribute, but they are not suitable role models. Many
a technical manager has gone astray on the path to power by emulating
the court jester.

These stratospheric positions are buttressed by a pyramid of lower
functionaries whose contribution to the management process can be summarized by the oft-heard dictum: "Shit gathers momentum as it rolls
downhill."

The Coin of the Realm

The unit of exchange in technological corporations is not technology or
even money. It is power. Power is related to money in two ways: first,
money (budgetary control or responsibility) can be used as a power tool
and second, there's only so much of each to go around. One executive's
power gain is another's loss. What is power? The ability to get things
done. This means the ability to control and direct the use of resources.
When there is a fixed amount or kind of resource, there is a fixed amount

of power. It is important to remember that unless an organization is growing substantially, your acquisition of power means someone else's loss, which in turn probably means you've made an enemy.

Information can be traded for power. Sometimes technical information can be traded for power, but usually not. Other types of useful information include: who's screwing whom (figuratively and otherwise), when the next power brokers' meeting will be held and who will attend, who has a drinking problem, who likes to gamble, who's getting a divorce, and other morsels of juicy gossip. Forget the admonition to Thumper you memorized as a child about not saying anything unless it's "nice." It is far more useful to remember that "nice guys don't win." Secretaries are a valuable and often overlooked source of information; so are marketeers. Both respond prolifically when treated with an iota of respect.

On Strategies and Style

Almost by definition women don't have the correct corporate style because they use the wrong restroom. Style, like beauty, is in the eye of the beholder. There is a list of perceptions of style that has made the rounds of many a corporate copying machine. It begins with the contrasts: "He's aggressive; she's a bitch. He's well dressed; she's a clothes horse."

If you don't dress like a hooker, you will be perceived as a threat and hence "inappropriately" dressed (so much for the "dress-for-success" theories). If, on the other hand, you dress like a hooker, you will be treated like one. Dress appropriately for business. If this seems too puzzling, stick to academic research. Disregard most advice from male colleagues and supervisors regarding dress.

Mentors have become a popular topic on the "management-for-women" circuit. The mentor notion is a polite way of saying that one must have friends at the top, because most of the advice one receives is not intended to be helpful. But before rushing out to collect mentors, it is vital to recall the story of Greeks bearing gifts. Advice, even that rare commodity of well-intentioned advice, often brings with it the cultural and sex-stereotyped biases of the giver. Be sure you understand what is expected in return. You may see yourself as a budding executive, but your mentor may not get past "budding" in your definition.

Short courses on managerial styles for women may provide useful techniques. But in the corporate world of titles, degrees count for much more. For women fighting the battle for recognition in high tech corporations, masters degrees and Ph.D.s in technical fields are a definite plus. They won't solve all the problems, but they will eliminate some of the constant need to prove that one really can do the things one has already done. MBAs are only of use in high tech corporations if they are backed up by at least a bachelor's degree in a technical subject.

Women have a delightful but often fatal tendency to see through the insanity of perks. They know they can do as much work in an office without a window as one with a window. If you are promoted to senior engineer and other senior engineers have window offices, don't be demure, don't be logical; demand a window office. No one will see you as a senior engineer if you don't have the window, which serves as the badge of rank. In fact you can't do as much work without a window because you will waste inordinate amounts of time convincing people that you really have the rank you have. In a corporate structure derived from feudal and military themes, it is inconceivable that a captain would willingly wear sergeant's stripes.

Team playing is an important and difficult subject. You must seem like you're doing it, even though everyone else is looking out for *numero uno* . This can be difficult when your own team doesn't want you to play. (It won't.) Rocking the boat or blowing the whistle is frequently the morally right action, but rarely a power strategy. You'll find that everyone else closes ranks leaving you on the outside. It is a good way to lose what few supporters you have, even those who seem to agree that the boat needs rocking.

Power is like jelly beans. You begin corporate life with a few jelly beans. Technical excellence gains you some jelly beans. Political savvy gains many more jelly beans. Working long hours does not gain you as many jelly beans as you think it does. Any difference of style from the local norm costs jelly beans. Any change costs jelly beans. Ignorance of the rules costs jelly beans. No one can tell you how to spend your jelly beans, but many will try. There are more ways to lose jelly beans than there are to gain them. You can't spend what you don't have.

If what I've said makes it sound like women can't win in high tech corporations, it will be refreshing to remember Lore Harp and Carol Ely, who started Vector Graphic, Inc. in 1979 in Los Angeles, using a spare bedroom, with a shower for their warehouse. They now run a multimillion dollar company whose advertising copy stresses the human side of the computers they design and sell. Information distributed to Vector Graphics' shareholders indicates that childcare and household help is a regular part of Harp's and Ely's compensation packages. Their company stands as a landmark in the progress of women succeeding in and changing the world of technology.

Notes

1. J. Fisk and R. Barron, *The Official MBA Handbook* (New York: Simon and Schuster, 1982).
2. Sally Hacker, "The Culture of Engineering: Woman, Workplace, and Machine," *Women's Studies International Quarterly* 4 (Summer 1981): 341-354.
3. Eduardo del Rio (Ruis), *Marx for Beginners* (New York: Pantheon, 1979).

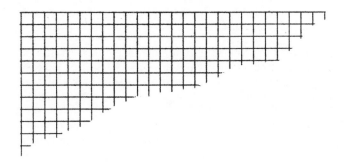

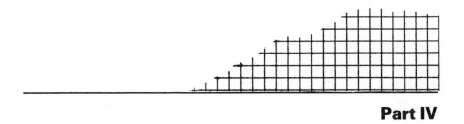

Part IV

The Politics of Tomorrow

It may seem puzzling that the first half of this section deals with reproduction and healthcare. But no issue is more central to the future than a woman's right to choose what happens in and to her body. As an intense political issue, reproductive control has already taken center stage in the bitter battle over abortion rights. The personal cannot become more political than this. Unfortunately the emotional rhetoric of the Right To Life movement has clouded the serious moral, legal, and medical issues of embryo development, genetic manipulation, forced sterilization, class-based childbearing, and eugenic control that will soon confront us as "engineered conception" becomes more widespread. The debates over new forms of parenthood may make the early twentieth century debates over birth control — not choosing parenthood — seem mild by comparison.

Two first-person stories indicate the intensity of these issues. Suzanne Rubin's anger blazes about the current practices of artificial insemination services; she passionately implores an end to the creation of children custom-made to meet their parents' needs. By contrast, Karen Smith, a surrogate mother, seems quite content with her choice to offer a child to another couple. In a fascinating, detailed report, Barbara Winters outlines the procedures and status of various forms of reproductive engineering, from *in vitro* fertilization to cloning. Her article challenges us to recognize that science fiction has already become reality; if women do not become involved in defining their reproductive interest, they will find that a mostly-male medical establishment has defined it for them.

In an all too brief survey of other issues affecting women's health, Alberta Parker describes the complex web of social and political decision makers who structure medical care options. Carefully outlining a wide variety of healthcare situations, from diseases of aging to electronic fetal monitoring and birth control, she, too, emphasizes that women must be involved in the setting of priorities for research and healthcare distribution; the political can be very personal. Sally Gearhart's analysis of feminist futures in science fiction touches directly on some of these topics as she discusses feminist utopias in which alternative reproductive technologies, among others, are central to creating alternative futures.

The second half of this section turns to explicit techniques for encouraging women to take hold of tomorrow. Because of the well-documented tendency of young women to turn away from math and science as they reach puberty, it is critical to reach them before they become what Judy Smith has called "math-anxious technophobes." Nancy Kreinberg and Elizabeth Stage provide some concrete suggestions for encouraging "computer literacy" in their illustration of the centrality of the computer to the future. Tish Sommers, a long-time political activist, puts her community organizing talents to work in a not-impossible fantasy of neighborhood block clubs as the backbone for human-scale, decentralized, locally-controlled technology. Her vision would empower all the currently disenfranchised members of society — women, the elderly, minorities, and children — to create a future that works for all of us.

Last, but not least, Pat Huckle takes on the futurists. Her feminist assessment of most projections about the future (look at who is making them) is coupled with an assessment of what feminism, as a political and social movement, can do to change those projections. More remains to be done in another volume about the very political interaction of the federal government with what Dwight Eisenhower first described as the military-industrial complex. The intertwined relationship of these entities goes far in determining the path of research and development, and thus future technology, long before the public is even aware that choices have been made. Particular attention needs to be paid to military technology, the most glaring and dangerous example of "the bigger the boys, the bigger the toys." Feminists need to find an answer to what makes the technology of death such an attractive seducer of male energy.

The Technological Woman has made it clear that technical design is a matter of choice, not natual law. Just because a technological innovation *can* be done, is no reason that it *must* be done. Technological choices have very different impacts according to gender, race, and class; women must act to ensure their place in the future. Perhaps a participant at a 1981 conference on Future, Technology and Woman summed it up best in her description of what she learned at the conference. "The future is now," she said, "and we'd better get involved."

Chapter 24

Reproductive Options I

A Spermdonor Baby Grows Up

by Suzanne Rubin

My name is Suzanne Rubin and I am the Los Angeles County Representative for Concerned United Birthparents (CUB). I am also a birthparent who searched and found my teenage daughter. Two weeks after I located my daughter, I learned that I was the product of artificial insemination by donor (AID). With great pain, my father told me what he felt I had a right to know — that he was not my father. He said he couldn't live with the lies anymore. Since my mother had died two years earlier, he felt he had the right to end their pact to keep the truth from me. Although the truth has caused both of us great pain, I am most grateful for finally receiving it. Many of my childhood mysteries are now solved. In the past year I have conducted my own research into AID, and have begun to solidify my feelings about being produced by AID. I would like to share with you what I've found out and just how I feel about being a 32-year old spermdonor baby.

Contrary to popular assumption, AID is not new. The technique itself was perfected in the eighteenth century in Europe. The first child born in the United States by AID was born in 1866. AID has operated in a legal and moral "no man's land" to a large degree since then. Some states have statutes covering AID, but most do not, and those statutes are often inconsistent. The issues involved are falsification of birth certificates, physician's liability in performing AID, illegitimacy of the child, inheritance rights, adultery, and, if the couple should divorce, does the husband have any right to custody of the child?

In the late 1940s in this country, California appears to have been a haven for infertile couples who wished to have children by AID. Doctors apparently could be found in California who would perform the insemination, and who were willing to sign a falsified birth certificate naming the mother's husband as the father of the child, completely eradicating the fact that AID had taken place. The legal status of these inseminations is still unchallenged. Who was there to challenge the procedure? Certainly not the physician — he was an accomplice. Certainly not the infertile couple — it would mean "coming out of the closet" forever. And certainly not the donor — he's anonymous. In some states (such as New York) AID was legal, but the original birth certificate named the donor as the natural father and the husband carried through with a step-parent adoption, thereby leaving a "legal trail" as far as the child's identity. California offered an option to couples which circumvented adoption — the issuance of a phony birth certificate — thus providing many couples with a way to live out their lives with *The Big Lie*.

At present, the more than 5,000 physicians who are willing to perform AID in the United States are bound by no moral, legal, or professional guidelines in the practice of AID. There are estimates that 10,000 children are born every year in the United States by this procedure. The number of those who are already walking around and who are the products of AID is extremely difficult to calculate due to a shroud of secrecy — estimates range from 50,000 to 1 million. Spermbanks are operating around the country with no external regulations. They operate under their own rules, and of course, are primarily operated as business enterprises. The more reputable spermbanks advertise for spermdonors primarily in college newspapers, and will screen their donors for medical and psychological problems. Such screening, however, is completely arbitrary. The records may or may not be maintained over a reasonably long period of time. Private physicians may solicit donors in any way they wish. Oftentimes, the physician himself is rumored to have been the donor.

The same ignorance, secrecy, and stigma which applied to adoption in the past, apply to AID today. Today's AID parents are advised to "never tell" their children the truth. In an obvious respect, the AID child is more a "natural" child of the family than an adopted child, but parents are encouraged to deceive the AID child but be truthful with the adopted child. There appears to be a genuine fear among AID practitioners that to reveal the truth to an AID child would create insurmountable social and psychological problems both for the family as a whole and for the child. It is only now, in light of an enlightened adoption community, that the deception necessary to keep the child in ignorance of his or her true origins is being questioned by a very few AID practitioners. Since spermbanks can be tremendously profitable businesses, it is sometimes most difficult for the AID practitioner to pay heed to the moral and ethical issues involved in AID, rather than just to the profit and loss statements that the business generates.

Many AID parents use the excuse of "protecting the child," while they are in fact protecting themselves — from the embarrassment of infertility, from the fear that their children will abandon them if there is no blood tie, and from the embarrassment of having a need for a child that is so strong that they are willing to take "genetic pot luck" from a total stranger. Surely the adoptee who learns her parents have voluntarily relinquished her to strangers has as difficult a time coming to terms with her origins as an AID child. The idea that a healthy family relationship could be built upon a foundation of deception and lies is absolutely ludicrous. In my own family, the lies warped the relationships and poisoned them beyond repair. There are also the moral and ethical questions as to whether parents have the right to deceive their own children about the truth of their origins. Is this really what parenthood is about? *I think not* .

It is my opinion that sexism is part of the reason AID has been allowed to flourish in such secrecy and with such conscious abandonment of the rights of the child produced. There is a brand of sexism which contends that women are the "babymakers and nurturers," and that one sperm-donor is as acceptable as the next. This assumes that just who is the "real Daddy" doesn't even matter, and really shouldn't. I believe this attitude to be ultimately demeaning to men and to all loving fathers. I believe that the fact that over 95 percent of the practicing physicians in this country are male has been another boon to AID. There almost seems to be a tacit agreement among the male doctor and the sterile husband to "keep it quiet" and "under wraps" — a sensitivity and shared belief in the pseudorelationship between a man's sperm count and his worth as a man. And, of course, biologically it's much easier to lie about who a child's father is than who its mother is.

Although I was not told of my true identity for more than 30 years, I always knew as a child that something wasn't "kosher" about my parentage. I resembled no one on either side of my family; my temperament, intellectual capacity, and interests did not seem to fit. I stuck out like a sore thumb. Being the only tall, blue-eyed redhead in a family of shortish brunettes didn't help. By the time I was five or six years old, I was conducting searches of the house looking for the "papers" I knew I would find if I were adopted. Although I searched and asked questions for years, I never found any proof to corroborate my feelings of not belonging. To this day, when people see my father and me together, they still remark, "Gee, where'd you get her? She sure doesn't look like you." At this point, I cannot begin to understand how my father weathered those remarks for all those years. He never has come to terms with his own infertility and is still unable to discuss it with anyone. I must have been a constant reminder to him that he was sterile, and for him that meant a shameful and embarrassing lack of manliness.

Although I was profoundly shocked by the truth of my origins, I have had more than a year to assess my reaction. Over time, my feelings may mellow, but I do not believe I will ever reconcile myself to my parents' decision to use AID. The one word which most correctly describes how I feel about being the product of AID is *anguished* . While I was conducting the search for my daughter and was reading about adoption and adoptees, I had an almost smug feeling that I, at least, knew who my parents were and although my childhood was an unhappy one, at least I "belonged" in my family. I knew where my connections were. I knew who my ancestors were. And it was an undeniably smug feeling. I was deeply saddened to learn of adoptees' pain in not knowing their origins, and I have a deep commitment to adoption reform since my daughter is an adoptee. But I did not realize just how gutwrenching it is to not know who your mother or father is.

Since I have learned of my own beginnings, I have been feeling just that pain. The words *bastard* and *illegitimate* have a new significance to me. I am an adult with a fully-formed identity and sense of self, and I have been shaken to the core by knowing that I was produced by AID. I used to be proud of my heritage — now I'm the bastard daughter of an unknown and amoral father.

I consider myself to be a religious and moral person with a strong sense of integrity. Sadly, it has become difficult for me to reconcile my religious and moral convictions with the fact that an act which I consider to be immoral, unethical, and adulterous produced me. How do I reconcile my sense of integrity with knowing that my father sold what was the essence of my life for $25 to a total stranger, and then walked away without a second look back? What kind of a man sells himself and his child so cheaply and so easily? What kind of a man separates his sperm from its procreative qualities so completely? That kind of a man is my father. I am enraged that any person could be so blase about my life and so uncaring. I have asked several AID practitioners why young males sell their sperm. To quote one of the directors of a large Los Angeles sperm-bank, "They do it for the bucks, Suzanne." How do I learn to live without profound pain and disappointment knowing that this man, who is my father and who is my flesh and blood, "did it for the bucks?"

I have begun the search for my biological father to find some answers. I have sufficient nonidentifying information to locate this man, and I will pursue the search to its conclusion. It is absolutely my rage and my pain that are fueling the search. It is most important for me to establish that my father was something more than an animal who procreated for money. Surely he has attributes other than his willingness to hire himself out for "stud service."

Since knowing the truth, my relationship with my father has deteriorated. And although my mother is dead, the knowledge that she deceived me all my life will never be forgotten. I feel that I was cruelly deceived. By lying to me all my life, my dignity as their child and their integrity as my parents was irreparably damaged. Because I was a child, my trust in them was exploited and used to cover up what they themselves considered "unpalatable" and of questionable morality.

Historically, AID was developed to meet the needs of the infertile couple. Priority was assigned to meeting the couple's need to have a child. *This must be challenged.* As in modern adoption practice, the child's needs must be recognized as having absolute priority. If prospective parents cannot put the child's long-term needs ahead of their own, then, by God, they should not be parents. AID children must be told at an early age the truth of their origins. Successful parent/child relationships are not confined to those where the biological tie exists. The only bonds that really hold are those of love and trust and mutual respect. Living *The Big Lie* destroys the trust that is so important in parent/child relationships. And, of course, it is a short-sighted and self-destructive fantasy to think that such a family secret can be forever maintained. Virtually all AID adults who have been interviewed sensed a "family secret" to which they were not privy.

When one begins to consider the child's needs, it is apparent that many AID practices must change. The AID child must have the same rights as an adopted child — to be told the truth, to have a legal status, to have a channel of information about the biological parent, and the provision for contact, if desired. The issuance of phony birth certificates is an absolute outrage and must be stopped. It is a shameful way for a law-abiding society to act — to legally sanction deceiving a child about its own father. Spermbanks and AID practitioners must be held accountable for their products and procedures.

I see AID becoming a more and more acceptable way to have a child in the future, and I do not believe the practice will be stopped. But we must have some legal and moral guidelines to follow, and we must have some faith and belief that this procedure is not so abominable that children will be aghast at what their parents have done.

Selling one's sperm — or for that matter, renting out one's womb — to create a life you do not want appears, at least to me, to be immoral, unethical, and alarmingly irresponsible. I do not believe every person has the God-given "right" to be a parent. For those couples who cannot have children any other way, I would suggest to them that there are thousands of children already walking this earth who desperately need loving parents and stable homes. I am deeply frightened by the manufacture of children to meet their parents' needs. We are creating countless numbers of children for parents who desperately need children — and somehow I don't think that's the way it's supposed to work.

More than 400 years ago, William Shakespeare said, "It's a wise father that knows his own child." It is an even wiser child who knows her own father.

Reproductive Options II

Surrogate Motherhood: An Interview

with Karen Smith

Surrogate parenting — just a few years ago, neither the term nor the practice existed; today, as defined by the Surrogate Parent Foundation, it means:

> an alternative method of childbearing for an infertile couple when the wife is unable to bear a child. In this procedure, a woman known as the surrogate agrees to be artificially inseminated with the husband's sperm and carry the baby for the couple. The surrogate further agrees to relinquish all parental rights. The husband, being the natural father, assumes custody with his wife, who then legally adopts the child.[1]

Karen Smith, who was 17 weeks pregnant — and showing — at the time of this interview, has two children of her own and was the first surrogate to sign a contract with the Surrogate Parent Foundation.

Q: Why did you choose to be a surrogate mother?
A: My first reason, I guess, was for the money — I'll be receiving $10,000. At the time (I decided) my daughter was going to be starting first grade at a private school and that would help pay three to four years of her tuition. Basically it was my Mom's and Dad's idea to do it; they came to my house and told me about it. They had seen the lawyer (from the Surrogate Parent Foundation) on a TV show and they talked to me about it and thought it would be great for me.

Q: Are you a single parent?
A: Yes, but I will be getting married soon.

Q: So your life circumstances had more to do with your decision than any feelings about this as an issue or a cause?
A: I wasn't even concerned about that. I was more concerned just about

myself and my family. How would my kids handle it? Or my family? Mainly how would I handle it? I still don't really care how anyone else feels about it.

Q: How have you been handling it? Have you found that there were awkward times?
A: No, I haven't yet. Everything has been so positive — overwhelmingly positive — it's surprising.

Q: Had you expected that there might be some negative response or questioning?
A: Yes, I thought I would run into a little bit more of the negative side of it. Because I'm a very open person, if anybody asks me anything, I tell them all about it. I kind of expected it, since it is a controversial thing.

Q: Do you think you'd have become a surrogate mother if you hadn't already had a child?
A: If I hadn't had a child? No, I wouldn't even consider it. I had been going to one psychiatrist first — because you do go to a psychiatrist through the whole thing — and I disagreed with her because she was accepting girls who were young and never had children.

Q: Have you heard stories, then, of younger women who've never been pregnant deciding not to give up the child?
A: Yes, I even have talked a few out of it (surrogating). It'll still be around in the next couple years — have a child first. See then if you want to do something like this. Now I go to another psychiatrist (I meet with a group of girls, of other surrogate ladies) and she will not accept anybody who hasn't had a child and who knows what they're going through. Who knows that the first three months they're going to be sick or tired. Or that the next to last five months they're going to be sick or whatever.

Q: Or maybe because they have their own child perhaps have less of —
A: — an attachment. Oh definitely. I just have to say that I don't even consider this child mine at all. I never have. If I ever had doubts, I would never have gone this far into the program. I've been in it for over a year now. I was pregnant once before and I miscarried in October (1981) with the same couple I'm pregnant with now.

Q: So even from the beginning you accepted that you were going to let the child go?
A: Oh yes, definitely. I think it's the only fair thing to do to yourself. I have heard other surrogates say, "Well, I think I could do it." But I say, you should never be sitting there if you're still in the process of thinking you *might* be able to do it. I feel you should have that all worked out within yourself *before* you get anywhere. That's what I felt I did. I couldn't imagine being pregnant and then saying "no, this is my child" after nine months. And having this couple who have been waiting for ten

years and now they're nine months closer — and then to say "no, no, no, I'm taking this away from you." That would destroy them.

Q: Have you met this couple?
A: Oh yes, quite a few times. I talk to them every time I'm at the doctor's. When I first found out I was pregnant after five months of trying, I called her up. She was just ecstatic — it was great.

Q: Do you have a sense that you will end up with a lifelong relationship to both the couple and the child?
A: Well, in a sense. We have agreed to keep in touch with the lawyer for 20-25 years; if I ever change my name or address or move or in case something happens genetically. Or if the child gets to an age that it would like to come and see me, its biological mother.

Q: This happens to be a very open couple in terms of wanting their child to know (about its biological parentage). Is that a requirement of the Surrogate Parent Foundation?
A: No, it isn't. It's worked out that way, which I think is the best way to do it, but it isn't a requirement. That's what's so different about this whole program. When I called my couple and told them we finally got pregnant, they couldn't wait to tell the grandparents, both sets of grandparents, and their friends, and everybody. You know, it's just like *she's* pregnant now. We're finally *all* pregnant. It makes it a whole different situation and, I think, a better situation. It's not such a heavy thing for either couple, because they've already worked it out within themselves to go into something like this. And already she's accepted that she's infertile.

Q: By having the kind of personal relationship you do with this couple, you don't feel like a "baby factory" then?
A: Oh, no. I first got into this program — I was the first surrogate for the foundation — that's why I was the one that went on **60 Minutes** and everything — because it *is* so personal. When I had the miscarriage, for example, the couple called me at the hospital; they sent me flowers. It makes it, I don't know, not easier, but worth it. You just don't feel that this couple is saying, "Well, let's hurry. Let's get this woman pregnant. Hurry up."

When I met my couple, I insisted that they had to be in the delivery room — I wouldn't have had them as my couple if they weren't. They were kind of shocked about it at first; they hadn't even thought about it. I told them they have to experience the childbirth. They have to be there to watch their child being born, especially the mother. And I told them the whole satisfaction of it all for me is watching them. Watching their faces. And I'll have the opportunity, if I want, to see the child in the nursery later. And I probably will go because I'm curious to see what the child looks like, what kind of a child I gave them.

Q: That seems natural. You can't just put down a shutter on your own feelings.
A: Right. And I wouldn't want to. But then I have my own life, my two kids. I hope to have another one.

Q: But that would be with your new husband? You wouldn't do the surrogate motherhood again?
A: That depends on my situation. Where I'm living, what my lifestyle is, what's going on.

Q: So you might consider it again. So far the experience has been positive enough?
A: Oh yes. I would only do it for the same couple though. We have talked about it. They have "first refusal" on me in my contract, if I do decide I'd like to do it again. To say "yes, we'd like another child" or "no, we wouldn't." It would be perfect; genetically, the kids would be exactly the same.

Q: Would you have accepted sperm from anyone or were you able to be selective about the kind of child you wanted to carry?
A: I think it's mainly that I wouldn't have accepted from a couple that I wasn't comfortable with. We sat and met for a couple hours the first time and first impressions mean a lot. If I was uncomfortable with them the first time, I would have said "no". They have a right to refuse a surrogate, just as a surrogate has the right to refuse a couple. No, I don't think it would be from just anybody.

Q: Did they do a lot of matching before you met the family, in terms of your appearance or religion or whatever?
A: No, not really. That's not a main factor in the whole thing. Fortunately, I don't know how it ever came about, but the lady I'm having the baby for happens to look more like my sister than my sister does. Same coloring of hair, same color eyes, same color complexion. I think they try to match you up somewhat, but a couple will meet surrogates and they may be totally different looking. You never know. The main thing is your mental state and your health; they're the most important things. And they do take you inside and out in both ways, which is really good.

Q: If the situation were reversed, would you want someone to do the same thing for you?
A: Oh definitely. I couldn't imagine going through life without any children at all. And if I had the opportunity and someone would do this for me, I would be so grateful.

Q: Why were you willing to publicize your involvement? I would imagine there are some other surrogate mothers who feel this is a very private decision.

A: Well, I feel so strongly about it, I'd like people to just get it out into the open and get it into our society and to realize it's not such a taboo, terrible, disgusting thing as some people think it is. You know, when I first was thinking about it, I would mention surrogating and some people didn't even know what the terminology meant; a majority of them didn't. So this way we get it out and in the next five years it'll be out there. It's a new, upcoming thing.

Q: Do you have anything else you'd like to add?
A: It's just that I know some people consider me to be a "baby seller." They want to know how I could do this to my body and myself. I say, "Well, it's *my* body, you know." I just want people to realize how important it is and how much it means to a lot of people and that it's really a beautiful thing. The giving of family, and birth, and children to someone who's without. It's great.

Notes

1. From the Surrogate Parent Foundation brochure, "Surrogate Parenting."

The Surrogate Parent Foundation, Inc., a California nonprofit organization, has been established to gather and disseminate current and accurate information on the many aspects of surrogate parenting. The Foundation also advises legislators and establishes ethical and procedural guidelines regarding new laws, protecting those involved.

For further information about surrogate parenting contact: The Surrogate Parent Foundation, 12435 Oxnard Street, North Hollywood, CA 91606, (213) 506-1804.

Chapter 25

Engineered Conception:

The New Parenthood

by Barbara Winters

In the past few years there have been dramatic breakthroughs in the ability of science to affect the process of conception. Through procedures like artificial insemination and the recently successful *in vitro* fertilization and embryo transfer, technology already has the power to alter radically the nature of reproduction. Conceivable developments in genetic modification, human cloning, and the artificial womb may offer choices that can affect all aspects of human life, from the nature of the family to the composition of future generations. These technological changes will have strong impacts on women, in whose bodies reproduction traditionally has occurred.

Some find the prospects that reproductive technology offers terrifying, others liberating. I want to explore some of the implications of these procedures, focusing especially on how women's interests may be affected. By describing the techniques in some detail, I hope to clear up some misconceptions and challenge the common view that the development of "test tube babies" signals the advent of Huxley's **Brave New World**.

I should say at the outset that I am not opposed to technology in principle; in particular, I resist arguments that all reproductive technology is evil because it is "unnatural." Arguments from "nature" to what is good are usually suspect; they have often been employed against women moving out of traditional roles.[1] So I recommend approaching these developments initially with cautious neutrality. Before accepting or rejecting them we must have a clear understanding of their social, moral, and legal ramifications.

I will focus primarily on three types of reproductive technology: one well-established — artificial insemination; one just beginning to be used — *in vitro* fertilization; and one not yet feasible — cloning.

Artificial Insemination

First performed at the end of the eighteenth century, artificial insemination is a technique in which semen, usually produced from masturbation by a donor, is injected by syringe in or near a woman's cervix at the time of ovulation. The donor can be the woman's husband (AIH: artificial insemination by husband), who for various reasons might be unsuccessful in accomplishing fertilization through intercourse. But the technique allows for more unconventional possibilities as well. In cases where the husband has sperm that are abnormal in shape or behavior, lacks sperm entirely, or carries a genetic defect, the wife may be inseminated with semen donated by a friend, relative, or stranger (AID: artificial insemination by donor). This option has always existed via "natural" means; however, AID allows for pregnancy without the psychological complications that intercourse outside marriage might involve. Artificial insemination has an estimated success rate of 50 to 85 percent over several trials and has resulted in 250,000 successful pregnancies (now about 10,000 per year) in the United States.

With the development of techniques to freeze semen while preserving fertilization capacity, sperm banks have been introduced in which donor semen of "high quality" — adequate sperm count, healthy sperm, and good semen volume — can be maintained over time for use in AID. While the donors have been primarily medical students (paid $20-$35 per "donation"), one firm that promises the "select" sperm of Nobel Laureates recently claimed its first birth. Sperm storage coupled with artificial insemination produces new possibilities that cannot be duplicated "naturally." It allows for impregnation in the case of couples separated by long distances, as was done in 1971 for wives of army personnel fighting in Vietnam. And it makes possible the storage of sperm, if of adequate quality, of men who wish to undergo vasectomy, therefore not precluding the possibility of later paternity.

AID also has implications for the possibility of pregnancy in cases of alternative lifestyles. Lesbian couples who desire children have chosen AID, sometimes using the semen of homosexual friends. It can enable single women to choose to become pregnant without sexual ties, making possible even "virgin birth." And AID has been used in conjunction with a "surrogate mother" — a woman who agrees to be impregnated artificially and relinquish the baby at birth — in the case of a couple where the female was a transexual.

While AID makes possible these new scenarios, legal restrictions and societal disapproval often remain obstacles. The child born of AID (as opposed to AIH) is considered illegitimate in Canada, Britain, and the majority of the United States. Some courts consider the husband the "natural" father if he consented to the procedure and view the donor as having no relation to the child. However, a suit is pending in California in which a donor is suing for paternity rights. Legislation is required to regularize the AID child's parentage and rights to support and inheritance.

The issue of control over and access to AID is also important. At present, doctors alone determine who will be able to use it. They usually will not perform AID on single women and require the husband's consent for those who are married. And most will not provide it in cases of alternative lifestyles; in a recent attempt to establish guidelines for access, it was argued that the British Medical Association should refuse to "satisfy the unusual desires of lesbian couples."[2] Deciding access according to the lifestyle preferences of physicians can be fundamentally unfair; unconventional modes of living are not necessarily incompatible with a child's welfare.

A final issue concerns the undesirability of certain administrative procedures of AID clinics. Most sperm banks do not perform genetic screening, thus thwarting the ends of couples who are not using the husband's sperm because he is known to have a genetic disease. Only one state, Oregon, has a law forbidding fertilization with sperm that have genetic defects or from donors with venereal disease. On the other hand, screening is conducted with respect to physical characteristics of the donors. Couples usually request a donor with certain qualities: he must be handsome, or blond and blue-eyed, or look just like the husband. And attempts are made to match racial and national characteristics.

Finally, record keeping is often deliberately poor in order to guarantee the anonymity of the donors. One survey found that one-third of physicians mixed together different donated sperm samples to accomplish this effect. The disguising of parentage can lead to obvious problems if it should later become important for the child to know more about or even locate the genetic parent, as when organ transplants are needed. It could also result in children of the same anonymous donor marrying and reproducing: not an unlikely possibility since same-sperm inseminations often occur in a specific geographical area and there are usually no limits on the number of times a particular donor may be used (one has served 50 times). In general, artificial insemination is conducted in an atmosphere of secrecy; many cases go unreported and there are few legal restrictions on practices. Such measures function to protect male donors, but they can involve a serious disregard for the welfare of inseminated mothers and their offspring.

Some of the options made possible by newer reproductive technology, such as the possibility of surrogate mothers, thus have been feasible for quite some time through artificial insemination. And many of the same social, moral, and legal consequences are involved. Artificial insemination has simply escaped the publicity some new developments have occasioned. But there are some genuinely novel possibilities that have been recently developed: some do not require, as does AID, that a surrogate childbearer be the genetic mother. I now turn to an examination of the most publicized technological change.

In Vitro Fertilization (IVF)

With the birth of Louise Brown in 1978, the world became aware that it is now possible to combine sperm and egg in a laboratory and then insert the developing embryo into the uterus where it can be carried successfully to term. Described more technically, the process involves making a very small incision in a woman's abdomen, usually under general anesthesia, inserting a laparoscope (a slender instrument containing fiberoptics, through which the physician can observe the ovaries and insert a hollow needle), sucking out one or more eggs, and placing it/them in a special nutrient solution in a test tube or petri dish (hence *in vitro*, literally, "in glass"). Then sperm are introduced, and usually fusion of an egg and sperm occurs. The now fertilized egg, which I will call the embryo, is developed outside the womb for about two days, at which point it has divided to the four-or eight-cell stage. It is then inserted into the uterus through the cervix, requiring minor dilation similar to that of many gynecological procedures. If all goes well, it implants in the uterine wall, and from then on, pregnancy follows its normal course.

At present, clinics in England, Australia, and South Africa, and in Virginia, Texas, and California in the United States, are performing IVF. Some 30 babies have now been born that were conceived in this way, including another for Mrs. Brown, with more than 100 on the way.

The procedure was developed to deal with a specific type of infertility. An increasing number of women, about 750,000 in the United States, cannot conceive due to abnormal oviducts, the tubes through which eggs travel from the ovaries and meet sperm in transit from the uterus.[3] Surgical correction is invasive, expensive, and successful in only about 25 percent of the cases in which the damage is due to disease. At least 520,000 women hampered only by this problem and desiring pregnancy will not be able to conceive even after surgery. For these women, IVF offers the only hope; it has been compared to a helicopter that transports the egg to the sperm since the bridge is closed.[4]

IVF can also assist in other types of infertility. It may allow pregnancy for some women with "hostile cervical mucus," a term used to describe improper consistency of the channels through which sperm swim, or the production of sperm antibodies. It may also remedy male infertility that is a function of low sperm count or semen volume where AIH has been unsuccessful. In the United States alone these conditions add another 540,000 people desiring children whose only prospect of fertility is through IVF.

Finally, because both the egg itself and later the fertilized egg can be microscopically examined, IVF can be used for early detection of defects manifested in abnormal size, shape, or speed of division.

Why should a "helicopter" arouse such controversy? Aside from the generalized fear of technological intervention in natural processes, there are concerns about the interests of the embryo, the safty of the women involved, access to the procedure, and desirability of some of the new options it offers.

IVF: Issues Affecting the Embryo

The moral status of a fertilized egg is a question that has, of course, been discussed at length, if often unproductively, in the context of the abortion debate: I shall not attempt to settle it here. Those who believe that the newly fertilized egg is a human being with the right to life — a "person," in the jargon — and that the right to life entails the right to be kept alive[5] have moral objections to IVF if it involves the disposal of embryos that are not implanted.

Problems of embryo disposal arise primarily in clinics where it is the practice to induce superovulation through drugs so that several eggs can be removed at once, increasing the odds of producing a successful candidate for implantation and minimizing the likelihood that the woman will have to undergo further laparoscopies. But what is to be done with the "surplus" fertilized eggs?[6] Even assuming the truth of the above view about the embryo's moral status, there are several ways to modify procedures to allow IVF. One is to avoid superovulation and fertilize only one egg at a time. A second is to freeze the excess eggs before fertilization, to thaw later if necessary. However, while some ova banks are presently maintained, it is not yet known whether thawed eggs will be fertilizable. Success here would also provide fertility insurance for women undergoing sterilization. A third option is to freeze the surplus fertilized eggs to implant them at a later time, possibly in another woman, if the first try is successful for the egg-donating mother. This method is now being developed by a number of doctors, creating its own problems in the prospect of "embryos on hold." As of now, no thawed embryos have implanted, but the number of attempts is too small to allow reliable extrapolation and this method has been successful in animals. Finally, all of the fertilized eggs can be implanted in the same woman, as is presently done in the Norfolk (Virginia) Clinic, with some chance of multiple births: several "test tube twins" have been born in Australia.

There is also embryo loss in the cases of those that do not successfully implant. Many proponents of IVF argue that embryo wastage in the same proportion that occurs naturally is acceptable; in normal reproduction, an estimated 70 percent of fertilized eggs spontaneously abort. The successful implantation rate in IVF is presently 16-20 percent, and one clinic believes 40-50 percent success rates are within grasp.

Another problem with respect to the embryo's interests concerns the possibility of producing defective babies. There are worries about the possibility of damaging the sperm or egg during the fertilization procedure or the embryo during transfer to the uterus. Some argue that even apart from damage, IVF has a greater chance of developing abnormal babies since it might use defective sperm that would normally not succeed in reaching the egg. The degree of risk of defects in IVF is not known at present; births have involved only one reported abnormality: a heart defect. Some argue that any risk at all renders IVF unacceptable, while others hold that some risk is acceptable if it is no greater than the chances in normal reproduction. For example, fertility drugs are given that have risks of fetal defects and of multiple births where one or more of the fetuses does not survive. There does not yet exist a clear policy on risk to the fetus.

In any case, the chances are low that a defective child would be the result of IVF. The egg prior to fertilization and the embryo before implantation are subjected to microscopic examination that will reveal the presence of some defects. Also, the body's normal tendency to spontaneously abort abnormal embryos will still be operative. Of course, implicit in this argument is the assumption that a defective life should be terminated at these early stages. This assumption also underlies the present use of amniocentesis, a procedure often used during normal gestation in which fluid surrounding the embryo is removed and its chromosomes examined for abnormalities.

IVF: Health and Access Issues

A second concern in the use of IVF is the health and safety of the women on whom the procedure is tried. IVF involves a number of risks: the administration of hormones when superovulation is induced, which can lead to ovarian cysts; possibly repeated laparoscopies usually under general anesthesia; a chance of tubal pregnancy if the embryo fails to implant in the uterus; extensive monitoring of the pregnancy, including amniocentesis; possibly greater than normal chances of spontaneous abortion; and delivery by Caesarean section in most cases. There is also concern that infertile women, desperate to have a biological child, will agree to any invasive procedure or degree of risk to accomplish this goal. And it is argued that their motivation must be a product of beliefs conditioned by sexism — that a woman is worthless if infertile or that the only meaningful life for women involves having children, since adoption is such an easier option. This position holds that a more appropriate response to infertility than undergoing IVF is psychotherapy or consciousness-raising.

There are several responses to this argument. First, while there can be bad reasons for wanting children, this desire is not necessarily a product of antifeminist dogma or societal brainwashing. Being able to love, protect, and share one's life with children as they develop into adults can be one of life's most enriching experiences; the parent-child relationship is sometimes the most intimate form of human contact we ever know. True, adoption can satisfy some aspects of this need. But the desire is often more specific: it is not just to have children but to have *our own* children, children who share our genes. Whether or not these are desires we should have, they are probably here to stay, and they are surely not entirely a product of social conditioning. The real issue is: should decisions be made about which motivations are "good," such that only the infertile are prevented from satisfying the "bad" ones, by being forbidden access to technological solutions?

It must be remembered that adoption is not a desirable and cost-free social solution to infertility. The surrounding circumstances include unwanted pregnancy due to ignorance, birth control failure, or rape; and the inability to keep the child because of the mother's age, the social stigma attached to unwed motherhood, or poverty. The psychic toll is considerable for a woman who, under these conditions, undergoes nine months of pregnancy and then gives up the child.

With respect to the possible dangers involved, respect for individual autonomy may require granting people freedom to incur risks, if they are aware of these possible outcomes, even if others doubt that the result is objectively worth it. People take risks similar to those involved in IVF for cosmetic purposes — plastic surgery — and greater ones for adventure — auto racing. There are strong arguments that a woman, supplied with the necessary information, should be free to make her own choice about whether to subject herself to risk for the end of reproduction.

A third problem is one of access to IVF. As in artificial insemination, the determination of who will be accepted is made solely by physicians on the basis of certain restrictive criteria. For example, at the Norfolk Clinic only childless women between 25 and 35 deemed to be in "stable marriages" are considered, and only the husband's sperm is used. Limitations may be understandable now, given the controversy surrounding the technique, but the arguments for eventual free and open access for those who can be helped are strong. Financial factors also play a role here. Since IVF is not covered by insurance, the cost (around $4,000 per trial at Norfolk) will rule out low-income women. But, it should be noted, so do other remedies for infertility, with private adoption costing $2,000-$3,000 and corrective surgery $6,000-$8,500 per trial, also not covered by insurance in most cases. There is worry that such expense may also serve as a *de facto* racial bar to access; at present all IVF babies apparently have been white.

IVF: Sex Selection

Further concerns arise about the possible effects of one of the options IVF offers: sex selection. Choosing the sex of the child can occur in two ways. Before conception, it is now possible to separate sperm on the basis of factors, like their weight and swimming ability, that determine whether they carry an X-chromosome, which would produce a female child, or a Y-chromosome, resulting in a male. Only those that will yield the desired sex would then be injected; this method could be used in conjunction with IVF or artificial insemination. However, sex determination is also possible without technology. In intercourse, how close to the cervix sperm are deposited and the degree of alkalinity of the vagina have an important influence on whether X- or Y-bearing sperm succeed in fertilizing the egg. Using this information, 85 percent of a sample of parents were successful in obtaining the desired sex.

Another method involves the destruction of or failure to implant embryos of the "wrong" sex. Through complicated microsurgery, the sex of fertilized rabbit eggs may be determined before implantation. This procedure has not yet been attempted in humans, but IVF will allow the necessary access. A presently available postconception method is amniocentesis followed by abortion, which has been chosen in some cases where no genetic defects were present simply because of the sex of the fetus. The moral issues raised by each type of method are different, in that destroying an already existing embryo, especially for such reasons, may require more justification than intentionally preventing conception of one of the undesired sex.

Sex selection can prevent the passing of sex-linked diseases; for example, carriers of hemophilia might choose only to implant or conceive female embryos to avoid having a hemophilic child. And it might ultimately reduce the birth rate, because parents would not have to keep trying to have a child of the desired sex. However, there is concern that sex determination will result in male children being chosen in disproportionate numbers, and speculation that those to whom sex is such an important criterion are operating with sex-stereotyped expectations of their children. Others argue that the sex balance would ultimately even out, but that the chances are high that if choice were possible, the first-born would be male in most cases. Since birth order has been shown to affect personality development, such results would have an important impact on sex-linked behavior. In contrast, some argue that sex selection would probably be used only for the second or third child. Since this option is presently available, we will have more knowledge about its impact in the near future.

IVF: Options for Parenthood

Until now I have been discussing IVF in cases where a wife's egg and husband's sperm are used, and the embryo is reimplanted in the wife's uterus. The moral status of this procedure is not significantly different from that of AIH. However, IVF allows for many other possible permutations, and it is these that perhaps arouse the greatest controversy. The chart below describes the various possibilities involving a married couple.

Let's begin with further cases where the wife is able and desires to carry the baby to term, option 1 having already been discussed. First, she need not use her husband's semen; he may be infertile or carry a genetic disease. With donated sperm (option 2) the process resembles AID. Next, she may be unable or unwilling to have one of her own eggs fertilized: she may carry a hereditary defect, be at risk for Down's syndrome, have no more eggs ("precocious menopause"), or have ovarian disorders that make it impossible to recover an egg. Such women could undergo IVF with a donor egg (option 3). Again the analogy to AID is obvious. Some infertility organizations have suggested that women undergoing hysterectomies might altruistically choose to donate their eggs to an ova bank for just such purposes, once it is technologically feasible. And of course the sperm used need not be the husband's in this case either (option 4), so it could be possible for a woman to carry to term a child toward which neither she nor her husband has contributed genetic material.

All of these options require that the wife be the gestator of the child. The benefits of this choice over adoption are that in options 1, 2, and 3 at least one member of the couple makes a genetic contribution, and even in 4 the couple shares the experience of pregnancy, with the concomitant bonding feelings, especially for the woman. Also there is increasing evidence that the embryo is affected by uterine conditions and by the gestator's activities, emotions, health, and diet during pregnancy. Her newborn may even recognize her voice. These options thus allow the couple a greater role in the process of child production than would otherwise be possible.

Figure 25.1
Possible Permutations: *In Vitro* **Fertilization**

Option	Wife's Womb	Surrogate's Womb	Wife's Egg	Donor's Egg	Husband's Sperm	Donor's Sperm
1	X		X		X	
2	X		X			X
3	X			X	X	
4	X			X		X
5		X	X		X	
6		X	X			X
7		X		X	X	
8		X	X			X

Surrogates

The second class of options involves women who are unable or unwilling to carry a pregnancy to term. Here one of the most dramatic consequences of IVF arises: the possibility of "surrogate mothers" who agree to gestate an embryo and relinquish it to the contracting parties after birth. Using a surrogate could be an attractive option for a woman with a partial hysterectomy, paralysis, uterine structural abnormality, endometriosis, fragile health, or a history of miscarriage. It could also be selected by women who are physically capable of childbearing but for other reasons decide against it: perhaps because of the career interruption, effects on appearance, or general inconvenience pregnancy entails. They may simply dislike pregnancy but still want to have a child.

Here again there are several options with respect to genetic contribution to the baby. If both the wife's and husband's sex cells were healthy, genetically desirable, and obtainable, they could be used to produce an embryo for implantation in the surrogate that would have the genes of both parents (option 5), an advantage over artificial insemination of the surrogate. However, if these conditions are not fulfilled, there are other possibilities. The wife's egg and donor sperm may be used (option 6): similar to AID of the wife, only with the addition of a surrogate gestator. Or a donor egg may be used in conjunction with the husband's sperm (option 7). Here the surrogate could have a genetic contribution if her own egg were used, although artificial or natural insemination of the surrogate with the husband's sperm seems an easier option.

Finally, the process could occur with no genetic contribution from the contracting couple, using donated sperm and egg (option 8); again the surrogate's egg could be used. Normally adoption would seem more desirable but the supply of available babies is decreasing, the wait may be very long, and the screening process for acceptable parents very restrictive. Alternately, one might like to have a child from known excellent genetic strains, perhaps preferable to one's own. With the separation of the gestational and genetic components one could select both sex cells from a possible future Nobel Laureates' Sperm and Egg Bank, and then choose a surrogate who has good gestational qualities. Finally, it should be noted that Figure 1 can be duplicated with respect to unmarried individuals. Adding all these options, the number of individuals in the United States desiring children who, given present technology, can be helped only by IVF is estimated at 1.94 million.

The possibility of "wombs to let" is horrifying to some, a reaction expressed by Leon Eisenberg: "As for the notion of a 'borrowed' or 'rented' uterus, I consider the proposal beneath contempt: women are not brood mares or sows."[7] This response is understandable; "using" another person is morally offensive. Consider an example of a kind of "natural surrogacy" that has always been possible: the Bible reports that Sarah, being unable to conceive, persuaded her husband Abraham to try to impregnate her slave girl Hagar so that Sarah could have a child, and Hagar bore Ishmael. There is no mention of Hagar's having had any say in the matter; she was simply "given" to Abraham. Women who are forced by social pressures to give up their babies for adoption might also be considered a kind of surrogate, again not by their choice. Both of these "natural" cases involve a type of compulsion that is morally abhorrent.

But this element of compulsion is not intrinsic to surrogacy. Women may be positively motivated to assume this role for a variety of reasons. A handful of surrogate services have developed across the country and are doing a profitable business, so far only using artificial insemination (since they have not been allowed access to IVF). It is reported that many women apply to be surrogates because they regard pregnancy as a creative and positive experience and want to help infertile couples. A number of private surrogates have served without pay. However, given the strong demand for such services (one Michigan attorney, after placing an ad, received 1,000 letters requesting access to a surrogate), the pool could not be filled solely by altruists; the financial factor is important for many. Surrogates in these clinics are paid $10,000-$15,000 plus all medical expenses (the contracting couple is charged as much as $25,000). A recent survey determined that over 40 percent of surrogate mothers were unemployed or on welfare.

Even if women freely apply for these positions, there still remain general social concerns about the possibility of *economic* compulsion. Worries have been expressed about the creation of a degraded class of childbearers, primarily from lower socioeconomic segments of society, in the wet nurse tradition. As one commentator pointed out, "It wouldn't be the first time that poor women found that their bodies are their one salable commodity."[8] To "prevent commercialism from affecting a mother's decision,"[9] states have enacted laws forbidding the sale of children for adoption; in some states the artificial insemination of paid surrogates has been held to be prohibited by such laws.

The argument that women should be legally prevented from allowing financial considerations to motivate them to become surrogates rests on the assumption that it is degrading to gestate *for pay* ; presumably surrogacy as an altruistic act would not be condemned. The arguments here are the same that are involved in whether compensation should be allowed for donating blood or body parts, volunteering as a subject for scientific experiments, or engaging in sex. The most important considerations here are really whether women's interests are adequately protected when they serve as surrogates. If they are well paid and their rights are not violated, surrogate mothers need not be regarded as an exploited class.

What rights might a surrogate need to have protected? The contract between her and the couple will presumably set out many stipulations about her activities during the pregnancy. It may specify, for example, that she not drink, smoke, take drugs, or have an abortion unless the couple agrees. It may require her to undergo extensive monitoring, including amniocentesis, and to terminate the pregnancy if genetic defects in the embryo are discovered. She may be held to assume all risks of pregnancy including death. Such an agreement favors the couple; the important issue is whether the surrogate can be forced to fulfill these conditions should she change her mind. Most legal commentators argue that specific performance could not be obtained: she could not be forced to have an abortion against her will, nor be prevented from having an early termination, though she may be held financially liable for damages. If so, her right of control over her body is presently legally protected. The issue of whether she can, in fact, be held to have assumed all risks of pregnancy, or might instead be entitled to compensation, for example, for damage to her liver that results from the pregnancy, also requires resolution.

Other legal remedies remain to be developed to determine who is responsible for the baby in problematic cases: if the contracting couple dies, or there are multiple births, or the baby has Down's syndrome and the surrogate refuses to abort. In general, serious legal and moral problems arise from permutations 2-8 of IVF concerning the child's parentage, legitimacy, and rights to support and inheritance from the contracting couple, any involved donor, and the surrogate. To consider just one aspect, the notion of "parent," especially "mother," now becomes unclear. Is the genetic or the gestational component more important in determining the *real* mother? Similar problems have existed for some time as the result of adoption and AID. Of special interest in this regard are two cases: option 8, where possibly none of the contracting parties has a genetic contribution (do gestational interests win?) and option 7, where the surrogate might make both a genetic and gestational contribution (do her interests thus overbalance the rights of the contracting couple?). The rights of sex-cell donors versus those of the childbearer require legal resolution as technology changes the concept of "parent."

Finally, the problem of access arises with surrogates as well. At present, the cost of $25,000 required for AID surrogate services is prohibitive for all but the wealthy. There is concern that pregnancy could become class-linked, with the richer segments of society choosing to have others bear their children. Insurance coverage and reduction in cost as more competitive clinics develop may prevent this. Still other problems arise from the screening criteria used by physicians. Some argue that surrogates should only be used in cases of medical need, not when career or aesthetic reasons are the motivation. But pregnancy has no trivial effect on many women's occupations, and even if a woman only wants to avoid stretch marks, why should she not be permitted access to technology that will spare her? The decisions about whether access should depend on motivation and, if so, what constitutes a "worthy" reason should not be left to physicians alone.

IVF thus raises important legal and moral questions regarding control and access, and protection of the rights of the child, the surrogate, and the couple. These must be faced immediately because the technology is now being used. I want to sketch briefly some future possibilities that will have even more dramatic implications.

Cloning

Cloning is a form of asexual reproduction in which the offspring is genetically identical to a single parent. It occurs naturally in plants and some lower animals. Artificially induced cloning of frogs has been successful, and recent experiments indicate that mouse embryos can be cloned. Human cloning has not been documented, ignoring the unsubstantiated claims in David Rorvik's In His Image: The Cloning of a Man, but the process would involve removing the nucleus from an egg and replacing it with the nucleus of an adult body cell. These materials need not be derived from the same individual. The renucleated egg, now with a full complement of chromosomes, would begin division and then be implanted in a uterus for normal gestation. The resulting child would be genetically identical to the individual whose body cell nucleus was used, since the genetic material of the egg has been removed. Every body cell thus would have the potential to develop into a new individual (and if such potentiality entailed "personhood," would have the right to life!). The possibilities discussed earlier with IVF are duplicated here, with certain additions, as described in the following chart.

Table 25.2
Possible Permutations: Cloning

Option	Womb		Egg		Body Cell Nucleus		
	Wife's	Surrogate's	Wife's	Donor's	Wife's	Husband's	Donor's
1	X		X		X		
2	X		X			X	
3	X		X				X
4	X			X	X		
5	X			X		X	
6	X			X			X
7		X	X		X		
8		X	X			X	
9		X	X				X
10		X		X	X		
11		X		X		X	
12		X		X			X

In cases of couples who carry a recessive genetic disease or where one or even both partners are sterile, cloning can offer a means of reproduction preserving at least half of their genetic heritage. Of course, AID (if sterility were due only to the husband) and IVF using a donor egg (in the case of the wife) would work as well when only one partner was sterile, but the couple might not want to have their child share a "stranger's" genes. Therefore, the options that involve replication of either the husband's or the wife's genotype (1, 2, 4, 5, 7, 8, 10, and 11) would presumably be the most frequently used. But those using a donor nucleus (3, 6, 9, and 12) could allow for the possibility of replicating another desirable genotype, say of a friend, an admired individual, or of a donor to a future Nobel Laureates' Nucleus Bank. So cloning could allow for a kind of positive eugenics, whereby exceptional individuals are replicated.

Cloning also would make possible sex determination in advance. It has one especially unorthodox application: it would allow a couple to "replace" a beloved child who is terminally ill by cloning it. Finally, cloning offers the possibility of an all-female world, since sperm would no longer be needed for reproduction; the all-male world is impossible so long as human wombs and eggs are still required.

One of the major confusions in most discussions of cloning concerns the moral status of the clone. There is a tendency to think of it as a kind of subhuman robot; proposals correspondingly have been made to regard clones as a type of property, to be used, for example, for human spare parts for transplants without rejection problems. Typical, if exaggerated for humor, is a newspaper column that queried:

> Can (a clone) do absolutely everything you can do, or just what you tell it to do? Or can it do nothing until you activate it? . . .. Where do you keep a clone? Surely not in the broom closet or the bathtub, two likely spots . . .. Under the bed might be OK . . .. (M)ust it be fed? Surely some sort of upkeep is required, even for such a genuine — if that's the word — article.[10]

Such misconceptions, while amusing, inhibit any kind of thoughtful or sensitive examination of the implications of cloning. For a clone, of course, is a human being like any other. It has the same genetic code that another human has, but in that respect it is no different from an identical twin. Its production is not entirely "natural," but it would be ludicrous to make such proposals with respect to the equally "unnatural" babies that result from AID or IVF. Neither its lack of genetic uniqueness nor its production by technological intervention alter its humanity, and it is entitled to the same rights and respect as anyone else. It would therefore be as morally unconscionable to use clones as transplant donors against their will as it would be to adopt Jonathan Swift's "Modest Proposal" to raise normally produced babies for food.

The tendency to regard clones as robots may result from a vision of a clonally-produced army of identical-looking men bred for strength, endurance, low intelligence, and the disposition to follow orders. In fact, most scientists believe that clones will differ markedly in appearance and behavior from their donors, even more than identical twins differ. Speculation is that cytoplasm, the material surrounding the nucleus in the egg, plays a role in embryo development. And it is known that uterine conditions are also crucial, even for determining appearance. Finally, the environmental factors are most important; the conditions that resulted in a Hitler or an Einstein cannot be duplicated. The genetic code merely sets up certain flexible tendencies: the seed that under certain conditions produces a giant maple tree can, under others, yield a bonsai. So clones of the same donor will neither look nor act exactly like each other or their donor.

Still, being aware of possessing a genetic structure identical to that of someone who has already lived may raise unique psychological obstacles for the clone. She might not feel that her future is entirely open; she might have unrealistic fears about psychological determinism. She would know what the life of someone with her genes was like and could see it as a blueprint or feel despair if she fails to live up to it. Education about nongenetic influences on character would be crucial to prevent such problems.

There are also worries about the effects of cloning on the structure of the family. Would the donor parent and his/her clone identify with each other and feel closer? Could problems of incestuous attraction arise as the cloned daughter comes to resemble her mother when young? How would a cloned child relate to "natural" siblings? These psychological issues would require sensitive handling.

Widespread use of cloning might produce different problems. Changes in the gene pool would result, with a sacrifice of the greater variety of genotypes gained by sexual reproduction. Restrictions might have to be placed on how many times one genetic code could be replicated, to prevent the production of millions of Farrah Fawcetts. And a legal copyright on a particular genetic pattern might be required to protect individuals from being cloned against their will, since it is fairly easy to obtain someone's body cells. Cloning, like other technological developments in reproduction, would require extensive social and legal changes.

Artificial Wombs

One of the most dramatic future scenarios is the development of technology that will enable the entire gestation of an embryo to occur outside the womb. At present almost one-half of the intrauterine growth of the fetus can take place outside the mother. The newly fertilized egg can be kept alive for at least six days, mid-term aborted fetuses have been maintained in culture for several days, and premature babies can survive through technology from 24 weeks. But it will be some time before all of pregnancy can be duplicated artificially.

The consequences of such a development would be extensive, and reactions to it range from regarding it as the ultimate horror to representing it as the most important step in the liberation of women. Feminists may be found on each side. Some argue that if women's bodies were no longer needed for reproduction and their eggs could be stored, men might choose to eliminate most of them. (Since the supply of eggs eventually would run out, a few egg-producers would always be needed.) Others find this worry needless, doubting that men have the power to do it or that women's only value to men lies in childbearing. Shulamith Firestone argues that only when women are no longer biologically forced to undergo pregnancy will they be able to assume a fully equal role in society.[11] The artificial womb could also do much to alleviate fetal and maternal morbidity and mortality and make possible the survival and eventual adoption of unwanted, naturally-conceived fetuses that are now aborted. The power of such a development is so great that it is difficult to conceive the full extent of its effects.

Implications for Tomorrow

Technology simply provides new options, some beneficial and some harmful: its effects depend on its use, which in turn depends on who controls it. I have not considered some of the possible misuses that could occur under a totalitarian regime, nor some of the more bizarre possible future developments. I will briefly mention a few and then discuss possible recommendations for control.

The field of genetic engineering permits the general possibilities of eugenics, both positive and negative. It is easy to imagine scenarios under a dictatorship where only certain gene strains are deemed acceptable for reproduction and carriers of others are forbidden to bear children. Of course, such a regime could produce similar effects through forced breeding, though with less certain results, especially in comparison to cloning.

As the ability to manipulate genetic material increases, science fiction possibilities of new forms of life may arise. "Chimeras" may be possible, whereby sperm and egg from different species are united to produce an interspecies hybrid. At present one method of testing male fertility involves injecting human sperm into hamster eggs to determine whether fertilization occurs, at which point the result is destroyed.

Similar to cloning are parthenogenesis and diploidization, in which an egg alone divides to form a new individual, genetically identical to itself, but not to the female whose egg it is, and necessarily female. These techniques, which have been tried with turkeys, mice, and several mammals, have not yet been attempted with human eggs.

Several possibilities with respect to embryo use arise from presently existing technology. "Surplus embryos" could be used for experimentation; human eggs could be used for more accurate, less costly fertility testing, and the resulting fertilized eggs discarded. And embryos could be used for "organ farms," as described earlier. Important and difficult problems about the moral status of the embryo thus require immediate resolution.

The most important issue raised by the new technology is control. Public policy in the form of requisite laws must be made immediately, so that technology is not used in any way it can be, simply because it exists. These decisions must be made openly and by society in general. At present it is primarily scientists and physicians alone who determine what developments will be pursued and who will have access to them. These professions are still predominately male, as was the group appointed in 1980 to develop suggested guidelines for use of IVF: the Ethics Advisory Board of the U.S. Department of Health and Human Services. Consisting of thirteen members, only two of whom were women, the Board recommended that access to IVF be restricted to married couples. Influence also has been wielded in these areas by organized religion; in Massachusetts recently IVF was forbidden primarily due to worries abut embryos' interests raised by religious groups. Women, the most dramatically affected by reproductive technology, need to become actively involved to ensure that their interests are respected. Some issues of special concern to women are access, information, and protection.

The beneficial aspects of reproductive technology result only to those given access to it. While the existence of an unequivocal "right to bear children" is controversial, arguments that certain people should not be permitted to conceive should apply equally to the fertile and infertile. Because the infertile need assistance that can be denied them, criteria for restricted access are easily employed. Applying such criteria to the fertile, on the other hand, would require preventing some from conceiving and probably would be unenforceable. Still, a test of fairness in these matters requires willingness to agree that any fertile individual who falls into a category that would be denied access to IVF *ought* not to bear children naturally. Applying this test, the only plausible justifications for restricted availability rely on arguments about the child's welfare. Therefore, I would argue against blanket denial of access to certain groups based on marital status or sexual preference; adoption criteria have been similarly liberalized in recent years.

Another aspect determining access is the cost of such technology. Women have strong interests in expenses being reduced or offset by insurance, so that solutions to infertility are not limited to the rich.

Reproductive technology makes possible the easy disguise of genetic parenthood. Paternity could always be doubted in the past; now this is true for genetic maternity as well. There are strong arguments for keeping careful records of genetic lineage and allowing open access to such information by the resulting children; such changes are becoming more common in adoption. Secrecy can be pernicious and may serve to imply that these procedures are morally unsavory.

Finally, protection of the rights of women using such technology, whether as donor, surrogate, or contracting mother, is crucial. Screening is required to eliminate insemination by donors with infectious diseases and genetic defects. And fully informed consent and compensation for damages must be ensured. One example that raises such concerns is that of a recent attempt to perfect a nonsurgical equivalent of IVF with a donor egg. Called "embryo transfer," it involves the artificial insemination of women volunteers by contracting husbands, followed by the "washing out" of the resulting embryo for implantation in their wives. The dilation of the cervix and irrigation of the uterus these volunteers undergo is painful and may potentially damage the cervix or tubes, leading to subsequent infertility. Their willingess to participate (they are paid only $50) has been explained by "their extraordinarily giving attitude. They think it's silly to waste an egg every month!"[12] Perhaps this explanation is accurate, but one wonders whether they were adequately informed of the possible future consequences of their benevolence.

Uniform application of a general moral view about all technology to particular individual developments becomes more difficult the more one comes to appreciate some of the complicated and subtle issues involved in different cases. Such general attitudes are difficult to justify in themselves: while technology has contributed antibiotics, organ transplants, and neonatal life support, it has also produced thalidomide, DES, and the Dalkon shield. With respect to the kinds of reproductive technology I've examined in detail, I have argued that neither blanket endorsement nor wholesale rejection is appropriate. Careful consideration of each is required to develop sane and sensitive, individually-tailored policies for the future.

Notes

1. See Christine Pierce, "Natural Law, Language and Women," in *Sex Equality*, ed. J. English (Englewood Cliffs, NJ: Prentice-Hall, 1977).
2. Dr. J. A. Hicklin, quoted in *British Medical Journal* (July 7, 1979): 70. This view did not prevail; the decision about access was left to individual physicians.
3. These and following statistics regarding incidence of types of infertility and possibilities of treatment by IVF are the result of a survey of scientific reports by Jacqueline Colby, "Infertility: Incidence, Etiology, and Prognosis," 1. Woshed paper, (La Jolla, CA: University of California at San Diego, Department of Philosophy, 1982).
4. A still experimental procedure, low tubal ovum transfer, may eventually provide an alternative to IVF for many, by making it possible to remove an egg and reinsert it after the point of blockage in the tube.
5. Well-developed arguments challenging each of these views are advanced in Laura Purdy and Michael Tooley, "Is Abortion Murder?" in *Abortion: Pro and Con*, ed. R. Perkins (Cambridge, MA: Schenkman, 1974); and Judith Jarvis Thomson, "A Defense of Abortion," in *The Problem of Abortion*, ed. J. Feinberg (Belmont, CA: Wadsworth, 1973).
6. I ignore here the moral issues involved in other possible uses, for example for fertility testing or experimentation.
7. Leon Eisenberg, "The Psychopathology of Clonal Man," in *Genetics and the Law*, eds. A. Milunsky and G. Annas (New York: Plenum Press, 1975), p. 392.
8. Caryl Rivers, "Genetic Engineers," *Ms.* 4 (1976): 50.
9. The language of *Doe v. Kelley*, quoted in Susan Lewis, "Surrogate Mothers: An Uncertain Legal Future," *Western Law Journal* 11 (1981): 10.
10. Lucretia Steiger, "Cloning Around," San Diego *Union*, October 7, 1978, p. D-1.
11. Shulamith Firestone, *The Dialectic of Sex* (New York: Bantam, 1972).
12. Dr. John Buster, quoted in H. Nelson, "Human Ova will be Transplanted," Los Angeles *Times*, June 16, 1982, Part I, p. 3.

I want to thank my research assistants, Jacqueline Colby and Laurie Shrage, for their invaluable assistance on this paper.

Chapter 26

Juggling Health Care Technology

And Women's Needs

by Alberta Parker

Innumerable technologies influence women's lives — many in positive ways, yet these technologies do not come without their own risks and negative effects. It is with the balance between these positive and negative effects that I am concerned, particularly with the large area of technology that is based on the biomedical sciences. This is because it, perhaps more than any other sector of technology, has the power of influencing how women come into being, develop, live, and die. At this point in time it is undergoing drastic change. The report of the Presidential Biomedical Research Panel in 1976 stated:

> Suddenly in the early 1950s the whole field began to expand in an explosion of new information, and the "biological revolution," as it is now called, was underway. During the last quarter of a century, the life sciences have extended into areas of human knowledge not known to exist before that time. Entirely new disciplines have emerged overnight. A research technology has evolved with the sophistication and power to match, almost, that achieved by the physical sciences. Because of all this, the profession of medicine has begun to experience a transformation unlike anything in the millennia of its existence.[1]

This explosion of information already has and will continue to create new opportunities and problems for women. But in assessing the new realities, we may overlook the inappropriate use of older, established technologies which create problems here and now, problems which will continue into the future unless changes are made today.

We cannot divide human history in pretechnological and technological epochs. Human beings, wherever they have been in time or place, have put to use knowledge, methods, and procedural systems. But there is something new, which has been described as "modern," "dvanced," "high," or "Western," and which differs in certain ways from the technology of the past. I would like to point out a few reasons why it is different.

First, modern technology is of unprecedented complexity. Not only are there multiple parts, but every part is built on complex knowledge and procedures, which are, in turn, part of many complex, intricate systems. Think of what is involved in the development of contraceptives and their use: the needs assessment process, the research, the development, and the distribution systems by which the technology is delivered. Think of the reaction and counter-reaction happening in our social system today over contraception, and one can see how system-embedded everything becomes.

Second, a close relationship between technology and the individual has developed. In fact, we have become servants of some technologies — for instance, the automobile. Third is the ubiquitous diffusion of technologies in present society. And fourth is that the procedural and organizational systems necessary in order to sustain the technology have become a part of it.[2]

All health care technology, no matter how simple or even how appropriate it seems, must be considered as part of modern technology because it shares these above characteristics. A good example is the recent flurry over menstrual tampons. Women have always had means of handling the menstrual flow, and they have often used insertables. But suddenly we have an example of technology that seems simple, yet meets all the criteria of modern technology. What happened? Advanced technology was first required to develop a superabsorbent tampon. Then, when toxic shock syndrome was recognized, all the complex procedural systems occurring in our society were called upon to respond, from the secretary of the Department of Health and Human Services (DHHS) to the Communicable Disease Center in Atlanta, to all kinds of epidemologic study groups, to the mass media. There were also intense industrial reverberations. Thus, even such a simple technology obviously exists in a very complex system.

Technologies based on the biomedical sciences are unique in certain ways. It has been pointed out that technology is not just a tool to be used in energy or agricultural production. People themselves are the subject of technology and are changed by it. Health care technologies are part of a system that is trusted, or has been trusted until the last ten or fifteen years, to do something good for us. It is considered "humane"; it has conquered disease and relieved suffering; and therefore, we have been not as likely to look at it closely. The price it exacts may not have been seen clearly enough.

Women's Different Health Conditions

There are three types of biomedical technologies that we must take into account: medical technologies having to do with life and death; those having to do with changing human potentialities, mainly exemplified by genetic engineering; and those having to do with human achievement or neurological manipulation. Great advances are being made in all three areas, but most of the advances in the last two — changing the genetic potential or changing the potential for human achievement — have a tendency to be subsumed by the medical profession as soon as they are developed. One of the few instances where this is not true is the promotion of health. Medicine has not been particularly interested in the promotion of health; it has remained primarily concerned with the prevention of disease and its treatment. Nevertheless, when we consider health care technologies, we should take into account the entire gamut of intervention, from prevention of disease, diagnosis, and treatment to rehabilitation.

In examining how these technologies affect women differently than they affect men, I have found it helpful to use a classification scheme based on health conditions of particular concern to women. When most people talk about women's health needs, they tend to think mainly about reproductive-related concerns. This is, however, only one of several areas in which women's health conditions differ in some way from those of men, due to their anatomy, physiology, or social roles. For example, related to reproduction are menstruation, menarche, contraception, pregnancy, lactation, uterine cancer, hysterectomy, and so on. In some cultures, however, women's unique social roles determine certain health conditions. For instance there are health conditions which arise because women gather the fuel, get the water, care for the children, or cook. In our culture, most of these functions are not exclusively performed by women, but in other cultures, these functions would be health factors.

Second are the conditions for which women have a higher risk than men. These conditions are not limited to women, but for any 1,000-member segment of the population, there will be a higher proportion of women suffering from them. These include iatrogenic diseases, those disease states caused by a doctor who prescribes some medication or procedure which creates a health problem. This happens more often to women because they go to the doctor more often than men, and so are at higher risk. Another example is mammary cancer. Men can get it, but women are more likely to do so. Obesity and diabetes, adolescent tuberculosis, and osteoporosis associated with aging are other examples.

Third are those conditions to which more women are subject because there are more women in the population. Most prominent in this regard are conditions associated with aging. Women make up a larger portion of the aged population because they live longer, on the average, than men. Because disease is associated with aging, it becomes a relevant women's issue. Examples are chronic disease, problems of the institutionalization of the aged, widowhood, and psychological isolation.

Last are those conditions where the risk to women is changing rapidly. These are often related to the fact that women are gaining equality with men, not always with good results as far as their health is concerned. More and more young women are smoking, and this is leading to an increase in lung cancer in women. As changes in life style occur, more women are being exposed to sexually-transmitted diseases. Forces which further liberation may cause stress among women — changing sex roles, meeting new challenges, having to live up to changing commitments, and ambivalence about new roles. It takes courage to say to your husband of 30 years, "look, I'm liberated."

When one considers any method, procedure, or drug that is used for any of these four types of health conditions, one is dealing with health care technology that relates specifically to women. Further, in considering these technologies there are three aspects we should be concerned with: development, distribution, and appropriateness.

Issues and Alternatives

The first issue is, by whom are the technologies being developed? Are women's needs being considered, or are they being overlooked? Are there gaps in technology that particularly affect women? This is an important problem. Patricia Harris, former secretary of DHHS, pointed out that although menstrual cramps cause a tremendous amount of lost labor hours, lost efficiency, and sheer discomfort, there is very little research activity being done on dysmenorrhea. Are male methods of contraception being thoroughly investigated? What is being done in developing male contraceptive devices so that the entire burden of contraception does not fall on women?

Support for the aged at home is another gap in health care technology that is not being addressed adequately. Although there are many different types of programs for the aged, few include all the services they require. Transportation to and from health care is a gap that particularly affects older women. Regardless of social or economic status, certain other aspects of health care delivery affect women more than men. Any woman who has had three children to take to the doctor, then to the lab, then to the X-ray, then to the pharmacy knows that health care services are not usually located conveniently at one site.

Another question is whether or not the technologies being developed, as well as older, established technologies, are being judged by their impact on women, including short- and long-term effects, and costs versus benefits. Those of us on Secretary Harris's Advisory Committee on the Rights and Responsibilities of Women felt that the impact was certainly not considered adequately at the federal level. One of our real responsibilities on the secretary's advisory committee was to try to institutionalize these concerns in some way. We knew that a secretary's committee could be easily dismantled, but we tried to see that people down the line bureaucratically, those not changing with every administration, were sensitized to women's issues so that as they began to implement programs, they would think about the effects on women.

We know from past experience that we should be conservative in technology development. Things develop rapidly in this country and sometimes things happen that one does not want to have happen. One example is the problem that has resulted from DES (diethylstilbestrol) usage.

Another element to consider is distribution. This means that every woman gets what she needs, but does not get what she does not need. And what applies to the individual applies equally to groups — groups of women need to get what they need, but not what they do not need. And many women in the United States have no access to medical care at all, particularly good primary care.

The last thing to consider is the appropriateness of the technology. Appropriateness does not mean only effectiveness and safety, although those are key elements. It also includes acceptability, cost, and feasibility — whether the technology can be used under the circumstances for which it was intended, and whether it is the simplest, most adequate solution. None of these criteria is an absolute. Any technology will represent a balance among them. For instance delivering a baby after a normal pregnancy with no evidence of high risk factors is attended by low morbidity and mortality. Therefore, anything introduced in the way of technology should accomplish an important objective, and should be very effective, very safe, low in cost, low in intrusiveness, and high in acceptability. If it is not all of these things, its use should be seriously questioned. On the other hand, a condition like breast cancer, which still has a high mortality rate, will meet these criteria of appropriateness in a different way. Much more leeway has to be allowed — less effectiveness, less safety, more intrusiveness, more destructive surgery, less acceptability.

An example of the inappropriate use of technology in pregnancy is electronic fetal monitoring. The last five or six years have seen the introduction and widespread use of electronic fetal monitoring, particularly the kind which uses an electrode screwed into the baby's scalp and attached by a wire to the monitoring apparatus. The procedure requires that the membranes be ruptured for the placement of the electrode. Some physicians believe this type of fetal monitoring should be used in all deliveries, and in some hospitals it is indeed used routinely with all women in labor, regardless of the risk status of the infant. Yet it has not even been demonstrated that this technology is highly effective in detecting fetal distress. It still has a high number of false positives, and some false negatives. Its use also seems to have contributed, at least in part, to the rising Caesarean rate, which has risen from some 5 percent to 15 percent or 16 percent and, in some hospitals, as high as 40 percent. In some situations it is almost the normal way of delivery.

Electronic fetal monitoring is intrusive. It changes a woman's perspective of herself and the task of delivery, and tends to remove some of the support systems — nurses may not stay with the mother, but rather run in and look at the monitor. Informed consent is also difficult to achieve. If a doctor says to a pregnant woman as he recommends fetal monitoring, "Don't you care about your baby?" of course she will agree to it.

The National Institute of Health has recommended that electronic fetal monitoring be used only in the case of high risk women. In spite of this, the use of this technology continues to grow, and the Caesarean section rate, at least partly in response, continues to rise. Pregnancy isn't that dangerous. Why is this technique being used so widely? One reason, I believe, is that physicians love mechanistic solutions and will use them if they can. Moreover, there is a monetary issue. Fetal monitoring is a product to be sold. Hospitals can include it in their cost of care. Defense against malpractice plays a role as well. And last, provider convenience is involved. Nurses and physicians can watch the monitor instead of attending the women in labor; although any woman who has had a baby knows the comfort provided by having somebody else in the room.

There are other issues related to the appropriateness of health care: the lack of home support for the aged, which results in premature institutionalization; the quality of long term care; and the issue of nursing homes and their control.

My suggestions on how to achieve equitability and appropriateness will not be new to you, as they apply to many other areas. First is the need to integrate women into the process. They must be involved in the development of health care technology in industry, in academic research, in government, and as consumers. They must be involved so the "soft effects" will be considered as part of the whole. They must be involved in the delivery systems, in the political process, and in the institutionalization of women's viewpoints through mass media.

Second, technology assessment activities need to be increased, with all aspects of medical technology, including the mode of delivery, taken into consideration. Both old and new technologies need to be examined, and information gathered through assessment must be widely disseminated.

Third, increased meaning must be given to informed consent. Women must have the knowledge required to make decisions, and must know the options in order to compare them realistically. This means that the relationship between physicians and female patients will have to change. More responsibility will have to rest with women.

With increased integration into the process, with assessment, and with more emphasis on informed consent by health care providers, women and society may be in a better position to insure that health care technology in the future minimizes risks to women, while optimizing benefits.

Notes

1. *Report of the Presidential Biomedical Research Panel* (Washington, DC: Department of Health and Human Services, 1976), p. 2.
2. N. Bruce Hannay and Robert E. McGinn, "Anatomy of Modern Technology: Prolegomenon to an Improved Public Policy for the Social Management of Technology," *Daedalus* (Winter 1980): 25-53.
See also:
   Leon R. Kass, "The New Biology: What Price Relieving Man's Estate?" *Science* 174 (November 19, 1971): 779-88.

Chapter 27

Female Futures in

Women's Science Fiction

by Sally Miller Gearhart

Without knowing why at the time, I found myself somehow physically sick when the moon landing took place. I have discovered the reason since then: it is that even to put a digging stick in my hand changes my relationship to the earth upon which I use that stick, for technology is not neutral. I am at the point of believing the human race is an evolutionary blunder; we are the only animals to have fouled our own nest so thoroughly that neither we nor anybody else can live in it. Granted there are rare moments of love, split seconds of real, true communication; granted there are precious experiences of compassion and caring that occasionally light our days, but none of these obliterates the violence we do to the earth and to one another. Neither the glories of Western civilization, nor the wonders of human consciousness, nor the ecstasies of human knowledge can in any way justify the cost of such achievements to our frantically enslaved and fear-ridden personal lives.

In my deepest moments, I believe it is time for us *homo sapiens* to fold up our tents and silently steal away; we are up past our bedtime. And we might note a lot of rejoicing in the stockyards and the zoos of the world at the departure of human beings from this earth. Imagine the singing of the trees, the rumble of relief from the hills and the valleys, and the joy of the fresh winds in the waters. But lest I become too heavy, let me add that some of my best friends are human beings. I think there is a shred of hope, and it is in that shred of hope that I am living the rest of my life, founded on the chance that we may be able to change ourselves as a human species before we blow ourselves asunder.

That change relies on something within ourselves that is not new. It is the principle of empathy which Doris Lessing calls the substance of "we feeling." It is the identification of ourselves with the earth, with animals, and with each other so that injury to any one of those things is also an injury to ourselves. And I see women, particularly feminist women, and particularly lesbian feminist women, as the vehicles for this return to empathy. I see women in that role because the values of empathy, cooperation, and collectivity are the values associated with them.

But we are not the only vehicles. Men are going to have to get cracking, too, if we want to survive as a species. The code of masculinity placed upon men, that code of "big gun/big man," has to be seen as the villain in world disintegration. Individualism per se, the inability to see beyond the self, denies empathy and epitomizes alienation. Man, particularly Western man, has somehow never emerged from boyhood or at least from adolescence; he is still a skin-encapsulated ego that has not moved to the collective mentality.

All of us, women included, have helped to romanticize the image and behavior in men of the eternal child. We excuse it, allowing men to stay forever in that irresponsible and violent stage. As individualism rapes the continents of this earth, we are saying "boys will be boys." As alienation escalates along with the prospect of all-out nuclear war, we are saying "boys will make war." People who have power are largely men with no sense of empathy, and indeed, it may even be true that in order to have the power, they must have no sense of empathy. Contrarily, people with empathy are largely women who have no power, and it may be true that in order to keep the empathy they must not have power.

Feminist Utopias

In science fiction, or more specifically, in feminist utopian novels, something amazing has been happening in the last ten years. Utopian novels — future fantasies about what society could and should be like — are coming from women in such numbers that, by comparison, men are writing no utopias at all.

In my definition a utopian novel is one that offers a comprehensive critique of our present values — economic, social, religious, political, and educational. It attempts to suggest the causes of our present ills and to provide solutions to poverty, disease, crime, slavery, and so on. A feminist utopia is that society in which women are at least equal to men. Some examples are Marion Zimmer Bradley's **The Ruins of Isis** and **The Shattered Chain**; Dorothy Bryant's **The Kin Of Ata Are Waiting for You**; Octavia Butler's **Kindred**; Suzy McKee Charnas's **Motherlines**; my own **The Wanderground: Stories of the Hill Women**; Charlotte Perkins Gilman's **Herland**; Ursula LeGuin's two books, **The Dispossessed** and **The Left Hand of Darkness**; Marge Piercy's **Woman on the Edge of Time**; Joanna Russ's **The Female Man**; Rochelle Singer's **The Demeter Flower**; Monique Wittig's **Les Guerilleres**; and Donna Young's **Retreat As It Was!**

When we look at these novels, we find some remarkable characteristics. There are several patterns or tendencies that distinguish these feminist utopias from male utopias, and indeed from all male science fiction writing in general. In these novels I see some symptoms that the hope of the world may, indeed, lie in women.

First of all, I see a movement toward collective values as opposed to the individual values male writers are always putting forth. Second, I see a movement toward empathy and identification as opposed to alienation in the works of male writers. With reference to collective values in these feminist novels, we find first a tendency for power to be less hierarchical, for decision making to be more consensual. Second, we find a tendency for the protagonist to be a group hero. Third, we find the female in control of reproduction for the good of the entire community.

Let us begin by looking at the power structure or the way in which decisions are made. It is not true that all of these novels have consensual decision making or that all of them are nonhierarchical. A few of them are still elitist and authoritarian; for example, there are monarchs in Ursula LeGuin's utopias. In **The Ruins of Isis** there is a matriarchy that is a class society, very hierarchical in its structure, and in **Herland** there is even an intellectual aristocracy. But aside from those three novels, the rest tend toward something that is at least a kind of participatory democracy, and at best that wonderful structure of collective sensitivity that is built on out-and-out anarchism. This is the paradox: the root of real collectivity is individual freedom or anarchism. Thus, when we talk about collectivity, we are not talking about mindlessly relinquishing our power or our personalities to some group. What we are actually talking about is the individual freedom underlying it all.

In these participatory democracies there is a fluid, regional, delegation order. In **Motherlines**, for example, it is the "tent," the family and the whole community, which makes decisions, dependent upon the participation of the people involved. That's very important. That people whose lives are going to be affected by a decision must be in on the decision making is a fundamental idea throughout all these books.

In some novels, power is rotated. The leader is the representative of the party and her actions are always open to question. Often there is struggle between the group and the individual. For example, in **The Wanderground** there is the rotation of the "long dozen" and the desire for a clear consensus. But that consensus again depends upon every woman's being able to walk away from the group and not be a part of it anymore; there is no coercion. The solutions of other books to problems of power are almost mystical. In **The Kin of Ata**, for instance, there is no governing body; dreams govern the people. And in **Les Guerilleres** we do not know the women who somehow energize the whole community; they are a great abstraction. Overall, then, there is a tendency in feminist utopias for decision making to be more collective.

Second of all, we note the emergence of a kind of group hero. In three of these novels, **The Wanderground, The Female Man**, and **Les Guerilleres**, there is a multiple or shared protagonist. In **The Female Man** there are four sides to Janet, the woman living in the utopia, Whileaway. All four split characters participate throughout the book; Janet is not any one person. And it would be hard to say who is the hero of **The Wanderground**, or of **Les Guerilleres** because all of the women are the hero. Even the titles of these books are collective. To find out who the protagonists are in a Greek tragedy, you look at the title of the play — if the play is named

"Antigone," you know Antigone is the hero or heroine. However, if you look at feminist titles, you find **Motherlines**, which has to do with the families Suzy McKee Charnas writes about; you find **Les Guerilleres**, the female guerrillas; you find **The Wanderground: Stories of the Hill Women** and **The Kin of Ata**, collective groups, and **Herland**, a woman's land.

In others of these books there is a single protagonist, though it is sometimes hard to decide who that single protagonist is. For instance, in **The Left Hand of Darkness** it is hard to know whether Genly Ai or Estraven is the hero or heroine, because both of those people share the reader's sympathies. In **Herland** there is not one person who is the protagonist; the role of protagonist is filled by all three of the couples. Thus, there is a tendency to use groups even in the titles and as protagonists of feminist science fiction.

Third, there is no doubt that these novels tend to say human affairs should be the prerogative of the female of the human species, as they are with other animals. The matter of reproduction, which is the bottom line when we talk about freedom for women, particularly stands out in this context. In these utopian novels, that freedom is actually the case and the whole group profits from women who take the helm in caring for the human race.

Alternative Values

In some of these novels, reproduction occurs in the usual heterosexual fashion, while in others there is the equivalent of the Amazon orgy. Once a year all of the women go out to find men and have a huge orgy. Of course they are all with child because they are all cyclically together in their menstrual periods, and the result of the orgy is that children come forth. Even in those societies which are not heterosexual, there are still heterosexual remnants. Marge Piercy's Mattapoisett uses technology and test tube babies as the way to reproduction; however, having one child requires three mothers. Those mothers may be men. Men in Mattapoisett do lactate and actually nurse the babies. There is another remarkable means of reproduction in **The Left Hand of Darkness** in which androgynes actually change into male or female, depending upon what the other partner has changed into. Every person in that society has the experience of being both mother and father — an incredible breakthrough in sex roles and reproduction.

Although some of these novels are heterosexually based, in the rest, reproduction takes place without the aid of men whatsoever through ovular merging or a kind of parthenogenesis. In **The Demeter Flower** women use herb tea made from the demeter flower itself, which makes possible the parthenogenesis. In **Herland** simply the desire of the woman to get pregnant makes it possible. If she doesn't desire to, she will not get pregnant. And in Suzy McKee Charnas's book, there is mating with stallions to stimulate the parthenogenic process. In nine of the fourteen novels, women have complete control over reproduction, and in five they have at least equal say.

With reference to empathy and violence, there are only two roles to play — violator or victim. By violence I mean the kind of violence that sometimes occurs between animals or people in some of these novels. Nowhere, in any of these novels, is warfare brought on by the women themselves; any violence is strictly self-defense. This is important to note. In the majority of novels, violence is associated with the male of the species, and in some cases they are virtually synonymous. For this reason, some of these groups form societies all their own, free from that kind of male energy which they understand to be violent. It is not something they, as women, want to perpetuate.

There is a certain attitude toward nature and technology, also having to do with empathy. In these societies, on the whole, people hold a "same" rather than "other" relationship to nature. Technology will be developed in line with that relationship, to a greater or lesser degree. In none of these novels is technology rampant. When there is high technology, like the induction helmet in **The Female Man**, it is of a highly selective nature. But in most of the books, the choice is not to have a high level of technology, because that in itself is an alienation from nature. Most of these women writers understand that just because something is possible does not mean it has to be done, which is something men have never understood. In **The Demeter Flower**, **The Wanderground**, **The Kin of Ata**, there is an almost total denial of technology, almost to the point of not using hand tools. Significantly, in five of these novels there are many relationships to animals, relationships never found broadly in the work of male writers.

Finally, it is very clear, at least according to these authors, that women are the hope of the world. It is all summed up in the general tendency in all of these novels to assert the superiority of women. The rightful role of women is as controllers of the affairs of human beings, and of the size and nature of the species itself. In these fourteen novels, only five insist simply on equality. One reverses sex roles, putting men in a servile position. In eight, there are no men at all.

Where, in all male writing, with the possible exception of **The Disappearance** by Philip Wylie, is there a society which excludes women? It can't happen because women are necessary, women are primary, and men in their hearts know it. Feminist utopian novels indicate ways we can begin to take steps toward returning the reproductive and erotic initiative to women. We need to make this return and with the Moral Majority on our backs, we need to begin very hard and very fast.

Although it is more dangerous to suggest, we must immediately, without delay, consider the reduction of the men of the human species — of course, there are many ramifications to that kind of proposal. Remember though, that the human species may be up past its bedtime — if there is any hope for us, it lies with women. I leave you with those two thoughts.

Notes

Marion Zimmer Bradley, *The Ruins of Isis* (New York: Pocket Books, 1978).
— , *The Shattered Chain* (New York: Daw Books, 1976).
Dorothy Bryant, *The Kin of Ata Are Waiting for You* (New York: Random House, 1976).
Octavia Butler, *Kindred* (Garden City, NY: Doubleday, 1979).
Suzy McKee Charnas, *Motherlines (New York: Berkeley, 1979).*
Sally Gearhart, The Wanderground: Stories of the Hill Women (Watertown, MA: Persephone Press, 1979).
Charlotte Perkins Gilman, *Herland: A Lost Feminist Utopian Novel* (New York: Pantheon Books, 1979, originally published 1916).
Ursula LeGuin, *The Dispossessed* (New York: Avon Books, 1974).
— , *The Left Hand of Darkness* (New York: Ace Books, 1976).
Marge Piercy, *Woman on the Edge of Time* (New York: Alfred Knopf, 1976).
Joanna Russ, *The Female Man* (Boston: Gregg, 1975).
Rochelle Singer, *The Demeter Flower* (New York: St. Martin's Press, 1980).
Monique Wittig, *Les Guerilleres* (New York: Avon Books, 1973).
Philip Wylie, *The Disappearance* (New York: Rinehart, 1951).
Donna Young, *Retreat: As It Was!* (Tallahassee, FL: Naiad Press, 1978).

Chapter 28

EQUALS in Computer Technology

by Nancy Kreinberg and Elizabeth K. Stage

By the mid-1980s, microcomputers are expected to be in 10 percent of all U.S. homes and to be considered a primary work tool for about 25 percent of all jobs. While it is clear that computers are already an influence on all of our lives, the increasing prominence of computers in the workplace will not be felt equally. Research conducted in Canada suggests that the impact of microelectronics will be so severe on traditional female jobs that unemployment rates in the clerical sector may reach 35 percent by 1990.[1] On the other hand, the shortage of computer professionals is such that salaries in data processing occupations increased by an average of 12.8 percent from 1980 to 1981, bringing the average salary offer to a computer science graduate up to $20,712 per year. While women are concentrated in the lower paying computer occupations, their salaries are closer to men's than in other scientific fields. Thus, computers and their increasing importance in the workplace pose a serious threat to those who are unprepared to use them and a tremendous opportunity to those who are prepared to control this new technology. Who will that be?

In this article we will outline the current answers to that question and discuss educational strategies that may alter that response. Changes must take place in schools and outside of schools so that women will have equal access to computer technology.

Stereotyped Expectations

The biggest barriers to women's taking advantage of the computer revolution are the myths and stereotypes about technology that are well established in children's minds at a very early age. Recently, teachers of fourth through twelfth graders were asked to have their students imagine they were 30-years old and describe how they would be using a computer. The responses were illuminating:

> When I am 30 I'll have a computer that has long arms that can clean the house and cook meals. And another computer that has a little slot that money comes out to pay for groceries and stuff. (6th-grade female)

When I have a computer I hope it will be a computer that
tells you how to do certain things and answers you. I hope
for my computer to also give me reports on the news so I
won't have to buy a paper. I also hope my computer could
create anything I want. Or do anything I wish or please, but
my computer would not be programmed for evil deeds, such
as stealing, cheating, or lying. I would like my machine to
be loyal and trustworthy. So my machine would be the
greatest machine around. (6th-grade female)

I would ask my computer to find me a perfect husband. I
would tell it to tell me where to find the prettiest clothes and
tell me where to get my hair done. Tell me where the most
famous restaurant is in the world. Then I would meet my
future husband, get married, have children — two, named
Ben and Angie — then I would get a divorce and raise my
children on my own till they're grown. And then it's just me
and my computer. All alone again. (7th-grade female)

The Math and Science Education Program for Women at the Lawrence
Hall of Science at The University of California, Berkeley, analyzed the
responses of 883 students (428 males and 455 females) to this question and
found that although both males and females imagined the computer taking over a major portion of their lives, females tended to focus far more
on the housework that the computer (robot) would do, while males
described way they would use the computer for finances, data processing, or games.

These findings confirmed an analysis of 5,000 earlier essays in which
students described a "typical Wednesday" in their lives at age 30. Sex differences in both career aspirations and attitudes toward family responsibilities were quite dramatic. Males expressed far more choices in their
intended careers, while females indicated a narrower and lower level of
career aspiration. The most frequently chosen occupation among
females, for example, was secretary! Not surprisingly, females devoted
more time to describing their family responsibilities and showed an acute
awareness of the realities of juggling work and home demands. One 16-
year old female described a typical Wednesday in her life at 30 as follows:

To start the day, I would get up at 6:00 in the morning. Making sure the kids were up and getting ready for school, I
would stumble out into the kitchen to get a cup of coffee.
After packing lunches, I would get dressed and wake my
husband up. At 6:45 I would leave the house to battle the
traffic through town to work. After arriving at the hospital I
would go to work in the lab. After work, I would come home
to a house full of kids and a mess to go with it. After an hour
of cleaning up, I would start preparing dinner. After dinner,

the kids and I would clean up and from 8:00 to 10:00 we would all relax, maybe watch TV or do something we enjoy. After 10:00 I would go to bed only to wake up to the same rat-race in the morning.

No wonder young women look forward to the age of computerized housework!

Unfortunately, these large sex differences in students' career aspirations are reflected in their patterns of course enrollment. For some time it has been evident that far greater numbers of females than males drop out of math and science once these courses become electives. National pre-calculus enrollments are about 60 percent male, for example, and there are indications that girls engage in fewer out-of-school activities that are related to the learning of science.[2] Girls' interest in computers seem equal to boys' in elementary school, but drops off during junior high.[3]

Studies are beginning to uncover data in high school computer science courses similar to math and science findings. For instance, in a 1981 statewide survey of computer programming courses in all California high schools, conducted by the California State Department of Education, the ratio of male to female enrollment was approximately 5:3 (11,441 males to 6,843 females). Enrollment in computer science courses at the University of California, Berkeley, is also heavily male-dominated beyond the introductory courses; only 23 percent of computer science majors at Berkeley are females.

This absence of young women from computer science courses in their precollege and postsecondary years can only result in another "critical filter" for women — a phrase coined in 1973 by sociologist Lucy Sells to describe the attrition of women from math and the subsequent barriers to their future participation in math-based fields of study and work. A comparable pattern is now emerging in computer science, but this time there are effective strategies to prevent computers from becoming a critical filter for girls and women.

Early Intervention

To encourage girls and young women to become interested in and proficient with computers, they must develop their interest in technology at an early age and be allowed continuous opportunities to increase their mastery with computers throughout their elementary and secondary school years. This involves a long-term commitment to computer education on the part of teachers, curriculum developers, science educators, school board members, teacher trainers, and parents.

Most elementary and secondary school teachers have had little experience with computers, in spite of a proliferation of computer courses.

A recent survey of teachers attending a mathematics in-service education program at the Lawrence Hall of Science revealed that of 81 teachers, representing grades kindergarten through twelve, 63 percent had no computer experience whatsoever, and the remaining 37 percent had only "some" or "a little" experience. All indicated, however, they wanted more information and practical, "hands-on" experience with computers.

Teachers are a potent influence on females' participation in computer courses. Parents and peers exert pressure, of course, but the school environment is potentially the most fruitful. If girls and young women are encouraged to explore, question, and imagine themselves mastering many skills, they will have a secure basis for achieving technical sophistication and awareness. Girls must learn to see computers as part of their future lives from the primary grades forward. There are a number of ways this can be accomplished in the schools through teacher education.

Teacher Education

Computers in the classroom are dependent upon a willing, able, and enthusiastic teacher who has acquired the basic information and skills to select the desired equipment, convinced administrators to purchase it, and then turned the computer into a teaching/learning tool for his or her students.

One program that enables teachers to promote the participation of girls and young women in computer science is EQUALS. A teacher education program at the Lawrence Hall of Science, EQUALS works with teachers, counselors, and administrators at all grade levels. The in-service program concentrates on three essential components: increasing awareness of the issues of computer education for females; providing instruction and materials that encourage confidence and competence in using computers; and creating a motivation toward computer-related occupations through the use of role models and activities.

Teachers and students both must understand the need for computer literacy and the implications of computer avoidance. EQUALS has collected data on male/female computer enrollments, the use of computers in occupations, salary ranges of workers in the computer industry, and opportunities for women in these fields. Teachers can use this information in parent meetings to promote discussions about the role of computer education, as well as in the classroom.

It is extremely important to follow awareness with actual computer experience; this is as true for teachers as for students. A strong program of computer education for teachers should be mounted in every school or district to help teachers develop an understanding of the uses for a computer, learn programming in BASIC, PILOT, or LOGO, and integrate the computer into their curricula.

To eliminate the stereotype that computers belong to the male domain, girls and young women need to meet and talk with role models of women who are working in many fields of technology. For instance the Math/Science Network, through its resource center located at Mills College in Oakland, California, sponsors "Expanding Your Horizons (EYH)" conferences for 7th- through 12th-grade women. The Network is an association of 1,000 scientists, engineers, educators, and citizens who work cooperatively to increase the participation of women in math and science. In March 1982, 43 EYH conferences were held on college and university campuses throughout California, in seven other states, and Australia. Over 14,000 young women and 4,000 parents and teachers heard the message — from role models and in workshops — that technology was a rewarding and challenging field for women.

Similar workshops are sponsored by the Mathematical Association of America, American Women in Science, and the American Association of University Women. There cannot be too many, and obviously, the schools cannot be the sole provider of computer activities for young women. Software developers, science centers, girl scout troops, and parents must also reinforce the school experience or take leadership where schools are lagging.

From Video Games to Software

Controversial as they are, video games constitute a large proportion of the computer experience of many children and adults. Starting with the development of "Pong" in 1972 to "Space Invaders" today, most video games have emphasized themes that appeal to young men more than they do to young women. The San Francisco regional contest for the International Asteroids Tournament attracted 400 youngsters, the overwhelming majority of whom were boys. "Boys like shoot-em ups; they like to see a thing blow up," explained Michael Moone, president of Atari's Consumer Electronic Division.

Thomas Malone, who studied sex-related differences in the interest of elementary school students in various games, observed that boys seemed to prefer scoring, competition, and bombing, while girls selected games with fantasy elements.[4] It should be noted, however, that the children had to choose from what was available, so that Malone's observations or the arcade observations of girls playing "Pacman" or "Frogger" have to be tempered with the realization that most games are created to appeal to their creators. Computer game creators have been drawn from a narrow, asocial segment of society; they are sometimes called "computer wonks," and only a few of them have gained social respectability due to their fantastic financial success.

There are, of course, computer programmers who are not "wonks" and who are interested in creating games and other software that has wide appeal. At the Center for Math Literacy at San Francisco State University, a group of programmers led by Bill Finzer has designed a number of programs that capitalize on the nonmilitary interests of females and males. "Pak-Jana," for example, is a dancer whose arms, legs, and head can be choreographed by writing a simple program. With a little imagination, graphics and music can be used constructively instead of destructively. Girls and boys respond well to programs that engage their curiosity and challenge them to develop strategies to solve interesting problems. Until educational and commercial suppliers routinely provide software that is engaging to all students, however, consumers need to make their desires known.

Other Out-Of-School Experiences

Many adults and children have their first computer experience at a science center or museum. It is time, however, that these centers become actively concerned that their computer classes are not attracting girls. When the Lawrence Hall of Science became aware that their after-school classes were not attracting as many girls as boys, a "Math for Girls" class was started to provide an environment in which girls were able to experience success in a cooperative group taught by a female role model, who was concerned with teaching them to take risks and to solve problems. Since 1974 over 1,000 girls have taken "Math for Girls" and the after-school classes have gone from 25 percent to 38 percent female. A similar strategy, "Computers for Girls," could provide a supportive environment while alerting parents to the importance of their daughters', as well as their sons', becoming computer literate.

The Girl Scouts also provide an opportunity for girls to learn about computers in an all-female environment where girls do not have to compete with boys for access to computers. Since 1979 Girl Scouts have been able to earn a computer badge by using a computer, finding out the names of computer languages and how computers are used in business and other areas, talking to people who use computers in their work, mastering a calculator, learning to count in the binary system, reading a science fiction book about computers or robots, and thinking about what they would like a computer to do. The San Francisco Bay Area Council holds a computer camp for 9- through 13- year olds.

Commercial groups also hold summer computer camps; Atari's Timbertech, for example, attracts children 9-17 from around the United States to Scotts Valley, California. Despite attempts to recruit young women through such groups as the Girl Scouts and the Math/Science Network, female enrollment is only one quarter to one third of the campers in any session. Camp director Monty Swiryn attributes this to parents, who make the decision to send their child to camp but aren't as likely to think of it for their daughters. Swiryn adds that once girls are put into the situation, they enjoy it and benefit from it as much as boys do.

Parents

The gap between the haves and the have-nots widens with every microcomputer brought into a home. Very young children playing computer games at home acquire a sophistication with computers that soon exceeds their teachers'. While it is true that a home computer may some day be as common as a television, it is not the case today. Children from affluent families are mastering the basic technology at home, while less advantaged children may not get to use a computer until high school, if at all.

In some areas, community computer centers have been established to provide access to computers to the public. ComputerTown USA! is a computer literacy project of the people of Menlo Park, California, the Menlo Park Public Library, and the People's Computer Company, a nonprofit educational corporation. They have identified more than 60 public access computer literacy projects in the United States and Europe whose aim is to give inexpensive access to computers to the public. At ComputerTown USA! the percentage of girls coming into the library to use the computers on a regular basis was only 15 percent, so a "Computer Day for Women and Girls" was held in 1981. Approximately 50 women and girls, most with no previous computer experience, were introduced to computers in a relaxed, friendly atmosphere. The aim, of course, was to encourage more women and girls to make use of the regular services.[5]

Further, children familiar with computers usually have a positive attitude toward them, as in this case:

> I would use the computer to find out answers for medical problems like my Dad. If I had a real problem I would punch it in the computer so I could try and cure the person. My Mom used the computer for answers for nursing school. I would use the computer for answers to hard questions or to study for a test. My uncle uses his computer for games. I like to go to his house and play the games. My friend's dad uses a computer to make crossword puzzles. I want to use a computer like all of them. (5th-grade female)

On the other hand, it doesn't always take:

> Right now I do not want to even hear about computers. My Dad has one at home and he is always working on it and that's all I hear every day is the little noises it makes. I know that I will not be working or doing anything with a computer when I'm 30 years old. I can't stand them! (7th-grade female)

The Future

Schools should consider offering parent education sessions focusing on the uses of computers at home and in school. Parents who are informed about the importance of computer literacy for themselves and for their children can become a valuable resource in raising money to purchase computers and software for schools. Family computer classes are currently being offered in science centers, but these reach only those families who have some interest in the technology. Families who have neutral or negative attitudes toward computers might be more willing to think about the educational advantages of owning one if their children's teachers were enthusiastic about computer use or if they had some first-hand experience themselves. As with other stereotypes that families share, deliberately or inadvertently, overcoming mothers' reticence about computers is probably even more important than fathers'.

The problems for women and computer technology at this point are primarily a lack of awareness of the importance of computer literacy and a lack of experience. It is important for girls and women to seize the opportunities for access to computers so that an inequitable distribution of knowledge and power does not result. Rather than invent a new phobia, "computer anxiety," a variety of constructive strategies that have been developed can influence this emerging field of education and employment. Teacher education, visibility of role models, development of interesting software and video games, family and other community experiences all offer promising avenues for increasing the participation of women in computer technology.

Many innovative programs to increase girls' and women's access to math, science, and technology were eliminated or severely curtailed by the Reagan Administration's funding policies. Elimination of the Science Education Directorate of the National Science Foundation stopped funds from that source, while Department of Education Programs such as Title IV of the Civil Rights Act and Women's Educational Equity Act have been cut drastically and/or made the object of political infighting. It is especially important to maintain high visibility efforts that encourage girls' participation in these fields, lest women lose the ground they gained in the 1970s. If each person reading this article worked on one of the goals below, we could ensure that girls and women will become equals in computer technology.

- Encourage teachers to promote computer literacy for all students by requiring that computer classes be 50 percent female and ensuring that all students have equal time using the terminals;
- Convince community organizations and science centers to offer opportunities for girls to learn about computers in a nonthreatening environment, or create a community computer center that will do so;

- Urge parents to try using a microcomputer, to consider seriously the advantages of purchasing one for their home, and to learn with their children how to use it;
- Learn to use a computer ourselves and each teach at least one girl or woman.

Notes

1. Heather Menzies, *Women and the Chip: Case studies on the Effects of Informatics on Employment in Canada* (Montreal: The Institute for Research on Public Policy, 1981).
2. J.B. Kahle and M.K. Lakes, *The Myth of Equality in Science Classrooms* (West Lafayette, IN: Purdue University, in preparation).
3. Dorothy K. Heller, "Computer Games for Women Stress Cooperation, Humor, Whimsy," *Infoworld* 4 (April 1982): 18-19.
4. Thomas Malone, "What Makes Things Fun to Learn? A Study of Intrinsically Motivating Computer Games," *Cognitive Science* 4 (1981): 333-369.
5. People's Computer Company, "A Computer Day for Women and Girls," *ComputerTown USA! News Bulletin* 2 (1981): 11-12.

See also:
Judy Askew, *The Sky's the Limit in Math-Related Careers* (Newton, MA: Educational Development Center, 1981).
Nancy Kreinberg, *1000 Teachers Later: Women, Mathematics, and the Components of Change* (Berkeley, CA: University of California, Institute of Governmental Studies, 1982).
Seymour Papert, *Mindstorms: Children, Computers and Powerful Ideas* (New York: Basic Books, 1980).

For information on the Math/Science Network, contact: Math/Science Resource Center, c/o Mills College, Oakland, CA 94613.

Chapter 29

The Next Move:

Organizing Women in the Office

by Judith Gregory

"We are on the brink of a second industrial revolution that will eliminate drudgery and boredom once and for all," business periodicals proclaim. The technological revolution "is creating more stimulating careers for office workers," a writer rejoiced in a special feature of U.S. News and World Report.[1] Examined more closely, however, American management's idea of the "office of the future" means little more than a recreation of the factory of the past. Today's office workers find themselves threatened with many of the same processes of job degradation that undermined the skills and dignity of an earlier generation of industrial workers (see Chapters 6 and 18). Without the pressure of clerical workers organized in their own behalf, the alienation of the assembly line may well be extended to the "electronic office." Organizations like 9 to 5, National Association of Working Women, are working to see that doesn't happen.

Clerical workers account for almost one in five of all U.S. workers and are among the least unionized and lowest paid members of the workforce. They are also on the front lines of office automation. The office jobs that are especially targeted for automation are dominated by women, who comprise 80 percent of the clerical employees, 99 percent of the secretaries, 93 percent of the bank tellers, and 95 percent of the typists and keypunchers.

New office technologies, because they are extremely versatile, offer a great potential to reverse this trend: to upgrade jobs, skills, and earnings, and to raise overall standards of living. Yet the opposite is occurring: jobs are being deskilled and devalued; working conditions are being degraded; promotional opportunities are declining; health risks are increasing; and large-scale job loss is possible in the not-so-distant future.

Furthermore, with the increase in automation, the things clerical workers like most about their jobs are threatened with elimination: a variety of tasks; the opportunity to learn new job skills; social contact with other workers; an overview of the office function; an opportunity to exercise judgment; and recognition for their work.

Women office workers must recognize the magnitude and urgency of the dangers they face. Computer consultants predict that in two to five years the adverse effects of technology may be "frozen" into place. Yet today only 15 percent of all women clericals in the United States are represented by unions.

The 9 to 5 movement seeks to create a common identity among women office workers as a major group of the workforce that is exploited by employers, who can clearly afford to treat them better. By joining 9 to 5, women take a first step in standing up for their rights. In March 1981, 9 to 5 joined with the Service Employees International Union (SEIU) to create District 925/SEIU, a new union for clerical workers that combines the strength of the Women's Movement with the strength of the trade union movement.

Both District 925 (the trade union) and 9 to 5 (the National Association of Working Women) are part of the strategy to create a movement among the nation's 20 million women office workers. Once empowered through organization, women clericals will represent a new political force, and office automation may well become the catalyst for that change. Let's look at the consequences that make automation such a critical issue for women office workers; each represents a new focus for organizing.

Potential Job Loss

The dynamic of computer technology is to reduce labor requirements (per volume of work) in any sector where it is applied — it is a labor-reducing technology. European studies predict enormous office displacement, estimating, for example, that by 1990 the need for clericals in the French finance industry could be reduced by 30 percent.[2] Eventually many managers hope to replace as many clericals as possible. As one bank manager told his fellow managers in a seminar on automation:

> The way I look at it, you've got your choice. You can have your two 'Suzie tellers' over here, with their vacation days, their sick children, their annual demands for cost-of-living raises and desires for promotions, or you can have your two automatic teller machines, which can work all night, never get sick or need a vacation, and which only need to be upgraded every five years. It's your choice.

Clerical work is still predicted to be the fastest-growing occupation in the United States in the 1980s. The U.S. Department of Labor estimates that there will be 4.6 million new jobs for clerical workers, nearly one in four of all new jobs anticipated in the coming decade. This continued need for clerical workers, however, masks the job-displacing effects of automation in office industries. In 10 to 15 years, there might still be a drastic reduction in the clerical workforce. This raises a long-term social concern: where will new jobs come from if employment in service industries slows down at the same time that manufacturing jobs decline? Public policy addressing these issues must be developed now.

Job Deskilling and Devaluation

When new computer systems are introduced, certain skills become obsolete, while new skills are often belittled and unrewarded, and variety is lost from work. Although office automation improves jobs for some, the majority of office workers' jobs are more closely supervised and increasingly specialized. Each person performs ever smaller fractions of the larger task. When this happens, each job requires less training and offers less chance for advancement.

Deskilling can occur in a variety of ways. In the midwest headquarters of a multinational corporation, secretarial jobs were broken down into component parts when word-processing equipment was brought into the department. As a result, one woman does electronic filing all day, another extracts data all day, one answers phones all day, another handles correspondence all day, and so on. The company requires that each woman complete a "tour of duty" of several months in each subtask in order to be considered for promotion. In other words, each woman must be promoted four times to get back to where she started! This is one example of how companies use new office technology as an excuse to wipe the slate clean and start over with new rules.

A recent study of Wall Street legal secretaries' jobs, among the most prestigious and highly skilled of clerical occupations, illustrates another way that skills are stripped away. Mary Murphree of Columbia University and City University of New York (CUNY) found that:

> . . . while early forms of office computerization served to upgrade and assist secretarial worklives . . . current innovations are striking at the heart of the traditional legal secretarial craft and creating a number of serious problems. The most challenging and responsible tasks traditionally in the legal secretarial domain are gradually being transferred away from the secretaries to *cadres* of professional and paraprofessional workers such as paralegal assistants, librarians, accountants, personnel specialists, and word-processing proofreaders, thereby reducing the secretarial function to one of merely 'telephone gatekeeper.' [3]

Women clericals now also find themselves doing more work for less pay, working faster, and for more people at once. A 1979 management survey found that fulltime video display terminal (VDT or CRT) operators earned only seven dollars more per week on average than conventional typists. Yet consultants estimate productivity gains from 50 to

500 percent when VDTs are used, depending on the type of document production involved. In some sunbelt cities, where office automation is likely to be installed at the outset, VDT typists actually earned less than conventional typists in 1979.

Office reorganization plans that put clericals into clusters or pools increase their workload, as well as breaking down work relations between clericals and managers, and in many cases among coworkers. "When they set up the administrative services center, they said it was more democratic," one woman explained. "We wouldn't have 'bosses' anymore, just 'clients.' But they were just trying to save money. A clerk gets $150 a week while a secretary gets $185 for serving just one person."[4]

Managers use production quotas and computerized monitoring of work performance to carry out speed-ups of awesome proportions in large clerical operations. Employers may even impose a "floating" rate of pay, which works like a treadmill. Rose re-entered the workforce after 20 years away. Her excellent typing skills quickly landed her a job as one of twelve CRT operators in a downtown Cleveland publishing company. She found that office work had changed a great deal while she was out of the workforce. She explains:

> The chairs were good and the machines adjustable, too. But I have never been confined to one place doing key entry at such a pace. The computer at one end of the room keeps track of the keystrokes you do. The more keystrokes, the more money you *might* get. At the end of the day, the figures for all of us are posted. You look at your speed, you look at everyone else's and you say. 'Tomorrow I'm going to do better.' They get you thinking just like they want to, you're really pushing hard.[5]

In addition, in order to use expensive, new office machines most efficiently, shiftwork and nightwork are being introduced more widely. Piece-rate work — pay-per-line-of-information processed — is also spreading, and there is even a clamor for "office homework," which suggests a return to the "cottage industry" concept of old. There is nothing new about speed-ups, piece-rate pay, or shiftwork. And there is nothing new about the drive to reduce labor costs while increasing management control over the workforce.

Increased Stress and Health Hazards

Evidence is mounting that the new equipment being used and the way work is being structured in the automated office pose serious hazards to the health of clerical workers, especially in the areas of occupational stress and exposure to VDTs. Research also points to a relationship between lack of control in the workplace and damage to physical and psychological health.[6] VDT operators report high rates of health problems, ranging from eyestrain, migraines, or insomnia, to severe muscular pain in the neck, back, and shoulders, to increased irritability, anxiety, depression, and decline in self-esteem and sociability.

Recent findings of the Framingham Heart Study show that women clerical workers with children and blue collar husbands developed coronary heart disease (CHD) at nearly twice the rate of men. The study also found that clerical women, regardless of marital status or family size, suffered nearly twice the rate of CHD as all other working women. The study found that clericals who developed CHD were more likely to have an unsupportive boss, to suppress feelings of anger, and to experience few job changes. The automated office exaggerates the very factors that lead to stress. And the computer is the ultimate unsupportive boss.

In February 1981, The National Institute for Occupational Safety and Health (NIOSH) released a report in which they found higher levels of job stress among VDT operators at Blue Shield's offices in San Francisco than they had ever found in any occupational group studied, including most air traffic controllers.[7] The NIOSH study also compared three groups — VDT clericals, "conventional clericals" doing the same work but with regular typewriters, pencil, and paper, and professionals using VDTs, mostly newspaper writers and editors. The research team found the highest stress among the VDT clericals, the "conventional clericals" in the middle, and the lowest stress among the professionals using VDTs. The differences, the researchers believe, are due to vastly different working conditions. The VDT "professionals" have more control on the job; they have more avenues for job satisfaction and pleasure from their work; they can decide how to meet a deadline; and they get credit for what they do. The clericals' jobs are completely rigid. This finding underscores the view that it is not the technology *per se* that causes these problems, but *how* the technology is used by management, and how workers are allowed to, or forced to, use it.

In interviews with office workers about the stress in their jobs, 9 to 5, National Association of Working Women, found that the inability or reluctance to express anger or frustration is related to the arbitrary environments in which clericals work — situations characterized by lack of grievance procedures (or ineffective procedures if they do exist), unfair supervisors, discrimination, and/or favoritism in promotions. Because clerical workers are overwhelmingly unorganized, it is difficult to challenge management to correct these problems.

The New Office Hierarchy

There is increasing concern over the danger of polarization of the office employment structure, with a small number of highly technical jobs at the uppermost level, a large number of deskilled jobs at the base, and between them a skills gap that is virtually impossible to bridge.[8] Writer Barbara Garson quotes a manager who describes this pattern succinctly:

We are moving from the pyramid shape to the Mae West. The employment chart of the future will show those swellings on the top and we'll never completely get rid of those big bulges of clerks on the bottom. What we're trying to do right now is pull in that waistline (expensive middle management and skilled secretaries).[9]

Office workers' worries about short career paths leading to dead-end jobs are justified indeed.

Office automation relies on a base of data entry jobs which involve repetitive, standardized, fast-paced, and accurate work. Jobs become more interchangeable as many different clerical functions are homogenized into information processing at computer terminals. The characteristics of a secondary labor market — low wages, low benefits, high turnover, and non-union, insecure, and semiskilled jobs — are extended to the office. Companies often permit or encourage deliberately high turnover rates in certain clerical operations. This practice gives them tremendous flexibility to reorganize office work as new technology is phased in. When jobs are made highly interchangeable and minimum wage clerks are hired to do them, the benefits of high turnover — avoidance of wage increases and retirement payments, and an unstable workforce less likely to unionize — outweigh any lost investment in job training for new workers.

Sex, race, and age discrimination continue and often are intensified as office hierarchies are revamped. Minority women especially are concentrated in "back office" data processing jobs, often working late-night or swing shifts. The clerical jobs that black women dominate — postal clerks, telephone operators, keypunchers, duplicating machine operators — are special targets of office automation.

Older women clerical workers also face exacerbated problems as their jobs undergo technological change. The notion that "older workers don't want to learn new things" is a prevalent stereotype. A 49-year old woman who talked to 9 to 5 during a lunch break from job hunting said, "First it started out as a rumor — that half of us were going to be replaced by new word processors and CRT machines. Well, within a month they had laid off me and four other girls, all of us with some number of years in towards our pension. Now they have two kids right out of high school running those machines." This contrasts sharply with promises to allow women to move up to fill new computer-related technical and professional jobs. Clerical workers complain that only a preselected few are chosen for training programs in new skills, and affordable community-based programs that teach appropriate courses are few and far between. This situation is compounded by employers' complaints that computer vendors are cutting back on training services and support, which were already minimal.

From Home Office to Offshore Office

The combination of telecommunications and microprocessor technology makes it possible for office work to be geographically dispersed and reorganized. Managers seek to use this new "office mobility" to reduce labor costs, to resist unionization, and, where there are unions, to undermine the traditional power of organized workers.

Electronic office "telework" — work done at a computer terminal and transmitted to another location via phone line or satellite — is heavily promoted in the press and management trade journals. These technological capabilities accelerate the restructuring of service industries. Some finance industry jobs, like textile jobs, already are moving to lower wage states that offer a "better business climate." This may trigger a competitive chain reaction similar to that which has developed over tax incentives to businesses in the manufacturing sector. Another spin-off effect of the new mobility of office work is increased subcontracting to firms specializing in "business services" such as data and word processing or computerized payrolls.

The "offshore office" provides yet another parallel to the manufacturing experience, in which "runaway" factories move overseas or to the sunbelt. A certain amount of bulk information processing has been performed outside the country for some time. In the past, this work was shipped to and from offshore locations by plane, but the advent of satellite communications links makes the practice more attractive. One entrepreneur, George R. Simpson, chairman of New York-based Satellite Data Corporation, relays printed materials by satellite to Barbados, where the work is done by data entry clerks whose pay averages about $1.50 per hour. In Simpson's words, "We can do the work in Barbados for less than it costs in New York to pay for floor space. . .. The economics are so compelling," he told **Business Week**, "that a company could take a whole building in Hartford, Connecticut, and transfer the whole function to India or Pakistan."

Communicating computers will have more personal implications, too. One business writer proclaimed that "portable terminals will be a special aid to homebound workers, such as mothers with small children," and then showed a photograph of a commodities investor lying on a Florida beach with his computer terminal beside him on the blanket. Still in an experimental stage, it is unclear how big a trend "telecommuting" might become. However, it is clear that the implications of electronic homework will vary depending on a worker's power and prestige. For professionals and executives, having a computer at home will be very convenient, giving them greater flexibility, whereas for clericals, work will be more rigidly monitored and will be paid by piece rates.

Office homework is often touted as an easy solution for the critical shortage of childcare for working parents. But work in the home is not the answer to the lack of childcare facilities — mothers still desire and need daycare centers whether they work at home or in an office, and they need the wages that enable them to pay for these services.

Implications for Organizing

The case for organizing is clear, yet unionization is not moving forward as rapidly as it must. About one in five of all clericals in both the public and private sectors is unionized. However, unionized clericals are particularly concentrated in the public sector; estimates are that less than one in ten private-sector clericals has union representation. In the finance industry, which employs one in four women clerical workers, the level of unionization is less than 3 percent.

But the office technologies of the 1970s and 1980s represent a qualitative leap over previous forms of mechanization. Workers suffering from abuses of new technologies are therefore more likely to seek union protection. The experiences of District 925/SEIU organizers discussed below indicate the complex effects of the new office technologies on union organizing. Two general points should be kept in mind: first, technology rarely is an issue in and of itself, but is integrally related to other problems which have long characterized office work; and second, the rate of introduction of office technologies varies among industries and companies. This is to say that the methods used by employers to change from the "social" to the "electronic" office are still in flux and vary greatly in degrees of subtlety or severity.

A District 925/SEIU organizer on the East Coast described the four ways word processors are brought into law firms: first, the company can hire new people at the minimum wage to work in word-processing pools, sometimes in large centers, other times in small departmental pools or "clusters" of two or more word-processing specialists; second, several legal secretaries can be trained on the new equipment and get raises for their new skills, which are integrated into their overall job duties; third, secretaries can be trained in word processing as an added part of their jobs without any additional pay; or fourth, the firm's secretaries can be redefined as word-processing specialists and moved laterally into word-processing pools or clusters. "The drift is towards the first one," the organizer says, "because there's tremendous logic for management to move as quickly as they can toward having minimum wage clerks doing these new, specialized jobs in a full-time way."

At one insurance company, an organizer believes that VDT work has had an important influence on how claims examiners see themselves as workers in need of a union. "They're all in one room, no one has a specialty, and they're very interchangeable. It's a national company — there's no union anywhere. These women see the need to fight organization with organization. They know they cannot make it on their own."

And another organizer in the Midwest related that "people are dying to get a chance to work on a VDT or CRT; they see it as a step up, as a new skill. They're not thinking about the health consequences, at least not yet."

Some tentative conclusions can be drawn from these organizing experiences. First, there are important differences among industries in how systems are brought in and how clerical workers perceive resultant changes. Organizers should research a company's local and national plans thoroughly, since extensive office automation requires a major financial investment and usually involves years of planning. "Showcase" or pilot projects may precede changes that will occur throughout a company or department. A "prototype" system for certain operations such as letters-of-credit, claims examination, or customer billing, may be developed at headquarters or a research center, and then implemented very rapidly elsewhere. Sometimes it is possible to find out about plans in the public sector by examining budget documents to identify major purchases of computer systems and the uses for which they are intended, which may include displacing staff.

Second, in discussing the issues raised by automation with clerical workers, it is important to distinguish between short-term gains and long-term problems. Learning to work on a new computer system often means an increase in pay and any step up is an important one when the average annual pay for clericals is less than $11,000. Nearly one in seven women office workers who headed families in 1980 earned income below the official poverty level of $8,450 for a family of four. It is useful for workers to understand that new technology may allow an employer to raise salaries slightly while still maintaining low wage ceilings overall. Additionally, VDT training frequently means training for another narrow, monotonous job. Once the skill is learned, the job becomes routine. Furthermore, employers may try to downgrade jobs at a later date, claiming they have re-assessed the value and skills of the job after computerization has taken place.

Third, it is crucial to organize around the opportunities that office automation represents. The intersection of office automation and pay equity demands — comparable worth for work of comparable value — provides a more dynamic way of looking at the effects of office automation on skills. Women clericals use so many "hidden" skills or "invisible knowledge " in performing their jobs, that job evaluation studies find secretaries typically underpaid by 40 percent. When office automation changes jobs, we need to identify which old skills are gone, which current skills are carried over, which new skills are developed, and whether or not the full range of skills is recognized and rewarded.

An article on prospects for pay equity in federal employment gives an example of how learning new technology is not carefully considered in job evaluation systems. Lyne Revo-Cohen writes that:

> . . . when the government re-audited jobs of clericals using word-processing equipment, the job classification was lowered (from GS-6). Word processors were informed that because their jobs required more than 75 percent typing, and because the end product of their work was a typed manuscript, the job series would top out at GS-4. This, contrary to the fact that the job had become more technical,

complicated, demanding, and productive. The impact on
morale and turnover has been highly negative and costly.
Another option might have been to take the job out of the
clerk-typist category, reclassify it as video-text operator,
and build in a broadened career ladder."[10]

Office automation opens up several other new avenues for discussion
with workers. There is some question as to whether new forms of work
reorganization actually achieve the stated goal of increased productivity.
This becomes a strategic point of discussion for *both* workers and consumers, as new systems in some cases decrease service quality or
availability.

Effects on Consumer Service

Factory-like speed-ups are conducted in the name of productivity, but
studies of automation, machine-pacing, and stress show that error roed
into thkesfrom 40 to 400 percent when control over the pace of work is
taken away from people and transferred to a machine system. Though
new office technologies do improve the speed of document production,
this emphasis on speed above accuracy, common in piece-rate and
machine-paced settings, is likely to have a detrimental effect on real productivity. The number of key strokes per hour or lines processed per day
typically is used to assess performance, but increased errors are not
necessarily deducted from this figure, which means that those
measurements are misleading. More importantly, the motivation to produce perfect work is diminished.

In an ongoing study of office work by Shoshonah Zuboff of the Harvard
Business School, one clerical worker explains, "When a person makes a
mistake with a computer, to try and get that mistake corrected is so
much red tape. So you tend to let it go. Maybe when they see how bad the
information is, they'll give us back our jobs."

Consumers as well as workers, therefore, will be affected by work
reorganization and computer technology. In European countries unions
are bargaining explicitly over these impacts of new technologies. For example, in research carried out in the Swedish State Social Insurance offices, 9,000 of 19,000 union members participated in study groups to
discuss the effects of new technology on their work. They commented on
their experience:

> Today our knowledge consists largely of how the machine
> works — how we can feed in the input data. . ..The risk in-
> volved in the new forms of knowledge is that our knowledge
> of insurance is pushed into the background. The chances of
> being able to provide adequate and correct information
> about insurance and its aims may be reduced. It becomes

difficult to give exact and detailed explanations of the decisions and other materials sent out by the computer.[11]

The Swedish Union of Insurance Employees worked with computer specialists and researchers from the Swedish Center for Working Life and conducted intensive education among its membership on how computers could be used to improve working conditions and service delivery. Among other provisions, the union's program of action asks:

- that work be arranged in a way that gives the personnel an understanding of the insured and enables them to provide information about insurance in a simple and easily understandable way;
- that personal contact with the insured be increased;
- that rather than centralizing work into larger offices, a number of smaller offices be created throughout the country so that offices are more accessible to the insured;
- that workers be given more training and that training for workers provide them with an overall view of the various types of insurance and a better understanding of the problems of the insured;
- that skilled jobs in social insurance not be computerized.

Thus, the union's proposal seeks to use the flexibility and geographical mobility provided by computer technology to the advantage of workers and the general public by improving both work and service to the consumer.

Organizing for Tomorrow

Clerical jobs, possibly because of their identification as "women's work," historically have been undervalued in terms of pay, status, and respect. The restructured, automated "office of the future" will not ease this tendency. In fact, as clerical jobs are broken down and deskilled and secretaries are redefined as " word processors," inequitable treatment will undoubtedly intensify.

As office working conditions become more monotonous, tightly controlled, and economically exploitative, the necessity for collective action in the form of unions should become as apparent to the clerical workers of the 1980s as it did to the industrial workers of the 1930s. These new workplace conditions will be interacting with the changing attitudes of many women workers about themselves — increased assertiveness and self-reliance, as well as a realization of the necessity for economic independence.

Both 9 to 5 and District 925/SEIU firmly believe that each problem posed by office automation can be turned on its head and transformed into an opportunity to improve the working conditions of today's female workforce and the workforce of tomorrow. The flexibility and versatility of computer technology make it uniquely possible to create better jobs, better working conditions, and better uses of human resources. Computers offer unprecedented chances to address and reduce discrimination by designing training programs that provide for "occupational bridging," to provide improved and more widely available services, and to increase employment by implementing new technologies with social criteria in mind.

Just as the office continues to change, so do the attitudes and concerns of women office workers. In the 1970s we began to organize for equal pay and equal opportunities. In the 1980s we will also organize to influence automation — while the technology is still in flux — to insure the health, well-being, and employment of women office workers. And by the 1990s we need to transform the momentum of the 9 to 5 movement into a new basis of institutional power in the office.

Notes

This article has been adapted from Judith Gregory, "Technological Change in the Office Workplace: Implications for Organizing," in *Labor and Technology: Union Response to Changing Environments* , eds. Donald Kennedy, Charles Craypo, and Mary Lehman (University Park, PA: Department of Labor Studies, Pennsylvania State University, 1982), pp. 83-101. Reprinted with permission.

The author wishes to thank the organizers of District 925/Service Employees International Union for sharing their experiences for this article.

1. *U.S. News and World Report* , September 18, 1978.
2. Simon Nora and Alain Minc, *Computerization of Society* (Cambridge, MA: MIT Press, 1980).
3. Mary Murphree, "Rationalization and Satisfaction in Clerical Work: A Case Study of Wall Street Legal Secretaries," Ph.D. dissertation, Columbia University, 1981.
4. Evelyn N. Glenn and Roslyn L. Feldberg, "Degraded and Deskilled: The Proletarianization of Clerical Work," *Social Problems* 25 (October 1977).
5. Interview in *Warning: Health Hazards for Office Workers* (Cleveland, OH: Women Working Education Fund, April 1981).
6. Robert A. Karasek, Jr., "Job Demands, Job Decision Latitude and Mental Strain: Implications for Job Redesign," *Administrative Science Quarterly* 24 (June 1979): 285-308.
7. U.S. Department of Health and Human Services, "Potential Health Hazards of Video Display Terminals," DHHS (NIOSH) Publication No. 81-129 (Cincinnati, OH, 1981).
8. Heather Menzies, *Women and the Chip* (Montreal: Institute for Research on Public Policy, 1981).

9. Barbara Garson, "The Electronic Sweatshop: Scanning the Office of the Future," *Mother Jones*, July 1981.
10. Lyne Revo-Cohen, *Federal Service Labor Relations Review* (in press).
11. Bo Goranzon and Kalle Makila, *Electronic Data Processing in the Social Insurance Offices: Programme of Action for the Swedish Union of Insurance Employees* (Stockholm: Swedish Union of Insurance Employees, 1981).

See Also:
   "Race Against Time: Automation of the Office" (Cleveland, OH: 9 to 5, April 1980).
   Leslie Schneider, "Words, Words, Only Words: How Word Processing Vendors Sell Their Wares in Norway" (Trondheim, Norway: Institute for Industrial Social Research, Norwegian Technical University, 1981).
   Harley Shaiken, "Computers as Strikebreakers," *Technology Review* (April 1982): 50-51.

The following publications are available from 9 to 5, National Association of Working Women, 1224 Huron Road, 3rd Floor, Cleveland, OH 44115. For a complete list of resources write the Working Women Education Fund at the above address.

   "9 to 5 Office Worker Survival Guide," 1982, $1.50.
   "Why Unionize and How to Do it," $.75.
   "Office Automation Workshop Guide," Summer 1980, $.50.
   "The Human Factor: 9 to 5 Consumer Guide for Word Processing Equipment," $1.50 individuals; $5.00 institutions.

For information on unionizing clerical workers, contact: District 925/SEIU, AFL-CIO, 2020 K Street NW, Washington, DC 20006, (202) 296-7345.

Chapter 30

Tomorrow Is a Woman's Issue

by Tish Sommers

My special interests are the concerns of older women, but that includes all of us who have the good fortune to be living, whether in our 20s, 40s, 60s, 80s, or whatever. There is an old Chinese proverb, "may you live in an interesting time," and we do indeed. What happens in the next ten or twenty years may decide the quality of life in old age for those who are still young, and determine whether those who are a little older will be alive at all. It could decide the quality of life for all of us, because the fate of one generation is inexorably linked with the welfare of all others. For tomorrow to be a woman's issue, first there must be a tomorrow, and that is not a certainty.

Here is one very gloomy script for the future. Suppose in the next few years things do not go well. The arms race speeds up, inflation is not contained, and oil supplies are periodically threatened. In order to increase defense spending, hard fought for benefits are nibbled away — first welfare and nutrition programs, then legal aid, CETA, Medicaid,unemployment benefits, disability insurance, housing programs, vocational education, schools, and the arts. These are all drastically cut, and gradually the federal government hands over the responsibility for social planning to local governments.

At the same time, the job market goes out of kilter with shortages of labor in some technical fields, and massive unemployment among the young, the old, poor, women, and all marginal workers. There is a growing backlash against older people supported by the media, and that leads to further curtailment of their earlier entitlements. Old people are just too expensive. They are getting more than their share, they are not productive, and they are too heavy a burden. They have had their turn. There is rising conflict in crime and neighborhoods deteriorate. Old people's self-imposed house arrest based on fear of the young becomes more common.

Rampant gerontophobia breeds further separation of the older population from the issues of society and from concern about the future. Well-organized voting blocks of seniors vote against school bonds, environmental issues, and any social programs from which they do not directly benefit. For the better-off segment of the aging population, there are well-planned ghettos called Leisure Worlds. But for the majority, especially widows, the situation is grim.

The "me first" mania becomes the accepted doctrine. Individual problems are no longer viewed as reflections of social ills, but are attributed to poor personal planning and bad luck. As social responsibility lessens, there is an ever-growing population of women, young and old, who are dependent, alienated, powerless, and poor, and who express their rage against each other. The intergenerational cold war is well entrenched.

Now suppose that oil supplies are cut off from the Middle East. In the name of honor, but really in the defense of the private automobile and the affected oil companies, the United States readies for battle. The era of limits is applied to everything — except goods and services destined for war. Nuclear war games and disruption of vital resources inevitably lead to an outbreak of hostilities, and more than ever, the large population of the aged is seen as a handicap.

At last there is a pharmaceutical breakthrough. A "death with dignity" pill, already tested on a large number of people who had been suffering from incurable diseases in developing countries, has been shown to act very quickly, and to cause no pain or suffering. It is available to any who want to take advantage of this technological advance and who do not want to be a burden on society. No one is to be pushed to take it, of course. Most religious denominations which had warned against the dangers of euthanasia are now in favor of its use, along with appropriate safeguards, of course, to be sure there is no undue coercion.

As the arms race escalates, the nation's resources are further depleted. As more and more young men and women are killed in the unwinnable conflict, pressure increases to eliminate the nonproductive elements in society — primarily old women. The president directs a special message to this constituency urging them to make a sacrifice for their country by taking the pill. Churches all over the land give comfort to those who answer the country's call, telling them of the mansions of heaven awaiting them.

If this scenario continued, the human race would come to an end, for sooner or later all stops would be pulled out and the atomic holocaust would begin. But I am an incurable optimist. I have not lived 65 years without noting that the pendulum swings. I cannot believe that the human race is speeding toward its own extinction like a Mount St. Helens ready to blow. All of us have a strong survival instinct — we may go up to the brink, but we won't jump over. A crisis may be precisely what we need to shake up our thinking and turn us around. Crises are the mother's milk of social change. They cause pain and suffering, but they appear to be the only way in which public opinion is sufficiently shaken to make major change possible.

A clear vision of an alternative future may speed that turnaround and provide sustenance when the going gets tough. Here are some ideas in that vein to help make tomorrow a woman's issue.

First, as life is recognized as a continuum from conception to death, those rigid life-span boxes of youth, adulthood, and old age with their corresponding functions of education, productive work, and leisure will no longer be viable. Barriers between generations will be reduced when all ages go to school, participate in productive life, and enjoy periodic leisure. Adolescence and young adulthood will be more rewarding and less drawn out, the middle years will become more precious when the burden is shared, and old age will be revalued in the process.

Models for the future in the market place are already being tested here or abroad. Work sabbaticals, long encouraged by academics, are gaining favor in management circles. But the concept could be greatly expanded so that everyone, regardless of age, could have the opportunity to take a year off to study, test new lifestyles, or perform community service. Once recognized as a socially desirable pattern, an adjustment in the rhythm of education, work, and leisure could become the recognized norm around which the workplace is organized.

To make this change of employment patterns workable, schools must be restructured to provide lifelong education. Since classes would necessarily be intergenerational, knowledge and skills could more easily be transferred from one generation to the next, reducing the load on the teachers. Schools could become centers of exploration and personal growth. There is already great interest in re-entry students and emeritus curricula, but these are just the opening wedges for a complete restructuring of the educational system.

Leisure needs restructuring, too. It holds the promise of revitalizing the spirit. When the "me" becomes the "we" generation, leisure time will focus upon enriching the lives of those around us. Volunteerism will take on new meaning when it is no longer the sole province of those with limited access to paid employment — namely, youth, women, and older persons. Volunteers can create their own jobs, take vacations at will, choose priorities, work on causes of deep concern, and select tasks for self-actualization. Such volunteerism provides a joyous occupation when life-span boxes have been eliminated. When all ages and all people have equal access to paid employment, volunteer work will become the pearl of leisure time activity.

But none of this will be possible unless there is a functioning full employment policy. The right to a job must become the most basic of civil rights, otherwise generations will be pitted against each other for paid employment. There will be no end to rationales for limiting competition for scarce jobs from the old, young, minorities, and women. Society can provide these jobs from the private sector, cooperatives, self-employment, and government as employer of last resort. There is no other way to go, and in the long run the social costs will be far less than maintaining and subduing an alienated population.

My vision also includes the U.S.U.S. — the United States Unarmed Services — an organization which recruits unemployed of all ages to provide auxiliary educational forces to work on energy conservation projects and to give primary health care. The U.S.U.S. believes strongly in equality of the sexes and is opposed to any age bias.

But none of this change can occur without basic shifts of power. Political parties will wither away and be replaced by regional councils which have a great deal to say about who is nominated to national governmental bodies. Neighborhood block organizations will make officials far more sensitive to local citizens and more fearful of the consequences of malfeasance.

Preventive care and health education will become the center of health care. A healthy block will become the cornerstone of neighborhood organization, encouraging healthy life styles, mutual help for primary care or minor diseases and injuries, and health screening. Each neighborhood or workplace unit will be linked with larger, more specialized centers for referral. Health care, like employment, will be considered a human right, with the fee-for-services process discarded as inflationary and leading to inequality of care. A national health service will be instituted to provide cradle-to-grave attention to physical well-being.

The neighborhood block organization will be facilitated by the Y.A.C., the Youth and Age Corps, a government-sponsored agency modeled after the Youth Corps of an earlier age. But because it will be nonsexist, putting emphasis on intergenerational teams with strong local support, it will be far more successful than its present model.

In my vision, block organization grows out of necessity. Lack of confidence in the monetary system is already leading to the rapid growth of barter. Older persons, especially women, usually manage these barter outlets. In the future, neighbors will have to meet more, trust, and trade with each other and in so doing, develop many more ideas for mutual help. Gardening will flourish as never before. Even urban areas will devise enormous roof solariums (as a side benefit to solar heating systems), which will augment a tremendous increase in home gardening and food processing stimulated by local organization.

The social workers, gerontologists, and service providers, most of whom are now without jobs, will find themselves in the same boat as their former clients, and will band together into S.H.E.O., the Society for Helping Each Other. They will prove to be effective organizers of survival schools, out of which will come some of the most innovative ideas of the period. S.H.E.O., a very age-integrated organization, will come up with a new kind of preretirement training. Rather than counsel retirees to make a shrinking budget stretch, the new counselors will initiate mutual help sessions dedicated to preparation for new creative freedoms and civic responsibilities.

Health, as we grow older, can no longer be taken for granted. The health counselors of tomorrow will assist in the organization of health co-ops to augment personal responsibility through exercise, diet, and positive health habits. For example, cigarettes will be available only through prescription to addicted persons, and not advertised in any manner.

To cope with the continued shortage of energy, specialists from the Home Conservation Corps will visit all types of organizations to collect ideas on how to reduce energy waste. These persons will serve as both information gatherers and promoters of conservation because people who contribute to a plan of action are far more committed to its success. Like Y.A.C., the Home Conservation Corps will be intergenerational, because all ages need to become involved to make it work.

Gone will be the concept of custodial care for frail elders. Instead, the Primary Care Givers will act as teachers to the patient, family members, and potential supporters, with maximum independence of patients as their goal. This job will be adequately paid. As alternatives to institutionalization, there will be cooperatives of persons needing care, shared living arrangements with peers or with other generations. With sufficient support systems, relatives or friends will be far more ready to bring people in need of care into their homes. Adult- as well as childcare centers will be available throughout the country.

An option to nursing homes will be The Last Perch, a live-in community of compatible people, some ambulatory and others living their last days in a joyous and beautiful setting. The key difference from present institutions is that the Perchers will hold onto control of their environment. They will select who is to be admitted, what type of food is served, what drinks are available at the bar, what the decor and social arrangements will be, as well as who will be admitted to study them in exchange for specific services. They will have access to a printing press, and a computer, of course, and perhaps they will produce their own television show. Their beautiful cooperative gardens will surround their last years with flowers. Last Perches will flourish across the country.

In the process of all these changes, the concept of the family will be broadened and redefined as consisting of two or more persons who share resources, goals, values, and lifestyles over time. It will become a network of responsibility and decision making which goes beyond blood, legal ties, adoption, and marriage. This will encourage revitalization of communities spurred on by intergenerational neighborhood co-ops. As family structure changes, there will be a greater sharing between the sexes concerning responsibilities for nurturing and care of the young and the infirm.

In my fantasy, a very significant thing will happen when the baby bulge crashes into middle age. When the number of women 45-years old and over swells, advertisers will turn their attention to the growing market and change their tune. The change will begin when the Miss America Contest is won by a 49-year old woman who later promotes a cosmetic line designed to augment mature beauty, including a special cream to put those lovely, sexy, brown spots on the hands.

But, how do we get from here to utopia? Only with painful struggle and much sustained hard work will these dreams come to pass.

Remember crises, the mother's milk? The 1980s will be full of crises, even if we avoid the gloomy script of war. There may be another great depression, or worldwide shortages. Gasoline prices could rise so high that automobile transportation will be brought virtually to a halt, except for the very wealthy and top bureaucrats; triple digit inflation could make the present rates seem normal. Anger and despair in the ghettos may reach such a level that destruction goes far beyond the riots of the 1960s.

But there are counterweights to all of this. As war creeps closer, the old peace movement is beginning to come to life in new form. As energy sources become scarcer, tighter conservation takes on a new urgency. And once that begins, wonders can be performed.

And there is a Women's Movement that will have enormous impact on the future. We certainly can't talk about aging without talking about women because the so-called problems of aging — loneliness, isolation, vulnerability to crime, and so forth — are in large part related to women's roles in society, especially dependency. But these will be changing in the next decades as women redefine themselves and develop more independence.

To get from here to utopia we cannot "go gentle" as Dylan Thomas said; we must go as revolutionaries. Older women must learn to rage as well as nurture. In the newly formed Older Women's League, we are redefining ourselves through action. We are selecting and organizing around those issues in which we can make progress, even in the worst of times, while laying the groundwork for the big push ahead. The major dangers are alienation and apathy, stemming from a loss of hope. But *Homo sapiens* are self-evolving mammals who can create their own long-term destiny.

All this seems a little scary to the young. But those of us who are old have seen changes in our lifetimes far greater than anything mentioned here. Future shock is less a problem for my generation because we have been shocked so much already. And as we grow older, we get more flexible and can cope with change better.

It is the young who will make tomorrow a woman's issue.

Notes

For more information contact: The Older Women's League, 3800 Harrison Street, Oakland, CA 94611, (415) 658-8700.

Chapter 31

Feminism:

A Catalyst for the Future

by Patricia Huckle

The future is not yet ours, as many of the articles in this book note. But women have begun to examine the multiple effects of advanced technology on their lives, and to organize themselves as participants in the public dialogue. This article is about some feminist dreams, about socioeconomic and political realities, and about their possible connection points. Enthusiasm, anger, and despair mix in our efforts to bring about change and to take a larger role in shaping the future. Feminists have a vital role to play in those efforts.

It is clear that societal structures today are not shaped by women. In fact, white middle-class men control resource allocation and decision making and have done so for much of history. The United States and other industrialized nations determine their economic and political future through diverse techniques: business forecasts, cumulative scientific research, and prognostications about housing, transportation, recreation, employment, communications, eugenic control, and environmental and military technology. Women need to develop a counter-vision of the future they wish to create.

Feminists of diverse perspectives have been concerning themselves with the central issues of economic survival, reproductive and sexual self-determination, and the struggle against social violence and coercion. Rich and inspirational as the feminist context is and has been, its consequences will be limited without integration into public regulations and policies that determine future options. My intention here is to identify some fruitful aspects of feminist thinking about the future, to sketch some aspects of the field called future studies, and to suggest strategies for developing a more feminist future — at the margin and at the center of society.

Past Into Future

As part of the search for a positive future, feminist scholars have begun to explore and expand women's historical experiences.[1] First, it is important to understand the historical roots of rule by men, and to extend the critique of current inequalities through a clear look at life patterns in the past. The past is also useful to point the way to the future. In revising traditional history, individuals or communities of women who did more than survive in a subordinate state can be found. For some, the historical search is for a "golden past," before male ownership of women, or for a woman-centered ideal society to serve as a model. Amazon myths (or attempts to recreate their reality) can serve the political purpose of providing a utopian direction. The idea of a matriarchal community, where women (or people) are in harmony with one another and the natural environment can serve to strengthen us today and give hope for tomorrow. Even where the practical replication is unlikely, there is value in these dreams.

Still others have studied the utopian socialist movement in the United States during the eighteenth and nineteenth centuries. Based on critiques of current social arrangements and belief in the perfectibility of "man," hundreds of social experiments developed in the United States and Europe at that time. Women played a part in these experiments, many of which held, at least in theory, to equality of the sexes. Although in most of these settings sexual division of labor and subordinate political roles for women were the norm, women often were able to develop technological innovations in domestic labor and did share in collective childrearing. From these communities we can learn of the strength and imagination of women architects and inventors, while still acknowledging the limits of their political power.[2]

In more recent history, there have been revivals of experiments in communal living.[3] During the 1960s, hundreds of communes were started in the United States. Some were organized in rage and despair at the environmental and political waste of human/natural energy in the larger society; some grew out of a naive idealism about the power of "love" to transform institutional structure. Many were anti-urban and antitechnology (except for stereo equipment). Women rapidly discovered — as they have in political groups across the spectrum — that the "good life," the simplified, "natural life" meant repetition of sex role specialization and oppression of women. In heterosexual communes, women were still sex objects and domestic servants. As "earth mothers," they were expected to live in harmony with nature while men controlled the tools, land, and decisions. Disillusioned, many women left, often to join other women.

Some feminists also saw rural communes as a way to escape male oppression and to develop as strong individuals in a collective context. June Arnold brilliantly chronicles this struggle in *The Cook and the Carpenter*, making us aware with laughter and pain of how difficult sharing power and responsibility can be.

A third thread in the historical pattern can be found in recent feminist scholarship on contemporary women's communities and relationships.[4]

Here the focus is on settings in which women live or work relatively isolated from men, or relate primarily to women. These settings include religious orders, both recent and ancient, as well as temporary living arrangements among women. Knowing that there have always been some women who resisted marriage and family, or who were able to control aspects of their lives can give each of us courage to try new models, new living arrangements. The point is not to idealize or romanticize women's past lives, but to use their strengths and innovations in structure and process to inform our own search.

These groups, historical and present, are our social experiments. Their attempts to blend theory and practice often have been painful and short-lived, but they were and continue to be valuable as refuges, as sources of renewal and energy, and as examples of daring to build toward a nonsexist future. Even for those of us who believe such separatist experiments are not a viable solution for a majority of women with varying age, class, and racial backgrounds, these groups can provide models for social change. It is interesting to note how many recent communal efforts are stimulated by or reflect the growing body of feminist speculative fiction.

Science Fiction: More Truth Than Fantasy?

Traditionally, science fiction has reflected "man's" attempt to escape from or control advanced technology.[5] Until recently, the genre has paid little attention to futures without sex role specialization or subordination of women. Feminist science fiction writers tend to deal with similar issues with respect to technology, but their work most often has been grounded in a sharp analysis of socioeconomic roles and of women's subordination. These novels, which provoke, challenge, and inspire creative response to new ways of relating and new possible forms of society, echo certain themes: a high value placed on equitable distribution of resources and authority; options in terms of the nature and place of work in individual lives; status based on individual worth; and a pastoral (or limited-technology) setting that is sensitive to ecological systems. Unlike most male or utopian fiction, these feminist novels also critique patriarchal power distribution and rigidly circumscribed relationships.

This literature reflects both aspirations and ideology. Women are freed from both the power and burden of reproduction. Children and women are fully integrated into society. Violence against women and social coercion toward heterosexuality or sexual subordination are eliminated. Cooperation either replaces competition, or competition is structured into marginal activities. No one owns anyone; in fact, both cooperative anarchy and collective decision making are the dominant forms of governance. Status and power come from being a valued member of a community, not from innate physical capabilities, or from sex, class, or race privilege. In these feminist visions, individuals are strong because the community is strong.

There are obvious benefits from this literary and historical effort to construct anew women's lives; but there are also hazards. To the extent that the urge to fantasize seduces us, we are less likely to continue active struggles in the present. Fictional assumptions that advanced technology will disappear without holocaust, or that technology can eliminate oppression seem naive. While we can develop new ways of seeing or break with traditional modes of thinking, we can also be trapped by wishful thinking and the urge to escape from all-too-present economic and social realities. No mythic past, spiritual ascendancy, psychic insight, former women's community, or literary construction should remove us for very long from the social/political/economic reality of women's lives throughout the world.

The personal search for fulfillment, the elation of worship, the healing sense of loving oneself and others, the mythic and mystical past and future have tremendous appeal. As feminists, we need this vital stream of exploration. Our communities flourish, erupt in conflict, collapse, and sometimes rebuild. New kinds of research develop in women's studies and in community efforts to find solutions to immediate problems. More traditionally trained and inclined scholars begin to raise feminist issues within their universities or government agencies. Each of these efforts needs to be nurtured and cherished. Each also needs the critical mind and heart. We can and should experiment and escape, but we must not mistake these efforts for the substance of change.

While we are about it, we must not forget that men continue to control access to leadership and management positions. In spite of media images portraying the advancement of women, white men continue to make the major political and economic decisions. This is particularly true in the areas of science and technology, where women represent only about ten percent of the researchers, and less than five percent of the managers. One reflection of that control is in the growing field of "future studies."

Gazing Through the Crystal Ball

Almost everyone in the private and public sector is concerned with planning for the future. There are many labels for these planners — futurists, forecasters, futurologists — who work in universities, government agencies, consulting firms, and corporations. They include novelists, economists, military strategists, political scientists, sociologists, urban planners, biological and physical scientists, environmentalists, psychic researchers, and architects. Their titles and their numbers continue to grow. One indication of growth is the membership of the World Future Society, which started with 200 members in 1967 and currently has more than 25,000 members. Another is the proliferation of journals, including: **Futures: The Journal of Forecasting and Planning, Long Range Planning, Technological Forecasting and Social Change, The Futurist, Journal of the International Society for Technological Assessment, Futurics, Footnotes to the Future,** and other periodical reports and bibliographies. It takes little research to discover the limited representation of women or women's issues in the field.[6]

Some of these planners are genuinely concerned about the quality of life and how ethical choices made now will affect the future. Visionaries push for an end to poverty, nuclear disarmament, a positive religious image, egalitarian politics and income distribution, and environmental harmony. Modern futures research has been traced to its roots in military planning, a product of which is the ubiquitous technique of systems analysis. Normative assumptions from the perspective of military defense are bound to represent beliefs on the "correct" use of power and control. The literature in this field thus often presents a posture of certainty about predicting the future. It assumes that planning and forecasting are not only essential, but possible. It also assumes that advanced technology can solve social and economic problems, often with the view that the North American or European pattern of industrial, or postindustrial development is both inevitable and beneficial for the rest of the world.

Critics of futures research point out both the technological and ideological limitations of current methodologies. A method like the Delphi technique, for example, which uses panels of "experts" to develop consensus patterns for forecasting, is obviously value-laden in its definition of "problems" and selection of "experts" who tend to confirm existing values. Future "scenarios," closely related to science fiction, again use "experts" to take a given present and invent the future. Trend extrapolation and cross-impact matrices use available, quantifiable data to identify alternative futures. Simulation modeling, simulation gaming, and technological forecasting also suffer from the limits of available data and ideological assumptions. Following an introductory claim of humility by the researcher, admitting the limits of the methods and the data, the planning proceeds.

Some of these problems and the potential hazards of male-dominated futures research are reflected in the areas of eugenic manipulation or reproductive control. Feminist writers have often taken for granted the need for scientific modification of the reproductive process. Some have predicted that technology could eliminate the tyranny of birth in women's lives, and novelists invent societies in which this is done. But it is not feminists who control biological/eugenic research or public policy. In the most pragmatic present, the ability to choose to terminate pregnancy is being restricted, while policies idealizing the limited nuclear family are before Congress and reflected in the media.

Uterine transfers of embryos, extra-uterine fertilization, cloning (if only of carrots and movie stars), and the billions of dollars spent each year on biomedical research are not controlled by women, nor are they conducted in the specific interest of women. Women do not yet have much access to science and technology, let alone the capability to control its future direction. They do not even participate extensively in the debate in the scientific community about the ethical issues involved. Male planners will do it without us; they will control the future if feminists are not participants, critics, and politicians offering alternatives.

Obviously, it is in the best interests of men to continue their control. The invention of the future as a way of affecting today's policies and practices has been based to date on the traditional, male-centered model. If women stay out, and continue to be kept out of the arena, the past will continue well into the future. It is encouraging to see the number of new women moving into scientific and technological fields; it is not encouraging to recognize how resistant the barriers continue to be.

Forging the Future

For such complex issues, multiple strategies are required. One, we need feminist visionaries — novelists, dreamers, separatists, and seers — to continue expanding women's potential and experience, and to build vibrant models based on feminist principles and critiques of patriarchy. Two, we need feminist scientists, technologists, planners, and blue collar workers who can survive and achieve in conventional settings, and who are willing and able to push for a feminist perspective in policy making. We need women willing to continue the difficult task of desegregating professional and blue collar occupations. We must support these women in their isolated, "breakthrough" work. Three, we need active political organization and pressure in every public arena to act on both immediate survival needs and long-range priorities; and we need to use a variety of strategies, including the media, to make our concerns public. Four, we need to build on the connections among activists in all these areas.

This last task, like the others, is difficult. Women of good will differ in ideology and priorities. Different levels of access to education and income, diverse ethnic and racial backgrounds, sexual preference, and age are more than categories for social analysis. Women (and sensitive men) genuinely see different political agendas with respect to technology. It takes great skill to listen and exchange so that very real differences of view can be legitimately expressed, explored, and expanded. It means giving substance to the rhetoric that there is "no one way," no monolithic solution to women's problems. It means patient coalitions, learning to speak one another's language, respect for diversity. With these, collective strength multiplies.

There are already many attempts to build this communication. Informal exchange goes on all the time as women move from one communal setting to another, or attend a seemingly endless number of regional and national conferences or cultural events. Summer workshops and living experiences, such as Califia or Willow in California, provide a setting for renewal and exchange across many boundaries. On a larger scale, the National Women's Agenda and the United Nations International Decade of Women provide a background for setting long-range priorities and developing communication networks for those involved. Conferences aimed at organizing female workers in hazardous industries or women office workers also provide a base, as does the burgeoning antinuclear movement.

Feminist periodicals offer another outlet for this dialogue; so do organizations involved in neighborhood support, health clinics, rape crisis centers, and shelters for battered women. Although all these sources are currently (1982) under attack by conservatives, and threatened by funding cuts, those involved are learning and sharing their political experience and ideas.

Women's Studies programs continue to enroll a wide range of students. They have a responsibility to serve as a connection between the public and scholars, and to seek out women involved in science and technology. We need to encourage Women's Studies to develop courses on the future and to establish ties with academic scientists, as well ask to retain a commitment to the "real world" of the nonschool community.

While we are talking about this building of connections and collective energy, we need to ask how the Wolf Creek women's farm or communes in Vermont and New Mexico relate to the "new towns" of Irvine or the arcologies of Paolo Soleri or the "Spaceship Earth" envisioned by Buckminster Fuller. The films and architectural designs of feminists are connected to, yet contrast with both traditional and avant-garde media and community plans. We need to generate feminist demographic predictions which look at how and why women decide to have babies and what that means or should mean to the preferred structure(s) of families. Access and political organization need to continue to be at the center of feminist strategies. Half in jest, a futurist once noted that the new golden rule is "he who has gold, makes the rules." If we accept at least some truth to the slogan, how do we alter our strategies?

We are fostering intense questioning and disciplined exploration of our past, present, and future. As feminists, we must keep our sights on the economic survival needs of most women, the presence of violence and social coercion in most women's lives, and the implications of forced pregnancy for women of diverse backgrounds. While we are about it, we must not assume that values and priorities of U.S. feminists are the same as those of women from other cultural and economic settings.

Priorities? All. To help the damaged now, ourselves and others. To nourish and support one another, to build root systems rather than pyramids. To settle in for the very long run required to generate major social change. To learn when compromise is required and useful, but to refuse to compromise on a feminist vision of a future society in harmony — without gender, sexual, class, age, race, or other levels of oppression or privilege.

Notes

1. Among others, see Merlin Stone, *When God Was a Woman* (New York: Harcourt Brace, 1978); Joan Bamberger, "The Myth of Matriarchy. . .," in

Women, Culture and Society , eds. Rosaldo, et al. (Palo Alto, CA: Stanford University Press, 1974), pp. 263-280; ARETHUSA 11, "Women in the Ancient World" (Buffalo, NY: SUNY Buffalo, Department of Classics, 1978); and Paula Webster, "Matriarchy: A Vision of Power," in *Toward an Anthropology of Women* , ed. R. Reiter (New York: Monthly Review Press, 1975).

2. See, for example, Walt Anderson, *A Place of Power* (Santa Monica: Goodyear, 1976); Dolores Hayden, *Seven American Utopias* (Cambridge, MA: MIT Press, 1976); Raymond Lee Muncy, *Sex and Marriage In Utopian Communities* (Bloomington, IN: Indiana University Press, 1973); and Charlotte Perkins Gilman, *Herland* (Westminster, MD: Pantheon, 1979).

3. Kathleen Kinkade, *A Walden Two Experiment: The First Five Years of Twin Oaks Community* (New York: William Morrow, 1973); Sherry Thomas and Jeanne Tetrault, *Country Women: A Handbook for the New Farmer* (New York: Anchor Books, 1976); Hugh Gardner, *The Children of Prosperity: Thirteen Modern American Communes* (New York: St. Martin's Press, 1978); Kenneth Rexroth, *Communalism: From Its Origins to the Twentieth Century* (New York: Seabury Press, 1974).

4. Gracia Clark, "The Beguines: A Medieval Women's Community," *Quest* 1 (Spring 1975): 72-80; C. S. Rosenberg, "The Female World of Love and Ritual," *Signs* 1 (Autumn 1975): 1-29; and Ernst McDonnel, *The Beguines and Beghards in Medieval Culture* (Chicago: University of Chicago Press, 1975). Also, Elise Boulding, *Women in the Twentieth Century World* (New York: Halstead Press, 1977).

5. See Sally Gearhart, Chapter 27, above.

6. U.S. Congress, Senate, Committee on Labor and Human Resources, *Hearing on Women in Science and Technology Equal Opportunity Act* (S568), 1980.

Index

About the Authors

Margaret Lowe Benston holds a joint appointment in Women's Studies and Computing at Simon Fraser University. The author of "The Political Economy of Women's Liberation" (1969) and many technical articles on chemistry, she now focuses her research on the social implications of technology. She and Marian Lowe are twins.

Philip L. Bereano is an Associate Professor in the Program for Social Management of Technology at the University of Washington, Seattle, where he holds adjunct appointments in Women's Studies and Civil Engineering. His research interests are concerned with how technological developments relate to social values in such areas as household technology, genetic engineering, energy, and telecommunications.

Christine E. Bose is Assistant Professor of Sociology at the State University of New York at Albany, where she also served as director of Women's Studies from 1978 to 1981. Her publications include studies on women's occupational prestige, wage differentials among retail clerks, the status of the housewife, the effects of technology on household division of labor, and determinants of women's work in 1900.

Sandra "Bambi" Emerson is the *nom de plume* of a woman in technical management who has served time in engineering academia, in small, rapidly-growing high tech companies, and in large multinational corporations that think (erroneously) they are on the cutting edge of technological change. A computer scientist, she has served as an instructor and counselor in several programs for women re-entering technical careers.

Maria Patricia Fernandez Kelly, a Research Scholar in U.S.-Mexican Studies at UC San Diego, is co-author of the forthcoming book, *Women, Men, and the International Division of Labor* , and author of a book tentatively titled *"For We Are Sold, I and My People": Women and Industry on Mexico's Frontier* . She holds doctorates in art history from Universidad Iberoamericana and in social anthropology from Rutgers.

Frances GABe is an artist/inventor by profession. She has had nine one-woman art shows and has patented 68 inventions comprising the Self-Cleaning House (SCH). Now 67 years old, she lives in the world's first SCH, which she built on her 7¼ acres of forested plateau near Newberg, Oregon. Frances GABe plans to manufacture and market the SCH and is writing her autobiography.

Sally Miller Gearhart is a lesbian-feminist activist who teaches Speech and Communication Studies at San Francisco State University. One of the participants in *Word Is Out* , a documentary about lesbians and gay men, she is co-author of *Loving Women/Loving Men: Gay Liberation and the Church* (1974) and *A Feminist Tarot* (1976). In 1979 she published her feminist utopian fantasy, *The Wanderground: Stories of the Hill Women* .

Genevieve Giuliano holds a joint research appointment in the School of Social Sciences and Institute of Transportation Studies at the University of California at Irvine. Her fields of specialization include public transit services evaluation, transportation planning, and the transportation needs of women. She received her Ph.D. in Social Science from U. C. Irvine in 1980.

Judith Gregory joined 9 to 5, National Association of Working Women, as research director in 1979. She speaks frequently on the issues of office automation and office workers' occupational health. The author of two major reports, *Race Against Time: Automation of the Office* (1980) and *Warning: Health Hazards for Office Workers* (1981), she received her B.A. in social research from Antioch College.

Barbara A. Gutek is Associate Professor of Psychology at Claremont Graduate School. Co-author of *Women and Work: A Psychological Perspective*, she is currently writing *Sexuality at Work: An Empirical Analysis*. Dr. Gutek has consulted for such organizations as Xerox, the Rand Corporation, and the Batelle Human Affairs Center.

Jaime Horwitz is writing her doctoral thesis on old and new images of working at home for the Environmental Psychology Program at the City University of New York. She also teaches at the New Jersey School of Architecture. Her background includes degrees in art and urban planning and many years of community advocacy design.

Patricia Huckle is Associate Professor and Chair of the Department of Women's Studies at San Diego State University. Her publications and research include work on "Women in Utopias," "Future Studies and Feminism," public service employment policies, and women in sports. She received her Ph.D. in urban studies from the University of Southern California in 1975.

Irmgard Hunt, an energy consultant, is a founding member and executive director of Consumer Action Now (CAN) and chairs the executive committee of the New York Energy Network. She transformed CAN from a group of women volunteers working on environmental and energy issues into a professional organization focusing on solar transition.

Katherine Jensen is an Assistant Professor of Sociology and director of the Women's Studies Program at the University of Wyoming. She grew up on a cattle ranch in western South Dakota and is collaborating on a book from the Wyoming women's oral history project. Dr. Jensen has published articles on Native American education, women and academia, and the contribution of oral history to quantitative research.

Natasha Josefowitz, Professor of Management at the College of Business, San Diego State University, is also a consultant to public and private organizations on male/female dynamics in the workplace. She is the author of two books: *Paths to Power: A Woman's Guide from First Job to Top Executive* (1980) and a volume of verse, *Is This Where I Was Going?* (1983).

Nancy Kreinberg is founder and director of the Math and Science Education Programs for Women at the Lawrence Hall of Science, University of California,

Berkeley. Her publication, *I'm Madly in Love with Electricity and Other Comments about Their Work by Women in Science and Engineering*, was one of the first career booklets designed to encourage young women to consider careers in the sciences.

Robin Tolmach Lakoff is Professor of Linguistics at the University of California, Berkeley. The author of *Language and Woman's Place* (1975) and of numerous scholarly articles, she received her doctorate in linguistics from Harvard University in 1967.

Ellen Levy has worked on an MT/ST for a board of education, Vydec 1400 and AM Comp/Edit at a major New York City bank; AM Comp/Edit and Comp/Set at various small type shops and a large publishing firm, and now works on an IBM OS/6 as part of a night pool at a university in Brooklyn.

Marian Lowe, an Associate Professor of Chemistry and co-director of the Women's Studies Program at Boston University, has done research on women and science and on the interaction of culture and biology. Dr. Lowe is co-editor, with Ruth Hubbard, of *Genes and Gender II: Pitfalls in Research on Sex and Gender*, and of a volume tentatively titled *Women's Nature: Rationalizations of Inequality*. She and Margaret Benston are twins.

Kristin Luker, a sociologist and demographer, is an Associate Professor of Sociology at the University of California at San Diego. The author of *Taking Chances: Abortion and the Decision Not to Contracept* (1976) and of *Abortion and the Politics of Motherhood* (1983), she received her Ph.D. in sociology from Yale University.

Ann R. Markusen is currently Assistant Professor of City and Regional Planning at the University of California, Berkeley. She has published articles on women's issues in *Signs*, *Quest*, *The Review of Radical Political Economics*, and *Frontiers*, in addition to numerous articles on regional and urban development. She recently taught a course on women and economics at the University of California at Los Angeles.

Carolyn Merchant is Associate Professor of Environmental History, Philosophy, and Ethics in the Department of Conservation and Resource Studies at the University of California, Berkeley. She is the author of *The Death of Nature: Women, Ecology and the Scientific Revolution* (1980) and formerly directed a pilot grant entitled "Technological Culture and the Human Prospect" at the University of San Francisco.

Rebecca Morales is an Assistant Professor of Urban and Regional Planning at the University of California at Los Angeles. Her research and publications have focused on the employment of undocumented workers in manufacturing and the changing economic structure of Los Angeles, with special attention to the role of women workers in these circumstances.

Sally Otos has worked on an IBM MT/ST at a print shop in Eugene, Oregon, and a Wang word processor at a Manhattan law firm. She now works on a Digital WT/78 word processor at an Ivy League university, where she is active in union organizing. She has also had temporary jobs in many, many types of offices.

Alberta Parker, Emeritus Clinical Professor of Community Health at the University of California, Berkeley, is a pediatrician and public health physician by training. An active organizer for primary care facilities both here and abroad, she has served as a consultant to the Office of Economic Opportunity and the World Health Organization. Since 1976 she has chaired the Health Task Force for the DHHS Advisory Committee on the Rights and Responsibilities of Women.

Diane Reynolds is Special Assistant to the Chief for the California Division of Apprenticeship Standards. She has been involved throughout her career with labor relations, employment, and training. Recently she was appointed by Governor Jerry Brown to the California Employment and Training Advisory Council.

Suzanne Rubin juggles her time between adoption-related activities for Concerned United Birthparents (CUB) and completion of her B.S. degree in accounting at California State University at Northridge. Ms. Rubin, who plans a career in public accounting, was reunited with her daughter Meredith in May 1982. Birthmother and daughter are reportedly doing well.

Judy Smith, who has a doctorate in zoology, has been an instructor of Women's Studies at Southern Oregon State University and director of the Women's Center at the University of Montana, Missoula. The author of several publications on women and technology, rural health, and birth control, she has directed numerous projects and conferences on rural women and coordinates the Women and Technology Network.

Karen Smith is the mother of two children, a 6-year old girl and a 3-year old boy. Involved with the Surrogate Parent Foundation since April 1981, she now speaks frequently on surrogate motherhood. Ms. Smith, who recently re-married, expects to deliver the child she is carrying in December 1982.

Tish Sommers, who calls herself a free-lance agitator, addresses the special issues of older women under the slogan, "Don't Agonize, Organize." Instrumental in developing employment opportunities for displaced homemakers, Ms. Sommers served on the California Commission on Aging from 1977-1979. She is the author of *The Not So Helpless Female* (1974) and a member of the national steering committee of the Gray Panthers, the board of directors of the National Council on Aging, and the president of the Older Women's League.

Elizabeth K. Stage is research evaluator for the Math and Science Education Programs for Women at the Lawrence Hall of Science, University of California, Berkeley, where she also conducts research on early adolescents' mathematical reasoning. Dr. Stage has taught junior high mathematics and science and has evaluated a number of programs designed to increase the participation of women and minorities in math, science, and computing.

Autumn Stanley is a free-lance scholar and writer doing research on women in technological history. She has previously published an asparagus cookbook, two children's books, and both scholarly and popular articles on various subjects. After her book, *Mothers of Invention: Women Inventors and Innovators Through the Ages* is published in 1983, she plans to collaborate with Martha Moore Trescott on a book about women entrepreneurs.

Mary Lindenstein Walshok is Dean of University Extension and Adjunct Associate Professor of Sociology at the University of California at San Diego. Her research into issues surrounding the employment needs and experiences of women recently culminated in the book *Blue-Collar Women: Pioneers on the Male Frontier* (1981).

Barbara Winters is an Associate Professor of Philosophy at the University of California at San Diego, where she teaches ethics, focusing on biomedical ethics and the moral implications of sex differences. She has published on ethics and the philosophy of mind and recently undertook additional studies in law at the University of California, Berkeley.

Jan Zimmerman directed the *Conference on Future, Technology and Woman* in 1981 at San Diego State University, where she is an adjunct faculty member of the Women's Studies Department. A writer and consultant in the fields of telecommunications, computers, and technology, she initiated the National Women's Agenda Satellite Project in 1977 to connect 100 women's organizations using a NASA satellite. In January 1980 she was named by *Ms.* magazine as one of "80 Women to Watch in the '80s."